UNDERSTANDING THE FUTURE

Well-respected in his field, Lyn Birkbeck has been a professional astrologer since 1979. He uses astrology as a tool for helping people to reconnect with their authentic and creative selves. He achieves this through one-to-one consultations, workshops, and the numerous books he has written.

Lyn lives in the Lake District in England. He is also a musician and poet.

Contact: www.lynbirkbeck.com

Understanding
The Future

The major astrological predictions from now to
2020 and how they will shape our world

A survivor's guide to riding the cosmic wave

LYN BIRKBECK

WATKINS PUBLISHING
LONDON

This edition published in the UK 2008 by
Watkins Publishing, Sixth Floor, Castle House,
75–76 Wells Street, London W1T 3QH

1 3 5 7 9 10 8 6 4 2

Designed by Jerry Goldie

Printed and bound in Great Britain

British Library Cataloguing-in-Publication Data Available

ISBN: 978-1-905857-63-0

www.watkinspublishing.co.uk

CONTENTS

Astro-Quantum Health Warning

E. Lorenz, a main originator of Chaos Theory, suggested that next month's weather ... could well be so delicately dependent on **conditions today** that it made sense to ask, "Does the flap of a butterfly's wings in Brazil set off a tornado in Texas" – this being the subtitle to his paper "Predictability" at 1979's meeting of the American Association for the Advancement of Science.

John Leslie, *The End of the World*

This Book is *not* about prediction. This book is about 'conditions today' as seen through the lens of past, present and future planetary motion and symbolism which is astrology, and of various theories in quantum physics, especially one called Observer Created Reality. Both, in real or metaphorical terms, state that how we are, and how we see it, is how we make it. In other words, and particularly with the help of these two subjects ...

We Make Our Own Future Now

Author's Note

The writing of *Understanding the Future* was completed in November 2007. Any events and developments which I describe or allude to that occurred between then and its publication late in 2008 – that is, while the book was in production – were therefore written before that time and not merely observed by me during it.

Lyn Birkbeck
3 March 2008
Lake District, England

Introduction

What Time Is It?

Turning away for a moment from such concerns as paying bills, sexual preoccupations, or whether you're too fat or too thin – do you feel frightened or powerless, or even morbidly fascinated, in the face of these current difficulties and threatening disasters?

- Global warming, including pollution and its attendant health and environmental hazards.
- Energy crises.
- International terrorism.
- Dangerous extremism; increasing crime and violence.
- Threat of nuclear war, this time possibly from rogue states.
- Dodgy science, like dangerous nuclear reactors, mutating chemicals in the food chain, GM crops, etc.
- An excessive use of and reliance upon technology that encourages laxity and emotional dysfunction on a human level (e.g. faceless and inefficient corporations and institutions, with computers failing to take the place of the human touch).
- Economic structures, philosophies and methods that are fast reaching their sell-by date.
- Escalating international air travel and worldwide emigration/immigration that increase the likelihood of accidents, pollution and the spread of disease and civil unrest.
- Various natural disasters that are overdue, such as the super volcano beneath Yellowstone Park. *Or is it because there's a city underground or are we underground?*

And have you noticed that the mental and emotional state of an increasing number of individuals is more confused and volatile than ever, fuelled by the consumer/advertising machine convincing them that they want and need things they don't really want and need? And when they find that such a 'dream' cannot be attained they have to resort to crime, drugs or alcohol to create or maintain the illusion of that dream.

Time to Find a Balance

This all begs the question: what is going on with human life on planet Earth? It would seem that we, as individuals and as the human race as a whole, have been striving towards something – peace, happiness, meaning – while all the time some other force seems to have been opposing this, plunging us into conflict, misery and pointlessness. At times we are forced to rise up and confront those who have power over us and have abused that power – like the French Revolution when the downtrodden or outraged exacted bloody revenge upon the ruling elite, or like the sixties, when we sued for a more loving, creative and peaceful way of liberation. But the sixties had its fair share of violence and insurrection; and the era of the French Revolution saw much innovation with the birth of automation, mass production, modern chemistry, and the whole philosophy of freedom and rights which we are so conscious of today – take for granted even. All this could be called the swing to the left.

Looked at from the opposite viewpoint, swinging to the right, it could be said that rebellious factions, in these and similar periods, went too far in challenging or destroying the existing order and that a repressive backlash of draconian measures was then taken to prevent anarchy and mob-rule – often by the 'liberators' themselves. What is more, this occurs along with a pendulum-swing back to materialism from idealism. For example, it has often been declared that we are paying now for the 'freedoms' of the sixties, with lax parenting, the breakdown of the family unit, misguided policies and social engineering, and a lack of spiritual direction with an accompanying moral vacuum creating social and cultural decay. Yet at the same time, the sixties are fondly remembered by many for their innocent idealism, and they still stand as an inspiration (especially musically and fashionwise).

So wouldn't it be good if we could find a balance between these extremes of left and right, of liberty and control? *Understanding The Future*, you will soon discover, is all about finding a balance through knowing precisely what is in the scales to *be* balanced.

Time for a Revolution!

Now some will say that we as a civilization are doomed, and the examples above could be seen to support this prediction. And yes, looking at the situation and the human condition in the same old way will get us into the same old mess – or rather a mess to end all messes. 'Necessity,' they say, 'is the mother of invention,' and by this token we are in need of the mother of *all* inventions! This invention has to be the equivalent of discovering fire, something which radically changes the way we live and see life. And yet, like a technical appliance that you never quite know how to use or connect, this 'invention' or 'discovery' has been around for quite some time now. Actually, it is more like *two* appliances that we have not yet been able to use in a way that does them both justice. Some have used them, but most have blinked at one or both of them with bafflement or incredulity – and maybe a bit of fascination.

These two 'appliances' are astrology and quantum physics. The first is so old as to be regarded by conventional minds as archaic at best or wacky at worst. The second is, in relative terms, so new that it is generally regarded as too abstract or abstruse to have any meaning or use in our everyday lives. But it is these two appliances – linked together as in fact they actually are, and called quantum astrology or just Astro-Quantum – that will give us that 'mother of all inventions', that fire to light the touchpaper of our future: a future worth striving towards.

Astro-Quantum: A Revolutionary Sense of Time and Reality

If any should think this is far-fetched, or crazy even, then let them remember that our old ways and paradigms are part of the problem, not part of the solution. This new way of seeing life and living it – as it actually is at its most fundamental level – is humbly now made available, to enable us to find a balance and a path through to a very different time – and a very different *sense* of time. Along with this revolutionary sense of time comes a revolutionary sense of reality itself; a new consciousness! This is how profound a time this is! Astrology and quantum physics here combine and take the form of the Cosmic Clock. And the Cosmic Clock is sounding an alarm in an attempt to wake us up. For the Cosmic Clock is that revolutionary sense of time and reality that is arising in the nick of time. More of how Astro-Quantum works will naturally unfold as we proceed, but if you wish to see the rudiments of it explained, go to Appendix 1 on page 236.

The Cosmic Clock

The planets of our solar system can be seen as a timepiece that tells us what is unfolding through time: the drama of life on planet Earth. When any two planets are at certain positions in the sky in relation to the Earth – much like the hour hand and the minute hand of an ordinary clock, with the Earth, as it were, at the centre – they indicate distinct times. And each of these 'times' has a particular quality or feeling that depends on the astrological meaning of the planets in question. We often refer to the 'mood of the times' or 'spirit of the age', or simply a 'good year' or a 'bad year'. And in much the same way that an ordinary clock can have different modes – like time, date, alarm, etc – the Cosmic Clock has different modes depending on which pair of planets we are looking at.

For example, when looking at the Cosmic Clock in 'Uranus and Pluto mode', we see that whenever these two planets were at specific angles to one another,

The Cosmic Clock: Uranus/Pluto Times

(this is just a sample, see Appendix 3 on page 243 for a more extensive record)

Uranus/Pluto Time Period	Key Events Occurring
74–65 BC	Spartacus's rebellion against Rome
1489–1507	Columbus rediscovers America
1592–1602	Shakespeare's works
1620–27	Mayflower sets sail for America
1705–16	Birth of the Industrial Revolution – the age of steam, coal and iron
1787–98	The French Revolution. Automation. Abolition of Slavery
1873–80	Advent of telephone and sound reproduction
1896–1907	Women's Militant Movements. Black Civil Rights Movements. First powered flight by Wright brothers. Quantum physics
1928–37	Atom split: birth of the nuclear age. Hitler, Stalin and Mao
1960–72	The sixties. The Pill. First man in space and Moon landing
2007–20 approx	These years could be make or break time for us as this mother wave comes with the 21st century attitude and environmental hazards.

You can see that Uranus/Pluto Times are epic, real history makers, as, to varying degrees, are the pairings of all the slower moving planets which, along with Uranus and Pluto, include Jupiter, Saturn and Neptune.

So When Is The Next Epic History Maker?
The next Uranus/Pluto Time was just beginning to show in 2007, and will last until approximately 2020.

then the historical periods and events shown in the list above occurred; periods which were charged with the qualities associated with these two planets. (See Appendix 2 on page 239 if you wish see Planetary Cycles more fully explained.) Uranus is the planet of liberation and equal rights, invention and innovation, evolution and revolution, whereas Pluto is the planet of intensification, depth, extremes, fate and power. So Uranus/Pluto 'times' are those of powerful inventions, drastic change, profound leaps forward, an intensified urge for freedom that can also invite a suppression of it, liberation of what lies deep within us, the best and the worst of human nature, and numerous other combinations of these two planets' qualities which we will explore.

Planet-Waves

We speak of waves of influence, of 'new waves', heatwaves, shockwaves, etc. and these planet-to-planet times can also be seen as waves – Planet-Waves. And just like waves they slowly swell, then peak, and finally ebb away – but leave in their wake whatever was the effect of their influence. They also regularly roll in and out again and again because waves come in succession. The Cosmic Clock can tell us when a particular wave is coming, and the size, quality and duration of the period of change that it brings. Furthermore, different planetary periods, or Planet-Waves, can occur simultaneously, weaving a kind of 'time tapestry' of mutually supportive influences, or of dangerous riptides created by conflicting currents, or combinations of both.

Saturn/Pluto Times – 9/11, Iraq, and World Wars One and Two

If we look at the Cosmic Clock in a different mode, like say Saturn and Pluto, then at certain times the qualities of Pluto would combine with Saturnian qualities such as authority, order, repression, boundaries, division, material reality, effort and discipline. So Saturn/Pluto Times would or could see events involving powerful repression, intensification of division, drastic measures to maintain order, transformation of the status quo, violation or annihilation of boundaries, or shows of powerful restraint and disciplined use of force, and the installing or uninstalling of deeply-seated structures. The last Saturn/Pluto Time or Wave was mid-2000 to mid-2004, peaking mid-2001 to mid-2002, which saw 9/11 and

Astro-Quantum Memo

Everything is waves. Thoughts are waves. Your thoughts are an expression of your consciousness. Your consciousness is a succession of waves. The waves go out and contribute to the creation of reality. So your state of consciousness has something to do with the state of the world. Planet-Waves are the consciousness of the solar system of which our Earth is a part. Feel, know and ride the Planet-Waves and your consciousness will be in sync with the greater consciousness that forms and transforms worlds.

Consciousness: the state of being conscious; awareness of one's own existence, sensations, thoughts, surroundings, etc. (Dictionary.com)

Consciousness is the currency

the invasion of Iraq and Afghanistan by US forces. Both World Wars began during the *peaks* of Saturn/Pluto Waves – 1914/15 and 1939/40 respectively.

There are three Saturn/Pluto Waves between 2007 and 2020, occurring simultaneously with the overarching 'mother-wave' made by Uranus and Pluto.

Planet-Wave Weather

A Planet-Wave also brings with it its own 'weather', depending on the nature of each planet and their positions in relationship to one another. Such Planet-Wave weather can be dark and stormy, like some of the waves or periods already mentioned, or present 'favourable winds' that help us to find solutions and create harmony. Then again, progress and advantage will be found also, or especially, in adversity. On the following pages we will see what Planet-Waves and weather are occurring during 2007–20 and beyond, and how if we ride the storms or surf the waves properly – in a balanced and informed way – we can transform rather than destroy, rise up rather than go under, resolve problems rather than create them. And we can do this on both personal and global levels. In fact, it will be shown how the one is inextricably connected to the many – how by individually surfing the waves right, or taking advantage of favourable winds, you help the world to do the same. How is this so?

Time to Find How You Personally Can Make a Difference

As you can see from the above, and possibly from your own experience, astrology and the planets' so-called influences are very real. But to understand how you personally can affect the state of the world and history, we need to appreciate what astrology actually is. An eminent quantum physicist called David Bohm posed the existence of a place out of which comes all of reality as we know and experience it. This place he called 'The Sea of Implicate Order' – implicate meaning *enfolded*; that is, waiting to be *unfolded*. This is similar to the bud that unfolds into a flower, or the potential of a male and a female to reproduce a child. So this sea is the Source of all life – which of course the actual sea is. Now the Cosmic Clock tells us what is unfolding or issuing forth from this Sea at any given time. This is what the Planet-Waves are. They are an *expression* of the Source before it has manifested as any event or human experience. What we make of it, what events, products and reality we create from them is up to us.

However, the Planet-Wave has a quality and intention of its own, depending upon the planets in question and their weather. What is more, and in accordance with something called Non Locality in quantum physics (see page 236 Astro-Quantum), doing or thinking something that is related to a planet's 'influence' has an immediate and corresponding effect in other places, near and far, and thereby affects the whole, either negatively or positively, depending on whether you are aligned with the bad or good energies of a Planet-Wave.

> *' Planet-Waves are expressions of the Source before it has manifested as any event or human experience. '*

Reading the Waves, Riding the Storms

Like a surfer, we have to read the wave if we are going to ride it right. We have to understand its nature and direction, to respect it as a living thing – and a living thing that is infinitely more powerful than the surfer riding it. Those who read the waves and ride them will be taken where those waves are *naturally* supposed to go, and will therefore have an infinitely better time of it, with a positive result to match. Those who do not read the waves will, sooner or later, *wipe-out*. With an unusually large and powerful wave, it becomes crucial that one reads it. You will either be taken far on an exhilarating voyage to a new time and place, or become exhausted, dumped or disappear.

The Uranus/Pluto Wave of 2007–20 is such a wave. Through showing you timing, direction and how to balance, *Understanding The Future* will guide you through this Planet-Wave and all the other Waves that form parts of it.

The Spiritual View: A Win–Win Situation

As I have already stated, some will say that we as a civilization are doomed. But by reading and therefore riding the Planet-Waves we can help the world to arrive at a better place, if there are enough surfers working together. This is because we will have allowed the Planet-Waves, that expression of the Sea of Implicate Order, to become what it naturally wants to become – something healthy and good because it is aligned with the Source, like an oak tree is aligned with the natural expression of an acorn! But if there are not enough surfing the Waves right and riding the storms, then disaster will descend upon the world.

From a purely materialistic worldview, this could appear depressing, and give rise to a sense of pointlessness and the question: why bother if it is quite possible everything could come to an end if not enough effort of the right kind is made by enough people? A great deal depends here upon your own individual beliefs concerning an afterlife, continuity of consciousness, karma, etc. But both astrology and quantum physics are essentially spiritual in their outlooks, as it is understood that life energy streams eternally from the Source and takes form as living things – which includes you and I – and then returns to stream forth and take form again, ad infinitum. Moreover, the quality of the form of expression given to that life energy – that is, in Astro-Quantum terms, how well one rides the Planet-Waves – has a great deal to do with the quality of the energy that returns to the Source and so, therefore, with the quality of what issues forth from it thereafter. In other words, even if the investment you make in helping to save the world by riding Planet-Waves right fails to do so, you will have contributed to raising the vibration or improving the quality of universal life energy. This means improving the quality of afterlife, the next life, consciousness, karma, other dimensions, or whatever you want to call the expression of *eternity*, something which is witnessed in astrology as the endless movement of heavenly bodies, and in quantum physics as the endless emission and interchange of waves and sub-atomic particles.

This is a decidedly spiritual or enlightened view, but that is precisely what this Uranus/Pluto Planet-Wave is forcing us to adopt, accept and become a lot clearer about. And let it be said that 'spiritual view' includes any approach to life that is guided by higher principles or higher beings, and not exclusively the planets and their waves.

The Cosmic Drama 2007–20

And so it is that at the time of writing, the hands of the Cosmic Clock in Uranus/Pluto mode indicate the approach of a Mother-Wave Major Storm – the last planetary weather of this kind occurred during the 1960s. And like the

---

Astro-Quantum Memo

Much has been said about quantum physics not actually supporting new models for living and thinking, such as those espoused by works like *What the Bleep Do We Know* and *The Secret* – and now here in *Understanding The Future*. All of these publications set great store by the idea that because quantum physics states that subatomic particles such as electrons only actually come into existence when they are being looked at, then in real life it is entirely up to us what we make our reality out to be. (see page 236 Astro-Quantum/Observer Created Reality).

The quantum physicist will argue that it is a machine that was doing the observing in the experiment, not human eyes and minds. But this is missing the point. Quantum physics is all about the inner reality of matter, and so therefore is analogous to the inner reality of our minds and lives, which is what astrology is all about. Human eyes see what the machine is doing and human minds made the machine – in their own image.

Quantum theory can be seen as a metaphor for mind-power

---

sixties, it will happen alongside numerous other Planet-Waves of lesser size, of both good and bad weather. These peaks and troughs, fierce typhoons and favourable breezes, will persist until what appears to be a 'point of departure' around the year 2020, after a distinct crisis between 2009 and 2017.

Additionally though, the *centre of the centre* of this period coincides with the end of the Mayan Calendar, 2012, a time which is predicted as the End of the World, or rather the End of *Time*, as we know it. If the significance of the Planet-Waves and Times down through history, as set out on these pages, is anything to go by, then these years do indeed appear to be a make or break time for us. This is because, unlike the sixties or any other Uranus/Pluto Wave in known history, *we are now confronted with an unprecedented set of 'current difficulties and threatening disasters'*. But are these calamities really coming from without, an 'opposing force', like some alien and aggressive foe? Or is the enemy within?

The Blame Game

Is there something in our own natures that is getting in the way of achieving a happier and healthier life, or suppressing a need to freely express ourselves? Is it just our personal inadequacies and inhibitions, and childish reactions and defensiveness born of childhood hurts, that we continually cause upset to attract aggression, and aggression to attract revenge, thus creating endless feuds and wars, be it between individuals or whole countries? A literally extreme example here is the terrorist who is hitting back at repression far closer to home than in the foreign realm or ideology he attacks. Or conversely, the leader who lashes out at terrorism when what he is really trying to do is suppress or hide (from) the terrorist within. (See page 60 Awakening the Underworld.)

Astro-Quantum Self-Rule

If, however, you get in tune and in time with the Cosmic Clock, then you are taking responsibility for any part, however small, you might have played or be playing that negatively affects your own and the collective situation. In this way, the chain of defensiveness–aggression–revenge is broken. This is called Astro-Quantum Self-Rule.

So when the Cosmic Clock says that it is time to liberate and police *ourselves* in due proportion; or to open up or contain *ourselves* as is appropriate; or to create any other kind of balance within *ourselves*, then by accomplishing or merely attempting this on a personal level, we are aligning ourselves with the direction any Planet-Wave wants to go, and towards positively changing the whole.

This is because the direction of the Planet-Wave is the natural and self-governing way, just as the planets stay true to their orbits and the solar system remains stable. This is somewhat like seeing litter in a public park and 'reading' this event as a call to dispose of that litter. It may not have been your litter, but by responding to the incident in such a way, you make the park a safer, cleaner and more pleasant place for everyone, including yourself. What is more, you will feel the power, buoyancy and spirit of any particular Planet-Wave coursing through you as you ride it, just as a surfer would experience an ordinary wave.

Synchronicity

Importantly, the Cosmic Clock can also show us that events that are seemingly 'accidental' or 'acts of God' are actually related to the human condition and human behaviour. This is a case of synchronicity, or the idea that separate incidents happening together in time are meaningfully related.

Take, for example, the Saturn/Neptune Wave that began in 2004 and by 2008 finally ebbs away, yet creates a lasting impression (for a full report on Saturn/Neptune Waves see page 135). The Neptune 'hand' of the Cosmic Clock indicates energies and influences that have, at one end of its spectrum, to do with dreams and ideals, and a sense of spirituality and oceanic oneness – but, at the other end of Neptune's spectrum, with illusions and subsequent disappointment, and being inundated by something beyond our control. And you will remember that Saturn indicates matters concerning quite the opposite, such as authority, material reality, order and boundaries.

Waves Within Waves

So 2004 saw a wave of immense public disillusionment with authority, evidenced most particularly in Bush's re-election, but also in disenchantment with politicians and government worldwide, not least of all Blair and his government in Great Britain. Yet at the same time there occurred a dissolution of boundaries, graphically displayed by the ocean in the form of the tsunami that inundated the coastlines of several Asian countries. And during the same Saturn/Neptune Wave or period, in 2005, we saw the flooding of New Orleans as a result of hurricane Katrina, along with the scandalously inept handling of this disaster by the authorities, not forgetting the bad design of the city itself.

If we go back to the Saturn/Neptune Wave preceding this one, 1987–91, we see again dissolution of boundaries and disillusionment with authority, with the coming down of the Berlin Wall and the end of the Soviet Union. Yet during the same year (1989) boundary-breaking 'accidents' or 'acts of God' occurred such as the Exxon Valdez oil spill off Alaska and a massive earthquake in the San Francisco Bay Area.

Yet another form of 'boundary dissolution' can be seen in the Spanish Pandemic of 1918 (death toll between 20 and 40 million), which happened during the Saturn/Neptune Wave of 1916–19, with the crossing of country boundaries, immune system boundaries, and species boundaries (as this was reckoned to be originally a bird flu that crossed over to humans). At the time of writing, during the Saturn/Neptune Wave of 2004–08, there is increasing alarm at the possibility of this happening again with the current spread of bird flu globally and foot and mouth disease in Europe. These are in addition to many other Saturn/Neptune issues that we will look at in the Saturn/Neptune Waves chapter beginning on page 135.

Whether or not a pandemic strikes during this time, or the next Saturn/Neptune Wave of 2014–2017, is down to how we ride the Saturn/Neptune Wave itself. It is a mystery as to why, in the same situation, one person will catch a disease and another won't. Just one of the Cosmic Clock's answers to this is that one has a well-balanced sense of boundaries (Saturn) and accessibility (Neptune), whereas the other does not. On a collective level this will, one way or

Astro-Quantum Memo

Go with the flow of where the wave wants to go

the other, register as a critical mass that can make the difference between a mild epidemic and a pandemic worse than 1918. (See page 156 The Butterfly Effect.)

In Time With Time

One more thing about synchronicity. By riding the Planet-Waves, you will eventually find that things in your life flow better as they are in rhythm and in tune with each other, or rather, because they are aligned with a common and binding theme. Good timing becomes the norm as so-called chance encounters and lucky coincidences occur quite naturally. This synchronicity then mushrooms into the collective becoming more harmonious and integrated. This is akin to a

Astro-Quantum Memo:
Resonating With Fate

Planet-Waves can be seen as 'Bringers of Fate'. Riding these Waves is simply what life is. We can fight their power and direction and get into trouble, or attune to them and go with their direction, use their power, like a surfer riding an ordinary wave. Quantum theory states that absolutely everything is fundamentally waves, as light and sound are waves. (See page 236 Astro-Quantum.) Our thoughts are waves. Waves can interact with one another in-phase or out-of-phase, harmoniously or discordantly.

Think of two people singing in or out of tune, or turbulence where a river meets the sea. So how your thoughts interact with what is happening, or appears to be about to happen, has everything to do with what occurs now or in the future. With this in mind, *Understanding The Future* is showing you what is fundamentally happening or possibly about to happen, rather like reading the wind itself instead of the objects that the wind is blowing about. Your mind is thereby given the opportunity to resonate with those Waves at their own level - having your thought-waves harmonize with the Planet-Waves. This produces a positive outcome or fate.

Understanding The Future
shows us how to co-operate with fate

'This Uranus/Pluto Mother-Wave 2007–20 has the potential to boost human mind-power and enable us to make 'course corrections' that will avert the disasters that threaten us.'

group of musicians playing well together because they are attuned to one another, and/or they are reading from the same score.

Awakening to Power

Finally, it has to be emphasized that the significant and beautiful thing about the Uranus/Pluto Mother-Wave of 2007–20 is that it is its core intention to awaken in us the power that we possess to shape our destiny. It wants us to discover just how much power our minds have over matter, that by having a conscious awareness of that incoming wave of history and reality in the making, we can influence the turn of events *at source*. This is the advent of Super-Mind-Power.

Indeed, as quantum physicists are becoming increasingly aware, we are co-creators of life. One could say that the planets which are the hands of the Cosmic Clock are pointing to what we need to know, and what we need to do, *before anything actually happens*. They reveal what issues are in the scales to be balanced, in the pot to be mixed and blended, or eliminated or refined, *before* its contents are served and consumed. It is saying that how and what we actually think in the present moment has everything to do with what is actually going to come about.

This too is in accordance with quantum physics – and with the ancient esoteric dictum 'energy follows thought'. But if we are asleep to this and what it poses, if we do not *awaken to our power*, then the powers that be – or rather ought *not* to be – will continue to have their way with us, and ultimately destroy us.

Astro-Quantum Memo: Simple Equations

Awareness of Waves = Appropriate Response = Bright Future

Ignorance of Waves = Blind Reaction or = Bleak Future
Non-Response

'By focusing on the future now, riding the
Planet-Waves and implementing Astro-Quantum
Self-Rule, we can change the future – now. '

CHAPTER 1

Surf's Up!

How to Live, Make and Use the Future Now

Reminders

The Cosmic Clock that is astrology tells us about the spirit of the time we are living through during any period in history. The nature and power of that time spirit, or *zeitgeist*, is indicated by the quality of particular pairs of planets, the hands of the Cosmic Clock. These planetary pairs create Planet-Waves that swell and surge through time and our lives.

So **Planet-Waves are 'Bringers of Fate'**. Riding these Waves is simply what life is. We can fight their power and direction and get into trouble, or attune to them and go with their direction, use their power, like a surfer riding an ordinary wave.

Two planets interacting make a Wave. A human metaphor for this is two very different and strong-minded people coming into contact and the best and the worst of each being brought out and magnified. But two planets do the same to one another on a cosmic scale.

Astro-Quantum – *Understanding The Future* compares and combines astrology with the rudiments of quantum physics. For example, a quantum physics discovery like non locality – where something occurring in one place happens instantaneously a very long way away – is one way of seeing how astrology works. It shows that if one person is riding a Wave right it will have a positive effect on the other side of the world straight away. And what is more, we can ride Waves that are still to come and change the future now!

Like a surfer, we have to read the Wave if we are going to ride it right. This is called *Awareness of Waves* and the rest of this book is a manual for just that.

The Planet-Wave Weather Chart and The Planet-Wave Timeline and Index

This manual begins with The Planet-Wave Weather Chart and the Planet-Wave Timeline and Index. These are your main maps, your guide to Planet-Wave surfing!

- **The Weather Chart** shows graphically all the Waves, and their weather types, during the Uranus/Pluto Mother-Wave 2007–20, along with the Mother-Wave itself. It also includes the start of the Aquarian age, and the end of the Mayan Calendar – all of which are explained in Appendix 4 on page 247.
- **The Planet-Wave Timeline and Index** shows the Weather Chart in tabular and chronological form, spelling out the actual duration, weather type, key-phrase and, most usefully, the page number(s) where you can find out all about any particular Wave.
- **And Beyond** – *Understanding The Future* not only shows you how to ride all of the Planet-Waves. It acts as a manual for any similar Planet-Waves occurring beyond 2020, and these can be determined by anyone with a little astrological ability.

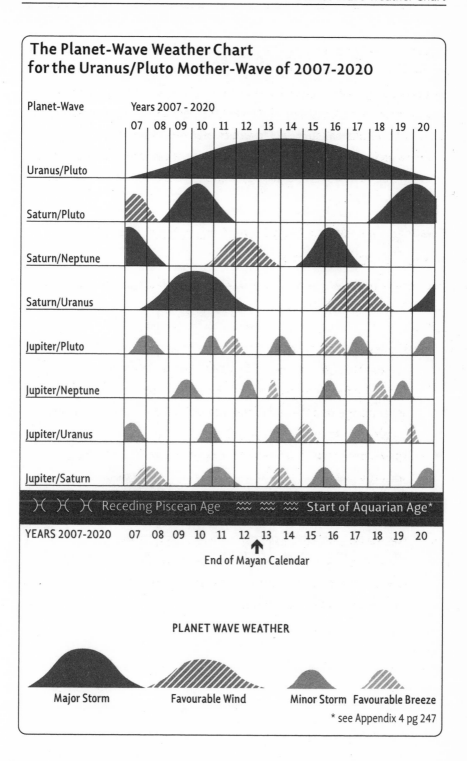

The Planet-Wave Weather Chart for the Uranus/Pluto Mother-Wave of 2007-2020

Planet-Wave   Years 2007 - 2020

Uranus/Pluto

Saturn/Pluto

Saturn/Neptune

Saturn/Uranus

Jupiter/Pluto

Jupiter/Neptune

Jupiter/Uranus

Jupiter/Saturn

)( )( )(Receding Piscean Age   ≋ ≋ ≋ Start of Aquarian Age*

YEARS 2007-2020   07 08 09 10 11 12 13 14 15 16 17 18 19 20

End of Mayan Calendar

PLANET WAVE WEATHER

Major Storm   Favourable Wind   Minor Storm Favourable Breeze

* see Appendix 4 pg 247

Planet-Wave Timeline and Index

#	Year(s)	Planet-Wave	Key Phrase	Weather	Page
1	2007–20	**Uranus/Pluto**	**Awakening To Power**	**Major Storm**	27–80
2	11/2004–8/2008	**Saturn/Neptune**	**Transcendence of Limitations**	**Major Storm**	123, 136–69 172–74, 177–85, 219
3	8/2006–8/2008	*Saturn/Pluto*	*Constructive Use of Power*	*Favourable Wind*	*119–23, 172, 220*
4	12/2006–11/2007	Jupiter/Uranus	Awakening Faith	Minor Storm	69, 220
5	1/2007–9/2008	Jupiter/Pluto	The Power of Belief	Minor Storm	69, 123
6	2/2007–1/2009	*Jupiter/Saturn*	*Benevolent Control*	*Favourable Breeze*	*123, 124 173, 220*
7	9/2007–7/2012	**Saturn/Uranus**	**The Old Versus the New**	**Major Storm**	123, 124, 173, 174, 188–216, 219–21, 224–30
8	11/2008–8/2011	**Saturn/Pluto**	**Power Struggles**	**Major Storm**	82–118, 124–25, 127–34, 174, 220
9	2/2009–3/2010	Jupiter/Neptune	Spiritual Vision or Pie-in-the-Sky	Minor Storm	173
10	3/2010–3/2012	Jupiter/Saturn	Growth versus Order	Minor Storm	124, 175, 221
11	3/2010–4/2011	Jupiter/Uranus	Awakening Faith 2	Minor Storm	69, 221
12	5/2010–4/2011	Jupiter/Pluto	The Power of Belief 2	Minor Storm	69, 124
13	12/2010–11/2013	*Saturn/Neptune*	*Practical Vision*	*Favourable Wind*	*124, 170–1, 174–75, 221*
14	5/2011–5/2012	*Jupiter/Pluto*	*Regeneration*	*Favourable Breeze*	*69, 124*
15	5/2012–8/2012	Jupiter/Neptune	Spiritual Vision or Pie-in-the-Sky 2	Minor Storm	175
16	6/2013–6/2014	*Jupiter/Saturn*	*Benevolent Control 2*	*Favourable Breeze*	175
17	6/2013–7/2014	Jupiter/Pluto	The Power of Belief 3	Minor Storm	70

Planet-Wave Timeline and Index cont.

#	Year(s)	Planet-Wave	Key Phrase	Weather	Page
18	6/2013–8/2013	*Jupiter/Neptune*	*Spiritual Growth*	*Favourable Breeze*	175
19	7/2013–6/2014	Jupiter/Uranus	Awakening Faith 3	Minor Storm	70
20	8/2014–8/2015	*Jupiter/Uranus*	*Getting Lucky*	*Favourable Breeze*	70
21	11/2014–9/2017	**Saturn/Neptune**	**Transcendence of Limitations 2**	**Major Storm**	136–69, 175–76, 177–85, 221
22	6/2015–7/2016	Jupiter/Saturn	Growth versus Order 2	Minor Storm	175, 222
23	8/2015–8/2016	*Jupiter/Pluto*	*Regeneration 2*	*Favourable Breeze*	70
24	7/2015–8/2016	Jupiter/Neptune	Spiritual Vision or Pie-in-the-Sky 3	Minor Storm	175
25	11/2015–12/2018	**Saturn/Uranus**	**Old Blends with New**	**Favourable Wind**	125, 176, 217–18, 221–22
26	10/2016–9/2017	Jupiter/Pluto	The Power of Belief 4	Minor Storm	71
27	10/2016–1/2018	Jupiter/Uranus	Awakening Faith 4	Minor Storm	71, 222
28	10/2017–10/2018	*Jupiter/Neptune*	*Spiritual Growth 2*	*Favourable Breeze*	176
29	1/2018–12/2021	**Saturn-Pluto**	**Power Struggles 2**	**Major Storm**	82–118, 125, 127–34, 222
30	11/2018–11/2019	Jupiter/Neptune	Spiritual Vision or Pie-in-the-Sky 4	Minor Storm	176
31	11/2019–1/2020	*Jupiter/Uranus*	*Getting Lucky 2*	*Favourable Breeze*	71
32	12/2019–4/2021	Jupiter/Saturn	Growth versus Order 3	Minor Storm	126, 223
33	1/2020–1/2021	Jupiter/Pluto	The Power of Belief 5	Minor Storm	71, 126
34	1/2020–10/2022	**Saturn/Uranus**	**The Old Versus the New 2**	**Major Storm**	126, 188–216, 222–30

Before You Get Your Toes Wet

Each Planet Wave chapter consists of several sections – chapters within chapters if you like; here's what you'll find in each one and what you'll need to know as you encounter them for real ...

Basic Wave Information

The Active Period, the type of Wave Weather, and the pages on How To Ride it.

What Time Is It?

What kind of Time or Times the Wave is bringing with it. The Energies in Play.

Previously and So Far

What happened previously with similar Waves since the beginning of the 20th century and with any Wave so far that is occurring at the time of writing (2007).

Astro-Quantum Memos

These keep you in mind of the basic nature of Planet-Wave surfing.

Stand-Alone Articles (◆)

These are inserts that feature important aspects of the Wave in question.

Surf It or Wipe-Out?

The Battle between the Spirit of the Time and the Devil of the Time, and the Conflicts, Trends and Possibilities these pose. Set out in life categories.

The Mood of the Time

This describes the emotional and psychological atmosphere of the Wave.

The Choice is Ours

A chart for easy surfing that affects everybody.

Favourable Winds

When these occur they provide a considerable opportunity to improve matters and ameliorate the effects of the Major Storms. Obviously, Favourable Winds are nowhere near as strong as Major Storms, and you have to 'set your sails right' in order to benefit from them. Major Storms sweep you up in their dynamic path whether you are thinking about them or not! This is a fact of astrology and a fact of life. It is easier to fall off a log than it is to climb a tree; it's easier to not make an effort than it is to make one. The Universe is a dynamic place that demands effort and awareness of all who want to function in it, especially on heavy-gravity planets like the one we are living on – that is, we are mostly obliged to 'climb trees' rather than just 'fall off logs'. The planet that governs gravity is Saturn; this is why most of the Major Storms involve Saturn, because they are phenomena born of gravity – weight and pressure and force of circumstances – working against the other planet in question, forcing their energies to manifest in the material world.

The Unfolding Story: Merging Waves and Jupiter Boosters

Merging Waves These notify you of other Major Storms and Favourable Winds occurring at the same time as the Wave in question. Merging Waves can be seen graphically on the Planet-Wave Weather Chart.

Jupiter Boosters As well as these Merging Waves there are Planet-Waves involving Jupiter that come into the picture of the Wave being looked at, and Jupiter kind of boosts whatever is happening, blowing things up so we cannot fail to notice problems or opportunities! As can be seen on the Planet-Wave Weather Chart on page 19 Jupiter Waves exist in their own right, and are responsible for Minor Storms and Favourable Breezes.

The Planet-Wave Chronicles Jupiter Boosters and Merging Waves can increase or modify the effects of any Major Storms and the Favourable Winds that are happening at the same time. Taken together, these Merging Waves and Jupiter Boosters dramatize and pace the overall course of them, rather like a storyteller would do, unfolding their stories in the process.

*❛ By describing Planet-Waves, **Understanding The Future** is showing you what is fundamentally happening or may be about to happen, rather like reading the wind itself instead of the objects that the wind is blowing about. ❜*

Personal Effect

As an individual, any Planet-Wave affects you and can be ridden successfully by **Surfing through the Houses**, managing **Relationships,** appreciating that **The Choice Is Yours** and the simplest surfing aid of all: **The Balance of Power Charts**. All of these personal aids are designed to also serve the whole, for this is what life and astrology are about. I would also advise you to get your individual chart read by an experienced astrologer, either for the first time or again.

Hotspots

These are times to be more on your toes, when there is the greatest likelihood of something happening. The Hotspots for all the Planet-Waves between 2007 and 2020 can be found in Appendix 6.

The Planet-Wave Year-By-Year Index

(See Appendix 7.) Go straight to what's going on during the year that interests you.

Reference and Relevance

Understanding The Future has been composed laterally as well as in a linear fashion. This means that you do not necessarily have to read it from beginning to end – although you can if you want – but that it goes forwards, backwards and sideways just like our minds and life itself. There are many places where you can leave the page you are on and go to another that connects with it in some way. When this is the case there is simply one of the following symbols: {>} or {<}, with

Astro-Quantum Memo:
Multiple Waves

When you see 🕐 followed by a page number and the name of another Planet-Wave chapter, this means that on the page given there is another Planet-Wave occurring at the same time which is similar in effect to the one you are reading about. The combined effect of these two or more Waves is far more likely to give rise to the events, trends or possibilities mentioned. Note that not all such events are cross-referenced like this, but only the most significant ones; otherwise it would clutter the text. Use the Planet-Wave Weather Chart to see a complete graphic overview.

Simultaneous and similar Planet-Wave effects mean that fate is speaking louder!

the name of the item and the page number you can hop to, back or ahead, if you want to see a fuller focus or another angle on what you are reading about.

Here Come The Planet-Waves – Get Ready!

CHAPTER 2

The Uranus/Pluto Mother-Wave

2007–20

What Kind Of Time Is This?
Time To Awaken To Our Power

Active Period	Wave Weather	How To Ride
2007–20	Mother-Wave Major Storm	Pages 28–80

The next Uranus/Pluto Mother-Wave is 2041–52

Recent ones going back to the beginning of the 20th century are reviewed below

Earlier Uranus/Pluto Mother-Waves are listed in Appendix 3 page 243

Energies in Play as we Ride this Wave

The energies of Uranus are interacting with the energies of Pluto, and everyone and everything on planet Earth will be subject to this interaction for the duration of its influence, as well as to the after-effects that follow upon this Planet-Wave. Remember that two planets interacting are rather like two very different and strong-minded people coming into contact and the best and the worst of each is brought out and magnified. But Uranus and Pluto do the same to one another on a cosmic scale, affecting us all!

 The character of **Uranus** is **Freedom and Innovation** and its energy is **Awakening and/or Disrupting**

 The character of **Pluto** is **Depths and Power** and its energy is **Empowering and/or Destroying**

Their combined effect is therefore ...

Awakening and/or Disrupting Depths and Power

Empowering and/or Destroying Freedom and Innovation

What Are We Human Beings Really About?

A Uranus/Pluto Mother-Wave churns to the surface all those things we have been sitting on, putting off or just denying. But it doesn't just do this for the hell of it, because it is all in aid of putting us more in touch with what it actually means to be a human being deep down – living as we do on a ball of earth and water spinning in space around an even bigger ball of fire! It wants us to feel free to be what we were destined to be, what we were really supposed to be.

The trouble is that by way of overcompensation this can either mean that we live to excess and destroy more than we liberate, or that certain forces clamp down heavily as we make our blows for freedom and a more satisfying and meaningful existence. These 'forces' can be internal in the form of fears and conditioning, or external in the form of authority, tradition or anyone who has some power over us. Either way, the more they resist or suppress our need to be who we truly are, the greater will be the measure of explosiveness, rebellion and upheaval that is unleashed in our bid to satisfy or merely recognize that need.

As you will constantly find as you read this book, this excess or suppression is now taking form in the actual physical condition of the planet we live upon. Our excesses coupled with our lack of awareness of what it actually means to be human have created in us appetites and habits that are destroying us and our environment. Merely suppressing or outlawing these excesses only increases them. We really must get to the bottom of why we are like we are – and find out *what* we are.

Using the language of astrology and some of the findings of quantum physics I will attempt to provide some answers to this monumental question. This applies to both the personal and global arenas, and most significantly to how powerfully the one affects the other. This we do by first looking at how some previous Uranus/Pluto Mother-Waves have affected us, and then by interpreting what this one itself, and other Planet-Waves occurring at the same time, are trying to tell us – and where they are trying to take us.

> *'Our excesses and lack of awareness are destroying us and our environment. '*

Dateline 2007: Previously, and So Far

Your Planet-Wave surfing can be greatly helped by knowing something of what happened during previous Uranus/Pluto Mother-Waves, as well as looking at what is happening with this one so far. If, however, you want to jump right into this Wave now, then go to page 44.

We open our review at the turn of the 20th century, but if you want to look even further back, refer to Appendix 3.

Uranus/Pluto Mother-Wave 1896-1907

In true Uranus/Pluto style, this Wave brought profound endings and beginnings. This doesn't just relate to the change from one century to the next, but to the Victorian Age. This ushered in what has been possibly the most progressive and changeful of eras, the 20th century. See how the Uranus/Pluto theme of powerful change – brought about by radical discoveries, revolutionary movements and deeply influential figures – arises especially at these times when this Mother-Wave is surging. {☉ 138 Saturn/Neptune}

Emancipation and Revolution

On the socio-political front, those classic Uranus/Pluto energies of power, freedom, depth and innovation found expression in the birth of the Socialist and Communist Parties – derived from Marx and Engels's *Communist Manifesto* produced during the previous Uranus/Pluto Wave in 1848. This 1896-1907 Wave also birthed women's movements such as the Women's Social and Political Union founded by Emmeline Pankhurst in England, and the anarchist monthly publication *Mother Earth* in America. Also during the Wave black civil rights assumed national status in America, initiated by W.E.B. Du Bois with his Niagara Movement. In India, Gandhi forged his civil disobedience philosophy of 'truth force' – which was very Uranus (truth)/Pluto (force)!

As well as these emancipatory movements, in Europe there was also the rise of Bohemian and neopagan subcultures, and in America the genesis of West Coast counterculture. Terpsichorean icon Isadora Duncan's dancing free from Puritanism was aptly described as the crest of this rebellious wave.

Scientific Progress

Technologically there were the gigantic leaps provided by the first powered flight by the Wright brothers, Einstein's Theory of Relativity, and the birth of quantum physics itself with Max Planck's discovery of the quantum in 1900. Also at this time physicist Ernest Rutherford actually predicted, along with the discovery of radioactivity in uranium, the nuclear age and how it could vanquish the world as we knew it. Sigmund Freud and other early mind-probers started to plumb the bottomless pit of depth psychology, ensuring that the human mind and our behaviour could never be seen in the same way again. {>60 Awakening the Underworld}. And all this was washed down with megalitres of worldwide upheavals.

Uranus /Pluto Mother-Wave 1928–37

With reliable and predictable might, Uranus and Pluto again deliver their dose of rights, reform and revolution, and iconic figures acting either for them or against them, depending on what side of the barricade they were on. {⊘87 Saturn/Pluto}{⊘138 Saturn/Neptune}. This time also saw the discovery of Pluto itself! {⊘190 Saturn/Uranus}.

Hitler, Mussolini, Stalin and Mao

The emergence of these figures asserts the Fascism, Marxism and radical socialism that are so typical of Uranus/Pluto, born as they are from some primal urge to gain freedom or power or both. Even that icon of such icons, Che Guevara, was born at this time. This Wave also brought with it the Spanish Civil War following upon the election of the Socialist Party with their anti-Church policies, matched by the atheistic existentialism of Jean-Paul Sartre, Simone de Beauvoir et al. {>41 Death and Rebirth of God}. And with the rise of Nazism, as with the previous Wave, there again occurred neopaganism – this time of Teutonic persuasion – such primal pre-Christian religions being a strong and persistent expression of Uranus/Pluto.

Unions, Gangsters and Protesters

In the United States there was radical reform as labour unions gained immense power, alongside the revolutionary economic theories of John Maynard Keynes which affected economic policy for the remainder of the century. A literal and particularly ugly expression of Uranus/Pluto was the rise of the gangster culture {>60 Awakening the Underworld}. Positively and creatively, power was lent to rebellion against social injustice and economic hardship in the life and works of singer-songwriter Woody Guthrie, who in turn became the inspiration for Bob Dylan who took on the mantle of protest singer during the following Wave between 1960 and 1972. In England, feminism found a leader and icon in Virginia Woolf with the success of her *A Room Of One's Own*.

The Nuclear Age

On the technological front, in 1932 Cockcroft and Watson made the first inroads into splitting the atom which gave rise to the achieving of nuclear fission by Enrico Fermi in 1934, thereby making real Rutherford's prediction of the Nuclear Age (see 1896–1907 above) with all that such has unleashed.

Crash and Depression

Economy certainly doesn't escape the upheavals that a Uranus/Pluto Mother-Wave can bring. Pluto is power, which equals money, and Uranus gives it a shock that is commensurate to any cracks that are already showing. And so it wasn't surprising (from an astrological viewpoint) that one of the greatest, if not *the* greatest, economic crises of all time occurred with the Wall Street stock collapse of October 1929. And this precipitated the Great Depression of the thirties.

Astro-Quantum Memo: Awareness of Waves

What is really important in viewing past Waves is the possible conclusion that often they could have been ridden a lot better! This was mainly because we didn't know how to ride them, for the simple reason that we didn't know where they were wanting to go, what their nature was, what they intended, when they were going to roll in, and, most of all, because we didn't know that such Waves even existed!

With *Understanding The Future* we can know what the future and the now have the potential to be. Ignorance is no longer an option – and neither are the disaster and distress that ignorance brings. This does not mean that we can know the exact outcome and events of a Planet-Wave, but we can be aware of what that Wave, that 'bringer of fate', is about – like a surfer senses the wave beneath his or her board. Nor does it say that there won't be collateral damage as we have difficulty letting go of old forms, beliefs, methods and attitudes – but with Awareness of Waves we will know or sense what needs letting go of, and why and how – as well as what to aim for.

With the Uranus/Pluto Mother-Wave it is the Power of Truth rolling in. We really need to go with that, not get in its way!

Uranus /Pluto Mother-Wave 1960–72

The period during which the last Uranus/Pluto Mother-Wave occurred was the much-maligned or much-missed, 'sixties', with its radicalism, protests and blows for freedom as expressed in music, fashion, literature, politics, race and feminism – activities all typical of this type of Wave. Also, because Saturn/Uranus Waves and Saturn/Pluto Waves were merging with it around its peak period, it was accompanied by something more literally earth-shattering ...

Three of the Biggest Earthquakes between 1900 and 2007

- October 13 1963: 8.6M earthquake in Kuril Islands {☾195 Saturn/ Uranus}.
- March 28 1964: 9.2M earthquake in Prince William Sound, Alaska {☾91 Saturn/Pluto and ☾195 Saturn/Uranus}.
- February 4 1965: 8.7M earthquake in Rat Islands, Alaska {☾91 Saturn/Pluto and ☾195 Saturn/Uranus}.

And among the many technological innovations – not least of all man's first landing on the Moon in 1969 – there was one in particular that chemically gave this Wave such a fundamental effect ...

The Pill

Possibly the most significant event at this time in a socio-cultural sense was the first widespread availability and use of an oral contraceptive, the Pill, for it had a profound effect upon the way we live our lives. For women in particular it triggered a very real sense of liberation – unwanted pregnancy having forever been what chained them to family and home. For men too it was liberating for they, along with women, could now enjoy sex for its own sake. But as we are now aware, such 'sexual liberation' had a sting in its tail. The downside revealed itself progressively as one-parent, usually fatherless, families. This, effectively the partial destruction of the family unit – and especially in countries with little moral/religious element in place – produced many young people who have little sense of belonging, structure or self-control. And this rootlessness particularly applies to those who are the children of those born in the Swinging Sixties.

Gang Culture

This in turn gave rise to a sharp increase in gang culture (just like the previous Wave) and all that it entails, particularly a sense of hierarchy and tribalism replacing that lack of belonging and structure. This has been largely negative because it is riddled with the anger and violence that is the result of feeling forsaken by parents, especially fathers, and society itself. Added to this is the drug-culture, the welling up of which was also a sixties phenomenon – and then the increase in criminal activity. The 2007–20 Uranus/Pluto Mother-Wave promises to bring the current offspring of this – the gangsta subculture – to a head.

Pandora's Box

This could all come under the Uranus/Pluto heading of 'Waking up to Sex and all that' {>60 Awakening the Underworld} which is ironic considering how many people were waking up to someone they'd just slept with and hardly knew! As the current 2007–20 Uranus/Pluto Wave rolls in – with AIDS and other sexually transmitted diseases threatening melt-down – the question still burns: how awake are we to what sex is all about? Typical of the sixties, like Pandora opening her mythical box of human afflictions, we leapt into a pool we didn't know the depth of, revealing a lack of respect for, or just plain ignorance of, the life-making force itself. Sex, the core of this force, is what the Pill made all too accessible; showing us that really there is no such thing as 'safe sex'.

Sex, like anything truly exciting, is inherently dangerous – which includes bringing a child into this world. As far as most people are concerned, there is nothing more exciting than sex. And it would have to be – otherwise we'd have died out long ago! {>105 Saturn/Pluto Waves where the illusion of 'safe sex' is explored further, along with the birth of AIDS}.

Genetic Engineering

The late 1960s and early 1970s witnessed the origin of genetic engineering, through experiments with bacteria, viruses and small free floating rings of DNA called plasmids, found in bacteria. This could be said to outbox Pandora's Box in terms of unleashing something that would damage or even destroy our natural environment if allowed to get out of control. GE – ironically the Greek name for the first and ultimate deity, Mother Earth, also known as Gaia, mother of Uranus {>60 Awakening the Underworld} – contains the potential to heal and feed the world, interestingly paralleling the only good thing in Pandora's Box, *Hope*. The problem is that if there is a way for something to get out of control it will; and there usually is! As poet Robert Frost put it, 'Something there is that doesn't love a wall'. Again, that Uranus/Pluto favourite activity, protest, will have more and more to demonstrate about regarding this 'hope' during the up and coming 2007–2020 Wave – *hopefully* before some monster does get out of the box!

Get Up, Stand Up, Stand Up for your Rights

Bob Marley's song, written at the very end of this Wave, neatly and poetically summed it up with respect to the oppressed finding their power and their voice – something so reliably predictable with Uranus/Pluto Waves – a classic case in point being Spartacus! Most prominently, there was Martin Luther King Jr. whose work and courage, along with black power movements like the Black Panthers, culminated in the Civil Rights Acts of 1965 and 1968. In Africa itself, the struggle for freedom and equality was championed by Nelson Mandela and the African National Congress. Protest against that most violent and outrageous of all human activities, war, was also more manifest than ever before, notably against the Vietnam War as it escalated during this time, particularly following the first air attacks upon this country by the US in 1965 {☯ 91 Saturn/Pluto Waves}.

A Close Nuclear Shave

Such protest against war was all the more justified, considering how close we came to global nuclear war with the Cuban Missile Crisis in October 1962. This occurred when the United States challenged Russia's installation of a nuclear missile base in the Caribbean, itself a response to US deployment of similar missiles in Turkey. It was only the intercession of the General Secretary of the United Nations that saved the day and, in the spirit of planetary lore, the effect of the collective horror and anti-war feelings that were burgeoning as this Uranus/Pluto Wave gathered momentum. It is also astro-relevant that China began its war against India on this very day, 28 October, and historians speculated that this was timed to occur at the same time as the missile crisis – but then there was a choice New Moon on that day, the astrological significance of which is something the Oriental mind is distinctly aware of.

Feminism

This was also a time of great resurgence of feminism with the appearance of many feminist groups, key figures and seminal works, from the publication of Betty Freidan's *The Feminine Mystique* in 1963 to the founding of the Women's Action Alliance in 1971. Feminism finds new power with every Uranus/Pluto Wave, most notably with the first great feminist manifesto *A Vindication of the Rights of Women* written by Mary Wollstonecraft in 1792 during the Uranus/Pluto Wave of that time.

Uranus/Pluto Mother-Wave 2007–20 So Far

In its early days as I write there are already signs typical of this Wave ...

Waking Up To Power: The Energy Issue 1

The idea that how you think – that thoughts themselves are like a force or energy that directly affects the actual circumstances of one's own and other people's lives – is nothing new. Everything from a traditional esoteric dictum like 'Energy follows thought' to the 'Observer Created Reality' of quantum physics {>236 Astro-Quantum} has asserted this idea. But now – like a testament to its own veracity – it is gaining momentum, and finding itself talked about and acted upon in the everyday world. Again, by its own law, the main instigators of this more widespread awareness – that thoughts are more powerful than was commonly believed – made their play a little before the technical or visible beginnings of this Uranus/Pluto Mother-Wave. These were the hugely, and unexpectedly popular, DVDs/books: *What The Bleep Do We Know* (2005) and *The Secret* (2006). Since then there have been several other publications of similar content, but seeing that it is early days in terms of this Uranus/Pluto Wave, these titles could be seen as (and have been criticized for) being rather naïve and simplistic, and this is explored in the panel on page 10. However, this is only natural when something is in its early stages of mass proliferation. A seedling is a rudimentary thing, but the potential is all there to be realized and developed, which is precisely what will happen as this Mother-Wave swells and does its birthing thing!

Waking Up To Power: The Energy Issue 2

The more common idea of what energy is, in human terms, is simply how energetic you actually feel on a day-to-day basis. It has been pointed out already that all Planet-Waves interact with one another, that they do not exist and influence us all on their own; they work in concert. This is particularly true with the issue of energy because many people have felt distinct drops in their energy, or an erratic supply of it, as a result of the Saturn/Neptune Wave that began in 2004 and ends in 2008. This is covered in the Saturn/Neptune Waves chapter beginning on page 135 and there the point is made that this Saturn/Neptune Wave acts as a prologue to the Uranus/Pluto Mother-Wave as it kind of primes us with the sense that energy has something to do with how we are thinking, and consequently what we are doing. This it does by *taking away energy* if our thoughts are not going in the right direction or if we are trying to go in two incompatible directions at once. This is like a surfer trying to go against the direction of the wave, with the result that he or she winds up exhausted and getting nowhere, or worse. So, Saturn/Neptune and Uranus/Pluto are both serving the same and supremely important end: to show us that our power or energy is dependent upon something both subtle and fundamental, upon *going with the flow and thinking the right thoughts.*

Waking Up To Power: The Energy Issue 3

With respect to fuel and electricity, etc, environment-friendly or renewable forms of energy are being sought, but the most popular versions, solar and wind power, are a long way from delivering the energy needed; indeed, wind power is not that acceptable in terms of visual and aural pollution. This Uranus/Pluto Wave promises to bring some profound innovations on the renewable energy front, but for now it is actually an energy form that is in itself Uranus/Pluto by nature – nuclear energy – because it is generated from Uranium and Plutonium. Britain has just decided to relaunch its nuclear energy programme, and not without resistance and protest from the greens.

Astrologically, the rise and return of nuclear power production during this Wave is an obvious and literal interpretation, and statistically, the fear of it is somewhat unfounded. Casualties caused in the production of energy are a well-known and accepted risk, but compared to those involved in the mining of fossil fuels – our greatest energy source to date – those caused by nuclear energy production are small. However, this is only a statistic based on the mere fifty years of the nuclear industry. As for the problem of disposing of nuclear products, this is something to which a solution is likely to be found as more investment is made into the use of nuclear power as the only pragmatically viable form of energy for the time being.

Another Chernobyl?

The risk of something sudden and enormous – like another Chernobyl, the most serious of all civil nuclear accidents – is not that computable. But astrologically, it is during this Uranus/Pluto Wave that there is a danger of one of these accidents occurring – big time. This is because there simultaneously occurs another type of Planet-Wave that is particularly 'vulnerable' regarding nuclear accidents, Chernobyl itself being such a one. This is the Saturn/Uranus Wave that arises from September 2007 through to July 2012 {⊕ 219 Saturn/Uranus Waves} – and bear in mind that when Saturn is part of a Planet-Wave it is probable that there is a lesson to be learnt, a brick wall run into. The one that was happening, actually just beginning to 'swell', at the time of Chernobyl, was late 1985 through to late 1990 – the actual day of the disaster being 26 April 1986. Interestingly, or ominously, the next Saturn/Uranus Wave after this one, and before this 2007–12 one, was that of 1998 to 2001 which saw Japan's worst nuclear accident on September 30, 1999. The last and only time during the existence of the nuclear industry that we had both a Uranus/Pluto Mother-Wave and a Saturn/Uranus Wave occurring together was back in the 1960s when there were no fewer that four nuclear accidents causing partial meltdowns and serious contaminations.

Nuclear Bomb Threat

Presently both Iran and North Korea are close to having nuclear weapons. As both these countries are, rightly or wrongly, dubbed 'rogue states' by those who already have nuclear capability, it raises the spectre of one or both of them dropping the bomb on some other country. It could be argued that countries that have had nuclear weapons for some time, the so-called superpowers, have grown a certain wisdom concerning the use of them – or rather the wisdom not to use them other than as a deterrent. But even as I write these words, news of US intentions to build missile defence systems near Russia's borders, and Russia threatening to aim its missiles at Europe in response, is already bringing back memories of the Cuban Missile Crisis at the heart of the Cold War, back in those precariously sensitive sixties. These rogue states, or rather their leaders, can be seen as having a 'nothing to lose' mentality or just a psychopathic, megalomaniacal one. However, the astrological point is that first, this combination of Uranus/Pluto Wave with Saturn/Uranus Wave is especially 'nuclear vulnerable' in the same way as it was for those previous nuclear accidents. Secondly, it was during the 1960s that we saw the most sustained and intense protest against nuclear weapons, something which had everything to do with stopping such a thing happening. So there promises to be a strong resurgence of 'Ban the Bomb' demonstrations of one kind or another, with a distinctly edgy 21st-century spin, as well as protests against various other matters that offend the people, all of which are a classic expression of Awakening to Our Power, *and using it positively,* the central quality of this Mother-Wave in a healthy sense.

Predictions of Doom

The very real sense of impending crises is and will be reflected more and more in the media as it focuses on all the things that could go pear-shaped (or mushroom-shaped!) in our world. This fuels a sense of caution, panic or hopelessness. In turn, all this can give rise, on the one hand, to denial that anything is afoot – as demonstrated below under The Mood of This Time – or to an all-pervading tension, the cause of which is hard to pinpoint because there is little awareness of what is actually going on and therefore what the individual can do about it. Government agencies will of course create new laws and guidelines

Astro-Quantum Memo

Being attuned to the energy of any Planet-Wave and endeavouring to surf it right will help to ensure the realization of its positive attributes and the avoidance of its negative ones, even in areas that are not directly connected. For example, riding a Wave well and thereby improving relations with friends, partners, neighbours, etc will automatically contribute to improving relations between one country and another. Everything and everyone is connected – instantaneously. This is reflected in how both astrology and quantum mechanics work. {> 236 Astro-Quantum}

As within so without – as above so below

concerning issues mainly of pollution, energy use, etc, but in the conventional world there will be little guidance as to how to identify, deal with and express what is really happening at a deeper and more meaningful, and essentially spiritual, level.

Such information will come from the spiritual and alternative or relatively fringe areas of socio-cultural activity, genuine astrology itself being one of these, with *Understanding The Future* addressing these issues of 'doom' head-on. Until such positive insights filter through to the general population, there is likely to be an increase in suicides and murders, especially of young people, as this 'doom' is sensed, while at the same time being oppressed by a society that has become dangerously performance- and image-orientated.

The Astro-Quantum solution to the above, that is, how we as ordinary individuals can help prevent such disasters, is to create and maintain a balance in all the ways suggested for all Planet-Waves throughout this period. This is because meltdowns, contaminations, panic and hopelessness are fundamentally and energetically the result of imbalance across the board. This is how critical it is.

✦

The Death and Rebirth of God as the New Super-Paradigm

In the language that is astrology, Pluto is death. This echoes what in science is called the Second Law of Physics – The Law of the Conservation of Energy. This simply states that energy is never born and never dies – it just changes the form it takes. So Pluto is Death is Transformation is Rebirth.

God, in astrological terms, is seen in the symbolism and existence of all heavenly bodies, particularly the Sun, as without it, the Generator of Life, nothing would be here at all. Uranus, however, is God in the sense of the idea that there is a Universal Mind, something which has an overview of all processes going on all the time, and says that there is a kind of *super-logic* to it all. If we can find the right symbols, equations or keys – and develop a pure enough intuition and judgement through using them – we can tap into what is in God's Mind, what is actually happening as distinct from what we subjectively think is happening when influenced, as we so often are, by hopes and fears, and the opinions of others we regard as being more powerful or knowledgeable than we are.

According to their own disciplines, both astrology and science do this – find and use symbols, equations and keys – at least, to the extent to which their practitioners are capable at any given time. Astrology has been succinctly called God's Skywriting, for the Universal Mind displays its state and intent and seasons through the movements of the heavenly bodies {<4 Introduction/ Cosmic Clock}. Presently, some quantum physicists – when they look at the inner reality of matter – see themselves as tapping into the Universal Mind, thereby obliging them to reconsider that the mysterious and infinite entity that we call God existed all along, despite previous scientific discoveries and conclusions to the contrary.

One could say that science started to kill off God with the discoveries and laws of the ironically deeply spiritual Sir Isaac Newton, the father of modern physics. This made reality out to be mechanical and measurable and without any divine presence ordering it. And since the turn of the 20th century, the time of an extremely powerful Uranus/Pluto Mother-Wave (see above), scientific discoveries – along with socio-sexual liberation – have even more effectively created the impression that there is no such thing as a divine or moral force, no such thing as God. The technological advances and social revolutions that were the product of a century that contained two world wars – and the Uranus/Pluto Waves discussed here – appeared to put power and freedom at the disposal of human intention and appetite.

The sixties put the lid on this – or rather took it off for good! Man setting foot on the Moon in 1969 was portrayed in such a way as to give the impression that this heavenly body was just another piece of real estate on which to play golf and plant a flag. Nothing could stop us now, it seemed. And the aforementioned Pill and genetic engineering saw to it that the choice to create life was even more in our own hands. What's more, in most of the Western world during the Swinging Sixties, preventing it also became easier with the legalization of abortion. Add to this medical science's further contributions of the morning-after pill, the ability to detect 'unwanted' babies such as those with Down's Syndrome, and the per-ceived, or illusory, power of freedom (from the hand of Fate) was well in place.

As ever, though, the pendulum swings, and Voltaire's words, slightly para-phrased, 'If God did not exist, it would be necessary to re-invent him' come back to haunt us in the form of religious fundamentalism of various persuasions, taking issue with the 'non-believers' with a 12th century vengeance as we begin the 21st. More healthily, quantum physics and the New Age movement have also rediscovered that there is still something totally powerful and inherently mysterious at the core of existence, and this is explored throughout *Understanding The Future.* In fact, it is the very core of it!

A point that the Uranus/Pluto Wave of 2007–20 is intent on forcefully making though, is that religious fundamentalism and the realization of the true power of human nature born of the reunion of science and metaphysics, are both reaching critical mass. Question is: Which will come out on top?

To this end, and in answer to this question, this Uranus/Pluto Mother-Wave also wants us to make the distinction between Religion and God or, more precisely, between the Church (of whatever religious denomination) and the teacher/avatar/prophet that it purportedly follows and espouses the doctrine of. Such deliberation should then lead us to one realization – that it is all a matter of *interpretation.* And that interpretation is all down to one thing:

Consciousness

Science too will arrive at, and in some respects is already coming to, this conclusion. Whereas before, science's 'super-paradigm' – that is, all-purpose and all-covering model of existence – was based in its concept of matter, space and time, it will now realize and ultimately prove (as science always has to in order to be true to itself) that the very thing that comes up with all concepts, scientific and otherwise, *is* consciousness. The New Super-Paradigm is Consciousness.

And science will find that consciousness has – like matter, space and time – its own laws. A key one – or possibly *the* one – is that there is something divine or supernatural that makes it possible in the first place. We are back to God or Spirit again – and the Devil!

Another of the New Super-Paradigm Laws science will find – but has always been known to any self-respecting mystic or seeker after truth, and by quantum physicists too – is that: **Everything is Interconnected**

Because of this interconnectedness there is an eternal, automatic and immaculate balancing process going on. For example, and back to the present subject, if you get one part of reality/consciousness – in the form of God-denying materialistic human beings believing that they can do whatever they like as long as they can get away with it – then you will get another, in the form of fundamentalist or militant believers, making it plain that you *cannot* get away with it. And of course this eternal, automatic and immaculate balancing process is seen only too clearly in ecology, Mother Nature's very own rule book and balance sheet!

In other words, according to the New Super-Paradigm, everything is just a reflection and manifestation of how balanced we are or are not, and how conscious we are of the necessity of being so, for our very survival. If we knew during past Uranus/Pluto Waves what we know now, how would we have ridden them? Or rather, how shall we ride the one we are on *now*, knowing what we know? In short, our state of consciousness is what determines our entire physical state, both present and future. Just ask yourself 'What is consciousness?' and you'll get the idea.

✦

Surf It or Wipe-Out?

The Uranus/Pluto Mother-Wave Major Storm

So which way are you, are we, going to go?
One path, riding the Wave or acting in the true Spirit of this
Time, will take us into a positive future – the other, giving in to
the Devil of this Time, will take us to a negative future.

The Spirit of This Time

Glad Awakening

Looking at the recent history of Uranus/Pluto Mother-Waves has given us a strong idea and sense of what they are about – the Power of Truth, that there is a *True Power* coursing through humanity, eternity, life on Earth and everywhere. There is a great story being told in which each and every one of us is playing our part, where something free and noble and quintessentially human is being sought after and fought for, and is trying to get free.

The Uranus/Pluto Mother-Wave 2007–20 is, more than ever, an awakening of the power to change our fate and put into effect our true destiny, to find the freedom to do just this, and to jog us into remembering that there is something fine and grand and ancient about being human. Practically, we are urged to put into effect inspiring ideas, feelings and dreams – be they your own or such as are expressed elsewhere – through recognizing the power that our very thoughts have. We can then utilize those thoughts, through visualization techniques, through prayer, and through small but influential words and acts, in both our work and personal lives, in ways that are aligned to making a better world. This means for both you personally and for the world as a whole. In fact, it will be found that we cannot now have the one without the other for this Wave makes it very clear that 'We must learn to live together as brothers or perish together as fools.' (Martin Luther King Jr.)

Having definite images of that 'better world' greatly assists this – like pulling in one rather than many directions. Inspired and guided by the power, love and intelligence that are inherent in the order and beauty of Astro-Quantum, *Understanding The Future* suggests visions and prospects that give you a sense of these images – while at the same time allowing you to interpret and express them in your own unique way. This is very much a part of what this 'Power of Freedom and Thought' zeitgeist is all about. Through envisioning a better world we automatically find new ways of eliminating the evils of the world. This is placing life within our own control. This is the way to surf into a positive new era. Valuable and revolutionary ideas erupt to the surface – especially when we dig down deep to find what saves the day – when our backs are against the wall. This will include waking up to misuse of power, like in politics and energy, and anything that blocks or disserves our attaining what is necessary to make that 'better world', that *healthy* world.

It is this Mother-Wave's intention to transport us to a very different time and place where we as humans discover that honesty truly is the best policy, and that to live and let live, and to do unto others as you would have them do to you, are the only ways *to* live.

Astro-Quantum Memo

· ·

Even the way you think will affect the future!

The Devil of This Time
Rude Awakening

This is the abuse of power, giving into negative influences or simply cynically denying and not tuning into the Spirit of the Time as described above. There could be powers unleashed that are destructive, possibly on a large scale. This would be placing life out of our control, with worst-case scenarios being nuclear war or a natural disaster, especially earthquakes and volcanoes, or anything cataclysmic or destructive that is described in this chapter and others. This would be telling us that we do not understand that each one of us has the power within us that contributes to making the world a better or worse place.

This Mother-Wave has the power to annihilate us, or most of us, if we persist with our old selfish and ignorant, guilty and greedy ways – or with thinking that if someone does not agree with us they therefore must be against us. Most of all it is the failure to realize that you as an individual have the power to influence the whole, in a small or great way – because the whole is made up of millions of individual wills and minds – that will contribute to the Devil of this Time getting its wicked way, or to the Spirit of the time prevailing, as is intended.

' Truly great power does not degenerate into mere force but remains inwardly united with the fundamental principles of right and justice. '

I Ching (Richard Wilhelm translation) hexagram 34

Conflicts, Trends and Possibilities

Spiritual
God and Science

As quantum physics and seekers of a New Super-Paradigm {<41 Death and Rebirth of God} make more and more inroads into understanding what truly comprises our reality and the nature of human consciousness, the sense and awareness that God and Science are not mutually exclusive become more evident and harder to ignore. A figure who embraces and embodies these two major aspects of reality is likely to appear, and will need to be divinely protected if they are not to be snuffed out before they begin to make a difference. Then again, such a 'second coming' is more likely to be that growing group of individuals who are giving expression to the New Super-Paradigm. When it reaches critical mass there will be a quantum leap in collective awareness, and then a shift in what our reality itself is.

Peak Experiences

In the same way that the Uranus/Pluto effect raises the incidence of mental illness and perceptual aberration (see below, Health) people will be more prone to epiphanic episodes, allowing them to directly experience the divine, giving rise to a quantum leap in understanding the nature of Spirit in their lives and in human life generally. In turn, they will be compelled to share such epiphanies which will trigger the same in others – albeit fancifully in some cases.

Socio-Cultural
Emotional Volcano

Society becomes wilder as if some emotional volcano is erupting. Something stirs and awakens way down in the depths. How this manifests has everything to do with the individual and his or her sense of what they feel – and more importantly, with what they believe they are allowed to feel. Angry people, those that simply and crudely take out their frustrations on others, will be more so – as will be the consumption of drugs and alcohol to fuel their rages and dissolve what inhibitions they have. Methods and agencies will (need to) be put in place to deal with this, either with harsher punishments or with treatment programmes that get to the bottom of such behaviour, or both.

At the other end of the social spectrum, those who have trouble expressing harder, perceivably anti-social feelings, are liable to suffer health problems as their bodies try to express the mounting tension and distress they are holding in. Educationally, all this could lead to teaching the rudiments of human psychology as part of secondary or even primary education so that children are aware of the unconscious mind and how it affects their lives. {>60 Awakening the Underworld}.

New Creative Wave

New and more outrageous forms of art, music and fashion abound. Images and sounds that give expression to the 'awakening spirit in monster's clothing' that is the visions, dreams and repressed urges that are in themselves the expression of all that is good, bad, intense and longing for liberation in the human frame. This Wave brings the revolutionary style in music, art and fashion that is the modern equivalent to what was around in the 1960s, the time of the last Uranus/Pluto Mother-Wave.

Trade and Industry

Economic and Environmental Changes

Overspending and borrowing, strikes and disputes, not to mention unplanned-for climate changes affecting crops and transport, all contribute to destabilizing the market. Psychologically, there is a danger of this creating a 'nervousness' with respect to buying and selling stock, thereby making the economic climate mirror the environmental one in more ways than one. However, in as much as the market has always been a reflection of the human condition, this is somewhat unavoidable.

People's hopes and fears are given a cosmic shakedown by this Uranus/Pluto Mother-Wave, meaning that panic-buying and selling could be the very thing that makes a bad situation a disastrous one. Witness the Wall Street Crash of 1929 {<32}. But then again, we are being shown that our materialistic worldview is drastically inadequate when it comes to creating or maintaining real stability. Bill Clinton's soundbite 'It's the economy, stupid' could be given a simple but critical twist. The survival of life on Earth, as painfully distinct from political survival, is about the *ecology*, stupid!

To this end demand for and implementation of measures that protect the 'small business' take existing practices like Fairtrade further still. Giant super-markets and producers co-operate – forcibly or voluntarily – in creating a just and ecologically sound system of trade and manufacture.

Environmental

Sod's Law

The trouble with Uranus/Pluto is that if a balloon is going to go up, or if a straw is going to break the camel's back, it's very likely to do so during one of its Mother-Waves. This, the 2007–20 one, has the added frisson of the dawning of the Aquarian Age and the end to the Mayan Calendar occurring during it {>247}. Added to all this is the purely statistical point that our environment is more under threat than it has been for a very long time, owing to our industrial and scientific age meddling with Nature and her sacred ways. Times when our environment is vulnerable to other, shorter, Planet-Waves must also be considered {⊕ 109 Saturn/Pluto, ⊕ 150 Saturn/Neptune, ⊕ 206 Saturn/Uranus}.

What's To Be Done?

Short of a miracle happening or it all being a false alarm (which it isn't), what can be done to prevent or minimize man-made disasters in the form of pollution and global warming affecting our climate, health and wellbeing to a far greater extent than before? What can be done about natural disasters such as a solar flare or a super-volcano drop-kicking us into a nuclear winter that lasts long enough to pretty well finish us off?

Short of trusting in a false alarm – which is a bit too close to the *denial* talked about a few pages from here – it would seem that a miracle is our best bet! But then 'miracle' is a relative term – it all depends on what you regard as possible. The combined effect of a critical number of human beings focusing their minds upon surfing this and other Planet-Waves in the right way is what will make the miracle happen. This doesn't mean to say that you even have to know about Planet-Waves to do this, to help a miracle occur, but it certainly lowers the odds of one or more happening.

The mean alternative is the one alluded to in the Introduction on page 9 under 'The Spiritual View: A Win-Win Situation': if you die, what happens to you has everything to do with how you have lived and surfed. And it is better to have lived and surfed than never to have surfed at all!

Miracle? What Miracle?

The word 'miracle' is derived from the Latin word for *something to be wondered at* – and so it is also born of wonder and wondering. So we need to wonder at the world of Nature and the world of our Minds, and at the combined effect of us all wondering at the potentials provided by quantum physics, astrology, and a very real faith in the existence of the divine and the human spirit. So in addition to conventional green, conservationist activities, through visualizing or envisioning these saving graces upon our collective horizon, and striving towards their real-ization, then – as if summoned forth from beyond – they will appear on that horizon. The miracles we love and long to believe in, and behold with delight when they appear on the silvery screen, we must believe to be real, and make real. The Uranus/Pluto Mother-Wave is calling us to wake up and wonder at the power of our very existence! {>154 Scientific/Proof of Oneness}.

Health

Electrical Complaints

The effect – upon health and the natural world – of power-lines and radio waves, for example mobile phone masts, reaches critical mass. Symptoms such as fitting and vomiting or subtler, curious disturbances become more and more common as radio waves increase and people are domiciled nearer to power-lines and stations. Generally, there is a proliferation of conditions that are hard to diagnose or give a label to, or ascertain the cause of. It could be said that as the Uranus/Pluto Wave empowers individuality, it also makes physical diseases more idiosyncratic.

Delayed Side Effects

Unexpected side-effects of earlier clinical treatments and methods start to show themselves with alarming frequency: anything from long-term drug reactions to defects in people who were born as the result of artificial fertility methods.

Mental Aberrations

Psychological and mental problems are more prevalent because Uranus/Pluto turns up the volume and intensity of human perception and sensitivity. This is why arriving at a New Super-Paradigm {<41 Death and Rebirth of God} is so important because it will give people a different set of reference points and values to measure and identify their reality with. But while this is being developed, many will find themselves between the devil and the deep blue sea as they experience thoughts and feelings they have no way of identifying or accepting.

Healing Revolution

Great healthcare breakthroughs are made, not only with respect to the likes of the above, but because of them inroads will be made into understanding what actually constitutes health in a holistic sense. Consequently, alternative/complementary disciplines start to dovetail with conventional methods in a far more comprehensive way. Radical surgery is used less and less and it is realized that often it is doing more harm than good. Stem-cell research and application moves ahead in leaps and bounds as it is found that this aspect of medicine is rubbing shoulders with the actual source of life itself, and therefore takes on a more spiritual connotation. There will, however, be commensurate objections and protest concerning all of this, from both medical and religious bodies, as will there be in the case of genetic engineering (see above).

More than anything else, the main advances and changes in the area of health and healing are down to realizing how much the mind can be used to heal the body, and how the body can be used to heal the mind. This is nothing new to alternative or even ancient methods, but the point is that medical science is able to confirm its veracity beyond doubt. As a result there is a revolution in the whole way healthcare bodies and practitioners operate. Again, this will not be without objection and resistance. {⊕ 188 Saturn/Uranus}

Scientific

Energy and Pollution Solutions

Advances and exciting discoveries and inventions can aid our energy and pollution problems {⊕ Saturn/Uranus Waves >187}. Some inventions or discoveries, it is found, have been around for some time, but the political will and the 'economic justification' were not present. Now, a steep case of 'needs must' rules the day. And just like with the gigantic technological efforts that took place during two world wars and the space programme, revolutions in technology will go some way, but not all the way, to heading global disasters off at the pass.

It is a single and extremely radical discovery that will really save the day. In fact, one that will actually create the New Day. This will employ certain natural processes that have always existed, giving rise to what could be called an accelerated form of symbiosis that kind of 'resets' the environment. The difficult bit – which if not accomplished would render it all in vain – will have something to do with using the mind power and willingness of a critical number of human beings. And this will take place, if at all, in the nick of time.

Flicker of Doubt

At the same time, scientists need to be extra careful when they think they are taking a step forward in their honourable and industrious attempts to remedy the ills they themselves have created in the name of making a 'better world' – as do politicians when heartily endorsing them to score votes. This is because the very urgency for devising lower and safer energy could take them one or two steps back. Already it has been found that energy-saving light bulbs – soon to be made compulsory in some countries during this Electric (Uranus)/Power(Pluto) Wave – have the disastrous side effect of triggering fits in epilepsy sufferers.

Egg On Face

Increasingly, technological innovations from the past are found to have serious downsides to public health. An early example of this is the research that reveals non-stick coatings, like Teflon, may prime the immune system to overreact to allergens like dust mites and animal hair. And it is just such damage to the immune system in particular that is found to be behind many rises in known health problems, such as asthma, and the appearance of new ones as well.

Internet Crisis

At the time of writing the World Wide Web is becoming stretched to breaking point, in a technical, commercial and moral sense. Unless a major shift occurs on all three of these levels, the Web is in great danger of becoming unworkable, unreliable, and unacceptably disruptive and corruptive. And it will probably have to get that way before there is a sea-change in its technology and management of its usage, thereby turning it into to something that unites the world like never before, as was always its promise and divine intent.

Political

Visionary Wanted: Only Real Thing Need Apply

The need for an inspirational political leader in the world, or more likely someone who inspires a political leader, is what sums up the state of affairs. The idea that when we need such a figure, he or she will appear, is quite likely to be the reality. This individual will have to be equally Uranian and Plutonian; that is, have both a genius mind and a powerful personality. It is therefore likely that he or she either created something of significance in the sixties, or was a child of that time, during the last Uranus/Pluto Wave, for this is often the case historically.

For example, one such iconic figure was Karl Marx who was born during one Mother-Wave (1818) and whose philosophy emerged in the following one (1845–56) and then really took off with the birth of the Socialist and Communist Parties during the one following that (1896–1907) {<30}. This is not to suggest that Marx got it right exactly, but the fact is that his influence was very powerful and marked the real beginning of how (in theory at least) to bring freedom (Uranus) and power (Pluto) to the masses.

The leader that is needed now has the task of uniting the world and its leaders towards the goal of global/species survival. For this reason he or she will have to be a deeply spiritual being. A second coming? (See Spiritual section above.)

The Mood of This Time

There is something in the air, for sure. Like anything could happen – from dangerous to miraculous! Doing something decisive or saying something insightful goes further than at other times, is more influential, reverberates more dramatically – be it on a personal or global level. At the same time, everything is exaggerated, so being outspoken or outlandish could get you more than you bargained for. Everyone, but especially those actually in any kind of power, is able to make differences and affect changes, for good or ill, more so than at times when there was no Uranus/Pluto Wave energy abounding.

A radically new horizon is felt to be beckoning – and it is. What appears on that horizon is down to all of us.. Is it a mushroom cloud or a revolutionary advance in the way we see and live our lives? Beneath all of this there is a mounting feeling that humanity and the world are in crisis. The issues described in the Introduction all point towards this, and towards what forms this sense of looming crisis is taking. If you've skipped the Introduction, then I strongly suggest you go back and read it, because it will also explain Planet-Waves generally, acting as a basic primer in how to ride them.

Denial

This is one of the most dangerous moods of this time and is born, ironically, of a quite natural fear of not surviving that mutates into various forms of denial that actually serve to make non-survival a probability, or at least a stronger possibility. This is a classic case of the power of thought – something which this Wave is all about waking us up to – but of the negative variety. A common form of denial is seen in the response to global warming, heavily fed by the confusion over what causes it or whether such a thing exists at all.

The two 'hottest' causes for global warming are: 1) the greenhouse effect caused by carbon emissions resulting from the burning of fossil fuels; and

2) solar flares that affect our clouds and climate regularly and quite dramatically at times. But it is misguided to believe that there is nothing to worry about with respect to such events as icebergs the size of Wales breaking off the Greenland ice sheet, purely because it is something that has 'happened before' and is just part of Earth cycles and evolution. Both of these causes are probably behind global warming, and some others to boot. Whatever the case, the fact remains that something is going on that is seriously affecting our lives.

The Wake-Up Call

From the Astro-Quantum viewpoint, everything is interconnected – and this means that we human beings do have something to do with the cause of global warming and any other condition or activity that is creating or threatening the fine ecological balance that supports life on planet Earth. To meet this with an attitude of 'Well, it's all happened before' is to miss the point. This *hasn't* happened before because this time and this Wave are about waking us up to the fact that as stewards of this planet we must now give actuality to the fact that everything is interconnected and a very important part of that interconnected-ness is US!

We could be seen as the crucial link in the chain of life – but the question is: are we the strongest or the weakest link? So this is the wake-up call to end all wake-up calls – possibly quite literally. In other words ... **we have got as far as we can get being in a state of denial about our part in the drama called Life on Earth**.

Along with other Planet-Waves occurring at the same time we are being forced or shown – depending on how dumb or bright we are – that we are co-creators and expressions of Life. {>236 Astro-Quantum}

Increase in Mental Illness

By burying our heads too deeply in the sand we could find our heads sticking out the other side of the Earth, or just suffocating. Such ostrich behaviour could be selected from an array of a million and one distractions or displacements, such as being obsessed with the size and shape of one's body rather than the state of the planetary body we live on, or rather than realizing that one's feelings about one's body are an expression of one's life and the way one lives it. Another choice could be doing some 'retail therapy' where one goes out to indulge oneself in the illusory sense that one is a functioning part of a dysfunctional world.

This means that this all too common mood of the time will also reach crisis point, with people losing all sense of what is going on and where they are as they drown in self-pity or self-induced ignorance; as they succumb to the ways of the dumbed down and overly materialistic world we have made or have allowed others to make for us. All this, along with other stresses of unnatural living, means that insanity could be on the increase. Remember, this is because the feeling of approaching crisis is *the* mood of this time – for the simple reason that we *are* reaching crisis point. As ever, the choice is ours ... be aware or be mad. Get your head round it or go round the bend. Be part of the solution or be part of the problem.

Denial, you could say, is an understandable reaction to such monumental crisis – that is, if there was nothing to be done about it or nothing to be learnt from it. However, there is something we can do and learn – but we need to take a radically different view of what we as humans actually are, or are in the process of becoming. This Uranus/Pluto Wave is especially effective in waking us up to just this, assisted by all the other Planet-Waves that are occurring throughout its time. These other, lesser Planet-Waves are far more potent than they are when they occur on their own. Rather than being just big waves, they are like big waves on top of a tsunami.

Panic

This is the other side of denial and involves two main responses to the Uranus/Pluto Wave. The first is just plain exaggeration of the threats to our welfare and survival by the very people who are warning us against them. But this is somewhat justified. For instance, many of the more serious effects of global warming, like the reduction of existing landmasses to mere archipelagos, could take hundreds of years – but we have to be shocked into stopping what causes it NOW! The trouble is, then, seeing that it isn't about to happen overnight, or at least within our lifetime, and jumping into the comfort of the denial zone described above. Then again – and this is a highly significant theme throughout *Understanding The Future* and in this Uranus/Pluto Wave chapter in particular – **everything potentially apocalyptic is going to happen a lot faster than has been mooted so far**.

As it happens, at the time of writing, there have been reports from scientists working in Antarctica that this faster rate is very much the case regarding global warming. As to how we actually affect the climate and weather, this is the province of Saturn/Neptune Waves which are explained and explored in that chapter beginning on page 135.

Future Shock

The second response to the Uranus/Pluto Wave that can create panic is, again ironically, the burgeoning of the very human faculty that is able to sense the future, particularly when it is life-threatening. For example, did you know that there are always fewer people on trains and planes that crash than on those that do not? In the case of the hijacked planes on 9/11, all four were carrying only half the number of passengers they usually do. As the intensity of what the Uranus/Pluto Wave is bringing mounts, then so too will more and more people be picking this up – with shows, on the negative side, of anxiety, foreboding and physical sickness (particularly stomach and gut upsets) as expressions of this, and on the positive side, of genuine and valuable insight and foresight.

Whether such presentiments of disaster can help us to avoid it or not depends on how conscious and constructive we are in responding to them, be it in ourselves or to others. In planetary symbolism this is simply stated as the Power (Pluto) to Predict (Uranus), something which Einstein himself always maintained was real, observing that the distinction between past, present and future was 'a stubbornly persistent illusion'. Or as the White Queen put it in Lewis Carroll's *Through The Looking Glass:* 'It's a poor sort of memory that only works backwards.'

However, it should be borne in mind that such presentiments are and will be purely emotional and on a gut level, rather than being a specific 'prediction' in the popular sense of the term. Again, to demonstrate what will become increasingly frequent, many people did not show up for work at the Twin Towers on 9/11, not because they knew what was going to happen – they just didn't feel like going, something deterred them. So this particular Mood of this Time could be presenting many with gut feelings that they would do well to obey, and share with others.

Power of Change

When all is said and done, it is the fact that this time is about the Power (Pluto) of Change (Uranus) that so strongly affects the Mood of this Time. Put simply, if you embrace and see the need for change at a quite fundamental, even life-changing level, then you will be set to ride this Mother-Wave right! You will feel the bigger story that is unfolding, the great adjustments that are necessary, and the various stages we have to go through in order to get through. If, however, you choose to entrench yourself and resist any kind of change at all, then expect to feel disquieted, anxious, even embattled.

Metaphorically, on the one hand it is like letting your senses take control as you surf a Wave, and surprising yourself and others with your powers of innovation and improvisation as you steer where and how the Wave wants to take you. On the other hand, it would be like insisting on taking control of a wild mustang that senses second by second where it must go in order to thrive and survive. You would have a very hard ride and probably fall off – or at least feel like that is what is going to happen any moment; paranoia in fact. In a phrase, *constructive or destructive uprooting* is the choice that makes the difference to the Mood you experience.

Remember that the scent of revolution is in the air. It will be unnerving and frightening at times, but focusing upon the objectives, and the 'Awareness of the Waves' in the ways that are described in these pages, will carry you and yours through to a very different time, and even place.

Astro-Quantum Memo

It is in our power, individually as well as collectively, to turn the Armageddon machine around. It mainly depends on waking up to this and following Planetary Lore and other mind-power methods to manifest positive change.

We do have the power to change,
but we must change to have the power

Powerful Coincidences

Something that will be fascinating, alarming, or sadly ignored, is an increased awareness of synchronicity – that is, meaningful coincidences occurring more often than usual. Such events can be regarded as:

> a) 'just coincidences' and paid no heed at all; as
>
> b) something very exciting and of exaggerated significance that floods one's normal sense of reality to the point of bothering yourself or boring others with it; or
>
> c) responded to as simply an 'agreement' that you are on the right track, or that something is trying to tell you something.

These last two ways of interpreting these coincidences are the right ones, but with b) they should be taken with a pinch of salt if you find yourself or others get spooked by them. Be matter of fact about them, then you won't jump to wrong or crazy conclusions. The frequency and intensity of these powerful coincidences will increase during Hotspots (see page 294).

✦

Awakening the Underworld

From Innuendo to In Your Face

The Underworld, of which Pluto is the Lord, is anything that lies beneath the surface of life or the everyday world. From this zone issue forth all those things that are regarded as dark and dirty, deep and intriguing, horrific and unmentionable, compelling and profound, occult and shamanic, sexy and beastly, cruel and criminal, creepy and crawly, gothic and ghastly. But it is also the very bowels of the Earth, and the putrefying, corpse-consuming, cosmic compost heap that causes Pluto, volcano-like, to grumble ...

> My realm wherein all rots and dies
> The beauty above ground belies.
> The blooms I feed, your world to grace
> But you dare not behold My face
> And lose yourselves in vain pretence.

But when the Great Awakener Uranus logs on to Pluto's site we really are forced to wake up and have a good look at his 'face' – at what we and life are like deep down – for a veritable volcano of Underworld contents spews all over our little day-to-day world of troubles, trivia, gossip, soaps and inconsequentialities.

This phenomenon was brilliantly dramatized in that most feted of books and films, JRR Tolkien's *The Lord of the Rings*. Its popularity, along with some lesser specimens of the sword and sorcery genre, is in some part down to the fact that it plays out what is going on all the time, but relatively out of sight (as is Pluto's usual style). And like many great works, *The Lord of the Rings* has a darkly prophetic quality about it, and a seam of profound and scary truth running through it.

So we have Hobbits living in the Shire – that is, little people living their little lives in relative peace in a rural idyll, complete with a good selection of creature comforts and cosy sentiments. Then from afar, something dark and threatening to that way of life looms in the form of the Dark Lord, his Dark Riders, and those hordes of malformed lowlifes, the Orcs – all classic negative Plutonian figures.

Successfully countering all this mayhem is the wizard Gandalf and his band of heroes comprised of individual members of the various races that exist in their world. This appeals to us because it has meaning. But that meaning is not always consciously grasped because, like the Hobbits, there is an unwillingness – at least, initially – to accept that there are dark and destructive forces abroad, and in turn a reluctance to accept the call to play a part in getting to the heart of them and thereby overthrowing them.

And now, as the Uranus/Pluto Mother-Wave of 2007–20 surges, we must accept that there are 'dark forces' abroad, identify them more closely, and do what must be done to make something positive out of the situation – which means to accept and understand what the 'dark' is all about. Mainly, this includes looking at our own shadows. Gandalf is the *shaman*, the one who knows the ways of dark forces and how to resist them, and how to turn them to his advantage. What critically equips him for this is an acute awareness of his own darkness; he was called Gandalf the Grey initially, evolving by the end to Gandalf the White.

Interestingly, it has been said that *The Lord of the Rings* was an allegory of the rise of Hitler and Nazism and the allies' resistance to, and ultimate victory over them – something which began during the Uranus/Pluto Wave of 1928–37. Tolkien himself denied this, but that does not discount the idea. Indeed, when a writer becomes too intent on making a point through allegory, his story winds up being self-conscious and contrived, which this book certainly is not. And whatever allegory was put there unconsciously, is all the more powerful.

In any event, and again interestingly from our Planet-Wave perspective, *The Lord of the Rings* did not actually take off and become a worldwide success until during the next Uranus/Pluto Wave of 1960–72, when the hippie culture made it its own. The allegory then became one of peace-loving folk versus the dark, straight and oppressive state.

So What is the Dark, and What Comes Out of it?

A deeply significant thing that comes out of the Dark, the Underworld, is reminiscent of what the philosopher Nietzsche called *will-to-power*. Nietzsche himself intended this to mean a potential of Nature that exists in *everything* to be what it fundamentally is to the max, and to not let anything inhibit or overrule it. And to indulge in it, celebrate it, create from it. So here we have a sense of depth, destiny and doom stoked up, often wrapped up in hedonism, and churned to the surface for all to see and experience. Although the urge to dominate is not what is meant by will-to-power – it being a perverted form of it – this is something which unfortunately also belches forth.

Let us examine then some of the expressions and forms that this Uranus/Pluto Mother-Wave will take, and is already taking, as the Dark is dealt out and delved into.

First, though, we have to remember that much Dark has already been let out of the bag during the 20th century – especially during the sixties – mostly because so many taboos have been broken; not least by the media showing the dead and the dying as a matter of course. Before the 1960s it was usually regarded as bad taste to do this. Likewise, raw sex and nudity now mostly bypass censorship; and hardcore pornography is accessible to anyone at the click of a mouse. Once such dark and very real things were only glimpsed at, or implied by innuendo. Now they are shoved right in our faces because it really is time we had a good look at them.

It would seem that true will-to-power, the urge to delve into and experience the extremes of what we really are, is now unavoidably linked to the degenerate, psychopathic and despotic. In *Lord of the Rings* language, there are no elves without orcs, no savers of the day without those that threaten to dominate and enslave. Uranus/Pluto can empower freedom or destroy it; cause us to dramatically rise or drastically fall. Everything depends on us recognizing and expressing power in a good way, or allowing it to be used in a bad way.

There is horror in the world because powerful feelings have been denied and allowed to fester, so that when they do erupt to the surface we are shocked and appalled, even though we have been dangerously desensitized by media exposure. Today as I write, I hear of a man who stabbed his partner 145 times. What kind of human volcano is that? And this is just an individual; think of what is bubbling under globally. But then, as this book is constantly at pains to point out, what goes on globally has everything to do with how each one of us is thinking, feeling and behaving – and with what goes on in this basement of our being. The threat of worldwide disaster – through nuclear war, disease, climate change, or whatever – is simply the collective volcano, and this may simply express itself as an actual volcano!

To turn our attention to the Underworld *now* and see and deal with what goes on down there will buy us a stay of execution, giving us the time and insight that would enable us to prevent the bowels of the Earth, the sump of all our unlooked-at shit and shadows, from bursting all over the place.

Another example of the Dark rising is paedophilia. There have always been child molesters, or smell-smocks as country people used to call them hundreds of years ago, but mostly the lid was either kept on their desires by a quaint thing called moral restraint, or it was covered up – particularly in areas where it was least expected to be, like the Church (ironically the source of such restraint). Now we have internet child-porn – again just a click away. Ease of access and little or no inhibiting factor equals an explosion. But here's the point: many paedophiles have also been victims of child abuse, and probably their abusers were abused too, ad nauseam. The vents of this particular type of human volcano run very deep, and it, like many other types, is fit to burst during this Wave. The need to purge and the need to forgive are two pleas that Uranus/Pluto flips to the surface, in that order.

And lest it be overlooked, some of the darkest shadows of all are the ones that are projected – especially because they can go undetected. It is all too easy to scorn and despise the degenerates of this world because they provide a convenient screen upon which to project and disown our own, albeit far lesser, dark and dubious feelings. As Hermann Hesse wrote in *Demian*:

> ❛ *If you hate a person, you hate something in him that is part of yourself. What isn't part of ourselves doesn't disturb us.* ❜

Yet another example is the predicament of computer video games obsessing and distorting the development of children. Exposing and subjecting young minds to the compelling nature of the dark images of the Underworld – quite literally with sinister products like *Grand Theft Auto* – is like putting a child behind the wheel of a very powerful car when they have no idea how to drive or of the true dangers of the area they have been lured into exploring. In fact, this is a valid metaphor for what such irresponsible or just plain ignorant exposure to the Underworld has done to all of us.

Most basically, this Uranus/Pluto Wave is again trying to wake us up to the very existence of the subconscious mind, for that is what the Underworld simply is in modern terminology. The actual 'discovery' and naming of the subconscious was, after all, made by Sigmund Freud during the Uranus/Pluto Wave of 1896–1907 {<30}. But generally people are still ignorant of it in a practical sense – they are not aware that they have a subconscious and that there are things lying down there they ought to know about before they leap out and do something desperate and destructive from which there is no going back! The point is that while this Uranus/Pluto Wave is rolling this is liable to happen with greater frequency and intensity. As far as the unconscious mind is concerned, either you go down there and take a good look, or it'll come up and get you.

Identifying, resisting and eradicating what is corrupting our world is the most important task. But like with our band of heroes in *The Lord of the Rings*, some of us will be sorely tempted to succumb to these powers in the form of fixations, addictions and lusts – mistakenly rationalizing them away as being harmless or consistent with human rights. This will bring us, on a personal level, to become undone, and on a public one, to be too soft on the peddlers and perpetrators of that corruption. Knowing when and how much to forgive or condemn is a real challenge of this Uranus/Pluto Wave. At one extreme, there is the danger of the 'moral backlash' of knee-jerk, black and white, pseudo-religious repression snowballing into a latter day witch-hunt. At the other extreme, there is a mindless and destructive indulgence posing as freedom, accelerating and intensifying the downward spiral that has already begun, progressively set in motion through previous ineptly surfed Uranus/Pluto Waves. Again we have to ask ourselves: knowing what we now know about past Uranus/Pluto Waves, how shall we ride this one?

As ever, the middle way is the one to aim for. Uranus/Pluto want us to discover and experience our will-to-power, to experiment and discover what we truly feel and want – often through crisis and being cruel to be kind – as opposed to what we have been led to believe we should feel and want. Most of all, though, in pursuing this truth of who and what we really are, we must let others do so too, without harming or judging. Pluto must have its due of will-to-power, but Uranus must exact its due of equal rights. This is the ultimate balancing act as we ride this Mother-Wave; a balancing act that in the end involves a personal journey into your own darkness, wherein lies your own truth.

> Delve in My moist and shady den
> And you will find true wealth within.
> Feel your darkness, feel your pain
> Fall to Me and rise again
> Immortals steeped in innocence.

✦

The Choice is Ours
Easy Surfing

The following chart shows us Positive Responses to the Uranus/Pluto Mother-Wave that collectively create Positive Effects. The Negative Responses need to be avoided in order to prevent the collective Negative Effects. Note the opposing qualities of the Negatives and Positives, and track back Negative or Positive Effects to the Responses that created them.

Astro-Quantum Memo

If you want to clean up the world,
clean up your own backyard

2007–20
The Collective Effect of The Uranus/Pluto Mother-Wave
The Choice is Ours

Negative Response	Positive Response
Refusal or failure to realize how significant and powerful a thing the group mind is. Leaving all decisions, objectives and values to the discretion of those supposedly in power.	Realization of people power, of how enough individuals acting, even thinking, in a deliberate, concerted and focused way can affect positive change globally.
Becoming increasingly tense and frustrated in direct proportion to refusing, or being denied the opportunity to change, experiment or discover ourselves.	Feeling that there is more to life than just the daily grind – and the escapism that compensates for it. Trying out new things, seeking self-knowledge.
Cynical indulgence, profligacy and weakness posing as being 'realistic' or 'pragmatic'. 'Fiddling while Rome burns' attitude.	Taking pride in our stewardship of the planet with respect to environment and energy issues. Realizing that taking care is a good idea.
Mindless and violent rebellion where patience and skill in negotiation have failed or been missing.	Demanding from those in power recognition of ideas and feelings and need for freedom.

SUPER MIND-POWER

Conflict between the people and those in power. Civil disorder. Negativity and nihilism running riot.	Official recognition of depth and originality of human potential; programmes installed to help realize it.
Failing to see the point in not trashing others' backyards simply means that your own backyard, and more, gets trashed.	Installation of green regimes and leaders. Bringing down or voting out anything or anyone whose priority is not the health of the planet.
Increase in crime and vandalism – and in drug and alcohol abuse in aid of escape or oblivion. More destruction than creativity producing strife worldwide.	Human creative potential being tapped and expressed, making for richer and more rewarding lifestyles and occupations. Solutions to world problems.
Matters going from bad to worse as a result of a collective negative outlook and the wrong people being in power. Major disasters occurring as an indirect expression of this.	People working in unison to aid the common good, in great and small ways. And so the global state improves, or at least shows signs of being brought around.
Negative Effect	**Positive Effect**

The Unfolding Story

⇉ Merging Waves and ⚡ Jupiter Boosters

This Mother-Wave acts like a powerful electromagnetic backdrop to all other lesser, but still very influential, Planet-Waves that merge with it over the course of its duration from 2007 to 2020, electrifying and intensifying their effects. In return, these have their own effects upon the Mother-Wave, and so they reverberate back and forth. The descriptions of these other Waves in the following chapters always take into account the effect of the Mother-Wave.

As well as these Merging Waves there are Planet-Waves involving Jupiter that come into the Uranus/Pluto picture, and Jupiter kind of boosts whatever is happening, blowing things up so we cannot fail to notice the problems or take advantage of opportunities! As can be seen on the Planet-Wave Weather Chart on page 19, Jupiter Waves exist in their own right, and are responsible for Minor Storms and Favourable Breezes, but are not covered here for reasons of time and space. Along with the Merging Waves they can increase or modify the effects of the Uranus/Pluto Mother-Wave.

The Planet-Wave Chronicles

Taken altogether, these Merging Waves and Jupiter Boosters kind of dramatize and pace the overall course of the Mother-Wave, rather like a storyteller would do, unfolding its story, and punctuated with Hotspots {>294}.

Here are the Jupiter Boosters that directly affect the Uranus/Pluto Mother-Wave:

✈ **Jupiter/Uranus Minor Storm – Dec 2006 to Nov 2007–**
Awakening Faith

✈ **Jupiter/Pluto Minor Storm – Jan 2007 to Sep 2008 –**
The Power of Belief

These Boosters kick-started the Mother-Wave, especially in areas to do
with morality over issues such as sex, religion, politics and the law.
People begin to feel more responsible or outraged about the state of
affairs. As these Boosters gather weight, we begin to see the writing on
the wall regarding global warming, primarily, and with respect to
indulgent and wasteful practises – especially as their effects become
more noticeable and faster than expected. There emerges a very real
emotional sense of us all being in the same boat and that we sink or
swim together. For example, people begin to actually take pride in their
recycling duties and skills.

✈ **Jupiter/Uranus Minor Storm – Mar 2010 to Apr 2011–**
Awakening Faith 2

✈ **Jupiter/Pluto Minor Storm – May 2010 to Apr 2011 –**
The Power of Belief 2

These Boosters are reiterating the last couple above. So it's a case of
matters appearing to improve as our resolve to do something radical
about the situation starts to have an observable effect, and we realize
that every little bit from every individual does make a difference. A
burgeoning faith in People Power, in fact. On the other hand, a failure to
sit up, take notice and act upon the last Boosters means an unexpected
and sudden worsening of the possible negative effects of the
Uranus/Pluto Mother-Wave. More trouble requires more faith and more
effort to bring it around. But it might be getting too late.

✈ **Jupiter/Pluto Favourable Breeze – May 2011 to May 2012–**
Regeneration

If we have responded positively to the last two Boosters, then this one
finds us going up a gear with respect to improving matters. This

particularly applies to physical and material regeneration. Here is a great opportunity to assist Mother Earth in her restoration. In fact, it is the very real sense of communion with her that makes such regeneration possible. But we are not out of the woods yet by any means. Making the most of this one is not some sort of bonus – it is absolutely essential!

✶ **Jupiter/Pluto Minor Storm – Jun 2013 to Jul 2014 –**
The Power of Belief 3

✶ **Jupiter/Uranus Minor Storm – Jul 2013 to Jun 2014 –**
Awakening Faith 3

These Boosters occur at the peak of the Uranus/Pluto Mother-Wave. So this time shows us the 'reckoning' in that it is plain that either we have missed our opportunity to turn matters around, or that we now have a fighting chance. Either the fire and/or water has got beyond our control, or a passionate resolution and persistence is firmly enough in place to make a difference.

✶ **Jupiter/Uranus Favourable Breeze – Aug 2014 to Aug 2015 –**
Getting Lucky

This could be the start of a beautiful recovery, a glorious ride on the Mother-Wave! Leaders of industry, countries and faiths work together towards a common goal with passion and enthusiasm. But this is only if we have already got to grips with the process and programme of recovery. Otherwise it would be a case of nothing being enough after too little and too late.

✶ **Jupiter/Pluto Favourable Breeze – Aug 2015 to Aug 2016 –**
Regeneration 2

All being well, we go from strength to strength now. Aid programmes and service agencies really get into their stride, regenerating the common welfare, guided by a fine sense of priorities. Again, however, only a miracle could deliver us if we have delayed a total reorganization of the way we live and manage life on Earth. Mind you, if a miracle is going to happen, this is one of the times that it could do so!

✗ **Jupiter/Pluto Minor Storm – Oct 2016 to Sep 2017 –**
The Power of Belief 4

✗ **Jupiter/Uranus Minor Storm – Oct 2016 to Jan 2018 –**
Awakening Faith 4

By now, our actions so far will be having a serious effect on the way things will turn out. Positively – that is, if we have managed to turn the tide, so to speak, or quench the flames – we find renewed resolve because there are setbacks as unforeseen forces or unconsidered elements come into play. We can find a way to deal with these contingencies. Negatively – matters go from horribly bad to even worse!

✗ **Jupiter/Uranus Favourable Breeze – Nov 2019 to Jan 2020 –**
Getting Lucky 2

This is such a short Booster that it takes a really sharp sense of opportunity and intuitive timing for it to make any difference. But it could provide the proverbial 'stitch in time'.

✗ **Jupiter/Pluto Minor Storm – Jan 2020 to Jan 2021 –**
The Power of Belief 5

This Booster signs off from the Uranus/Pluto Mother-Wave and hops on to the Saturn/Pluto Wave that began in 2018. This means that, on the one hand, a very new time is embarked upon with a strong sense of world order – which simply incorporates a practical vision of what truly constitutes such a thing. On the other hand, there is a form of order, a regime, that is horribly limiting and repressive, or a global state that is more of an end than a beginning.

Personal Effect

This is how, as an individual, the Uranus/Pluto Mother-Wave can affect you, and be ridden successfully by you, for its duration, particularly around the times when it is peaking between 2011 and 2016.

Surfing with Uranus and Pluto Through the Houses

These effects are based upon the two Houses in your chart through which Uranus and Pluto are passing or 'transiting' at any time while the Mother-Wave is active. As it is a case of a need for Change and Innovation where Uranus is concerned, and for Empowerment, Elimination and Transformation where Pluto is concerned, knowing these positions will help you to manage the energies of each respective planet in an appropriate way, enabling you to find the right balance and surf successfully!

There are two ways to use this aid:

1 **Off-The-Peg** This is using the Uranus and Pluto positions according to what is known as your Birth Sign, Sun Sign or Star Sign. This looks at what Solar Houses Uranus and Pluto are transiting through while the Uranus/Pluto Mother-Wave is active. So using the **Planet House Transit Guide** (beginning on page 254), first go to the **Uranus: House Ready-Reckoner** on page 270. Next, look at the left-hand column for the time Period you are interested in, then look along the row until you get to

the column of your Birth Sign. There you will see the number of the House being transited by Uranus – 1st, 2nd, 3rd, etc – and just below it the number of the page where you can read the description of possible situations and actions you can take. Straight after this, do the same thing for Pluto – that is, go to **Pluto: House Ready-Reckoner** and use that table in the same way that you used the Uranus one. Now you can get a feel for how the two planet positions compare. All this can be very useful and accurate, but remember that it is only based on your Sun Sign.

2 **Made-To-Measure** This is using the Uranus and Pluto positions according to your individual birth chart which would have to be calculated correctly from a reliably accurate birth time. So if you do know your birth time and have your birth chart accurately drawn up, then anyone with a basic knowledge of planetary positions will be able to tell you which Houses in your personal chart are occupied by Uranus and Pluto at any given time between 2007 and 2020. Then simply find and consult the readings for those Houses in the **Planet House Transit Guide** (page 254). For example, if your astrologer or your own astrological calculation told you that Uranus was transiting your Twelfth House and Pluto was transiting your Ninth House, then you would find these interpretations on the pages indicated in the Planet House Transit Guide by using the **Index** on the first page of it. So for our example the Index would send you to page 276 for Uranus transiting the Twelfth House, and to page 291 for Pluto transiting the Ninth House.

Note: you do *not* use the Ready-Reckoner when using Made-To-Measure.

The Uranus/Pluto Mother-Wave Effect Upon Relationships

Closer Together or Further Apart and Nothing Much in Between

There is likely to be an increase in crises in relationships, especially close ones. This is because the influence of Uranus is that of freedom, which causes you to want more space to do your own thing, while Pluto's weight is towards bringing us closer, creating greater depth and intimacy. So the two planetary energies seem to work against one another. But their combined process can be seen to be this: through giving each other more space, or by detaching from emotional issues long enough to get a really good look at them, then a new and deeper intimacy is found. Of course, such detached emotional observation – or not being able to accomplish just that – can also have the opposite result of finding that the two of you are just not compatible or mature enough to forge a closer bond. This may turn out to be the very reason that one or both of you resists finding a closer intimacy – because you suspect that through looking at issues more intently, you might find out why this is not possible.

So there is either a parting or a closer union, or a parting followed by a reunion. But with the unpredictability of Uranus and the unfathomability of Pluto it is hard to say which will happen until you have been through the process. Remember that, after all, this Mother-Wave is all about Awakening Depths and Empowering Freedom – on both collective and personal levels. And the 'Will-to-Power' aspect of Uranus/Pluto (»60 Awakening to the Underworld) means that a more meaningful and intense sense of relatedness is what is required, born of a stronger awareness of your own individual needs and desires. But if one or both of you is not willing to commit and immerse him- or herself in this way, then that could mean an end to the relationship. The Uranus/Pluto Mother-Wave has no middle ground; it's a case of deeper and freer or nothing at all, or a relationship in name only.

On your own? All of the above would apply to you if you had no close relationship to speak of. That is, if you want an intimate relationship, Uranus and Pluto will cause one to materialize more readily than at other times, but they'll demand that you step outside of your comfort zone and be prepared to plunge into the unknown, while at the same time being open and honest enough to admit that you might well have some catching up to do in the emotional maturation department.

The Choice is Yours
Easy Surfing

The chart on the next page shows us Positive Responses to the Uranus/Pluto Mother-Wave that create Positive Effects for you personally and ultimately for everyone. The Negative Responses need to be avoided in order to prevent the Negative Effects in your own life. Note the opposing qualities of the Negatives and Positives, and track back Negative or Positive Effects to the Responses that created them.

2007–20
The Personal Effect of The Uranus/Pluto Mother-Wave
The Choice is Yours

Negative Response	Positive Response
Denying or hiding from what, deep down, is true about you and your life, even when the evidence is staring you in the face. Outing or mocking others' dark sides instead.	Realization that the more you discover and reveal of the truth about who and what you are, the more personal power and influence you find you possess and experience.
Seeing life as an impossibly difficult and meaningless passage from birth to death. Being just out for yourself as a miserable consequence of this.	Seeing life as a river that flows powerfully and inevitably from source to source; swimming underwater sometimes. Knowing your special place in creation.
Feelings of self-righteousness or elitism disguise themselves as feelings of being unloved or misunderstood.	Appreciating how most people are just like you deep down, despite – or rather because of – feeling desperately alone at times.
Stubbornly resisting the need for change. Denial of anything that is not yet known or scientifically provable.	Sensing change and acting upon it. Reassured that as one door closes another one opens.

THE POWER OF TRUTH

Negative Response	Positive Response
Depression and being stuck with someone or something. 'An atheist is a man with no visible means of support.'	Unexpectedly positive life transformations happen as if by magic. All's well that ends well.
Lost in a dark well of self-pity and impotence. Only thoughts of revenge for company, which if served would leave you even colder.	Finding friends you never thought you'd have or had. Loyal support between kindred spirits, and its mutual furtherance.
Difficult becomes impossible; meaningless becomes empty and dead. The more you pursue material gain and reasons for being, the emptier you feel.	The satisfaction of feeling and being on course with your own destiny. Mutually advantageous encounters occur, in flow with the current of your life.
Those who do not want to know the truth fail to recognize it. Feeling alienated and isolated as you hide from it; hounded and paranoid as you run from it.	Attracting powerful and successful people and situations. Satisfaction in areas relating to intimate relationships, money and health. Greater clarity and motivation.

Negative Effect	Positive Effect

The Uranus/Pluto Balance of Power

The following pages provide two wonderfully basic ways to ride the Uranus/Pluto Mother-Wave. For a simple way to surf this Planet-Wave, and ride it to where it wants to get to – as shown in 'The Spirit of this Time' – and at the same time bypass 'The Devil of this Time', use the Uranus/Pluto Balance of Power chart on the next two pages.

On the first page, you will see in the left-hand column various symptoms that you could be experiencing if you are leaning too much in the Uranus direction; that is, over-emphasizing ideas, theories, principles, liberties, etc. The right-hand column then suggests various ways of redressing the balance with Plutonian remedies, which mainly involve getting in touch with your most genuine, intimate and down-to-earth feelings.

On the second page the left-hand column lists symptoms resulting from overdoing Pluto – with obsessions, dark thoughts, etc – and the right-hand column suggests Uranian remedies that encourage ways of taking a step back, chilling out, or seeing things from a higher, more open or esoteric, perspective.

As a rule, each numbered item is balanced by the equivalent numbered item in the right column, but not always – there are crossovers.

The second basic way to ride the Uranus/Pluto Mother-Wave is the meditation on page 80

The Uranus/Pluto Balance of Power 1

Too Much Uranus and not Enough Pluto

If this is the case, you could be experiencing some of these symptoms.

1. Getting out of touch with everyday physical and emotional needs and values – manifesting as health and/or relationship problems – as a result of trying to live up to some impossible ideal or something that looks good in theory.

2. Losing sight of what is practical or in tune with human nature due to being too politically correct.

3. Others turning off in your presence, feeling that you are not being appreciated, or that you no longer know how you genuinely feel – only how you think you ought to feel – all as a result of being too 'esoterically correct' and trying to follow too closely some spiritual or psychological doctrine.

4. Chaos and confusion – expressed for example in feelings such as jealousy and alienation – as a consequence of sexual or social experimentation or foolishness.

5. Being too open and finding yourself compromised, or exposing others' private truths with similar results.

6. The Rights Blight. Confusing lack of self-control for freedom, and mistaking plain difference for inequality. This just leads to personal turmoil and civil disorder.

Plutonian Remedies

Adopt one or more of these remedies to offset and relieve the symptoms of 'too much Uranus'.

1. Be emotionally honest with yourself and focus upon what it is you actually feel and desire, in spite of what you think is right or wrong, and communicate or express this.

2. Consult someone of good reputation who specializes in connecting with and treating the deepest layers of one's being, and thereby puts you in touch with what genuinely motivates and influences you.

3. Focus upon your gut and pelvic region, 'listen' to what is going down there, particularly around your perineum or base chakra. This will balance out too much 'head stuff' and align you with what is stable and fundamental about yourself and your life.

4. Make an effort to 'debrief', that is, to talk openly about your feelings, even though this might appear uncool, naff, weak or just plain embarrassing. That way you'll get to understand how you really feel, and the real reason for doing what you did, or for thinking what you think, as distinct from what you thought was the reason – or what you assumed had no reason at all.

5. Use and respect secrecy as distinct from being merely secretive – which is merely hiding (from) something. Despite ideas and opinions which say that everything should be open and above board, there are obviously situations where a lid should be kept on things, for the good of both yourself and others.

6. Know that freedom and rights are often dependent upon your own hard-won awareness and authenticity.

Note: It is quite possible to experience both too much Uranus and too much Pluto at the same time.

The Uranus/Pluto Balance of Power 2

Too Much Pluto and not Enough Uranus

If this is the case, you could be experiencing some of these symptoms.

1. Physical and/or emotional extremism that inevitably gives rise to physical or emotional damage, with nothing gained or resolved – or worse.

2. Obsessive behaviour born of fears or desires that you appear to have no control over. Justifying bloody-mindedness even though you are not happy, let alone anybody else.

3. Being filled with doom and gloom because you are convinced that is where everything is unavoidably going.

4. Overwhelmed with the feeling that something dark and menacing is out to get you; or that there is an 'evil' in you.

5. Being frightened that someone has an ulterior motive against you.

6. Great pain and discomfort caused by someone obsessing over you, or stalking or spying on you. Resorting to hiding or revenge only makes matters worse.

7. Alienation or frustration caused by obsessively digging for an answer or secret in the wrong place – possibly for fear of finding something you won't like.

8. Making yourself unpopular, being avoided or getting rejected because of interrogating and trying to 'police' everyone, possibly because of a deep-seated distrust.

Uranian Remedies

Adopt one or more of these remedies to offset and relieve the symptoms of 'too much Pluto'.

1. Detach from your emotions and impulses long enough for them to change into something else, especially if you have the strength to concentrate on what would be best for all concerned.

2. If you are obsessed you are a prisoner to a feeling or idea that you haven't looked at properly, and seen for what it actually is. When you have you will be free.

3. When on the edge of an abyss, don't look down, take a step back and look up! Giving into doom is the ultimate self-fulfilling prophecy.

4. Get to know better what or who you see as oppressive. Making friends with what you fear transforms it or them into something astonishingly different.

5. Be bold enough to confess your fears while at the same time being open to the unexpected. You will be refreshingly surprised!

6. Your own unlooked-at dark or dubious feelings have taken external form. Honestly expose your truths and fears, rather than hide your lies.

7. Before digging, any self-respecting prospector surveys a large area thoroughly and dispassionately. Only when they have found the right spot do they start digging.

8. Trust things to unfold as they will. If need be, identify what it was earlier in your life that made it hard for you to trust.

Note: It is quite possible to experience both too much Uranus and too much Pluto at the same time.

Uranus/Pluto Mother-Wave Meditation

This is the simplest and the best: a Meditation or Prayer for the Spirit of this Time. Sit quietly with it and gaze at the symbols, alone or with others, while inwardly or outwardly uttering the invocation as many times and for as long as you wish. It is especially recommended that you perform this ritual during any Hotspots involving the Uranus/Pluto Mother-Wave (see page 294).

My fellow beings and I
Find new powers of mind
That liberate the truth
And the beauty of our humanness.
We pledge that these shine forth,
Unfolding endlessly.

CHAPTER 3

Saturn/Pluto Waves
2007–21

What Kind Of Times Are These?
Times of Power Stuggles,
and of Constructive Use of Power

Active Periods	Wave Weather	How To Ride
August 2006– August 2008	Favourable Wind	Pages 119–21
November 2008– August 2011	Major Storm	Pages 82–118, 121–34
January 2018– December 2021	Major Storm	Pages 82–118, 121–34

Saturn/Pluto Major Storms
November 2008–August 2011
January 2018–December 2021

What Kind Of Times Are These?
Times of Power Struggles

Energies in Play as we Ride These Waves

The energies of Saturn are interacting with the energies of Pluto and everyone and everything on planet Earth will be subject to these interactions for the duration of their influence, as well as to the after-effects that follow upon these Planet-Waves. Remember that two planets interacting is rather like two very different and strong-minded people coming into contact and the best and the worst of each is brought out and magnified. But Saturn and Pluto do the same to one another on a cosmic scale, and this affects us all!

ℏ The character of **Saturn** is **Territory and Stability** and its energy is **Suppressing and/or Ordering**

♇ The character of **Pluto** is **Depth and Power** and its energy is **Empowering and/or Destroying**

Their combined effect is therefore...

Suppressing and/or Ordering Deeply and Powerfully
Empowering and/or Destroying Territory and Stability

82

Territory and Power

The Basic and Primitive Territorial Nature of Man

Of all the Planet-Waves, Saturn/Pluto Major Storms are the hardest and potentially the most destructive. They have set us at odds with one another since man first laid claim to this land. This has led to defensiveness, closely followed by disputes over territory, and the inevitable theft of land from any other tribe that was deemed a threat, or weaker and more vulnerable by virtue of geography or inferior strength and numbers. The national boundaries we have today are the result so far of this process, and when Saturn/Pluto Major Storms are raging these boundaries are abused, altered or ratified. In the process, nations die and are born.

In fact, these Storms generally make for endings and beginnings in a concrete fashion, as do Saturn/Neptune Storms in a manner of dissolution or surrender {>136 Saturn/Neptune Waves} and Saturn/Uranus Storms in a sudden way or because of something new replacing the old {>188 Saturn/Uranus Waves}.

Astro-Quantum

The whole issue regarding respect for another's property and person is the microcosmic representation of the above macrocosmic issue of national boundaries and territories. If greed or old scores are allowed to escalate into conflict between family, friends and especially neighbours, then we shouldn't be surprised that the same happens between nations too. After all, political or military leaders appeal to these rapacious, fearful and defensive instincts with the result that we go to war – for war is unfortunately what humanity has usually made of Saturn/Pluto Major Storms. As for endings, this of course has to be – everything must pass – but the challenge is to end what needs to be ended because it is not serving a purpose anymore, or is destabilizing the whole by way of being decadent, corrupt or inefficient.

Shadowlands

The great trouble with human nature – and definitely something we *should* end – is our unconscious inclination to psychologically project our shadow – that is, our dark and fearful side – on to whoever or whatever is found in its path. So what is common to both sides of any issue is, ironically, what promotes a sense of separateness. The persistence of such divisiveness is what creates conflict and war, and the strife, horror and death that they bring. As long as an individual is projecting fears and negativity on to someone or something else, then they are contributing to what makes war between nations, races or religions possible.

A testament to this bad habit is how we project an entire 'personality type' on to a whole race, religion or nation, but then find, if we are honest, that when we meet an individual from such a race, religion or nation they are not usually the embodiment of that group's supposed personality, but someone in their own right. Where their 'racial, religious or national type' does become evident is simply where it grates against our own assumed one. So from this it could also be said that assuming our own national, religious or racial type indicates that we suffer from an inability to be our own person.

The Cold War

The all-too-bleak example of Shadowlands, the projection of a collective dark side on to another, was the Cold War. This began in 1946/47 with the beginning of a new cycle of Saturn/Pluto Waves. (See Appendix 2 on page 239 if you wish to see to Planetary Cycles explained.) The Americans were obsessed with their image of the Soviet Union as the great demon that threatened the freedom of the Western way of life – giving rise to McCarthy witch-hunts, and 'reds in the bed' and 'domino theory' attitudes. On the other side the Russians believed the US wanted to Americanize the world, making them a threat to Communism and its 'freedom'. Within both nations the people were constantly encouraged to accept these stereotypical views. This wasn't hard to do because of our basically paranoid human nature, and it was easier for an individual to have someone or something 'over there' to blame rather than someone or something closer to home. Such was the propaganda of both countries.

Excessive materialism is reaching critical mass. The impending global economic collapse is a sign that either we must kill it or it will kill us.

But in truth, and sadly, if any one American met any one Russian, with the aid of a decent interpreter, they would have found each other to be just what they were: people. The Cold War, this globally institutionalized paranoia, persisted until its dissolution around 1989 with the breaking up of the Soviet Union and the symbolic fall of the Berlin Wall, courtesy of the Saturn/Neptune Wave of that time. {>142 Saturn/Neptune Waves} But unfortunately, as we shall see later, it never really went away, and with the bellicose table-thumping of both sides since the last Saturn/Pluto Major Storm of 2000–04, and with the not so-far-off and audible roar of the 2008–11 Saturn/Pluto Major Storm, we can sense that the Cold War is in danger of coming back with a typical vengeance.

Astro-Quantum Memo

If you wish to have Peace in the World
You must first have Peace in your Life.
If you wish to have Peace in your Life
You must first have Peace in your Heart.

Peace be unto you

Materialism and Power

Economic crises are likely during Saturn/Pluto Major Storms, not least of all because of the war and strife they create. However, all things considered, the two Storms occurring during the 2007–20 Uranus/Pluto Mother-Wave could spell out something far more fundamental, simply because our world has become so materialistic that some kind of limit or ceiling is going to be hit. We've gone too far.

The Benefits of Boundaries

None of this means to say that boundaries themselves are a bad thing. It's only disrespecting them that is so negative. This would also apply to not having boundaries and limitations that are firm enough. Wherever we, personally or collectively, have been too liberal, open and accepting, then Saturn/Pluto Waves force us to 'swing to the right' and be stricter, more conservative, and come down harder on anyone who 'crosses the line'. This is particularly so when the easy-going influence of Neptune, or the freedom and rights of Uranus, have gone too far. This is especially relevant with the 2008–11 Saturn/Pluto Major Storm, as it occurs immediately after the 2004–08 Saturn/Neptune Major Storm, and during the 2007–12 Saturn/Uranus Major Storm, both of which concern the dissolving or freeing up of boundaries and limitations, but possibly too much so. {>136 Saturn/Neptune Waves} {>188 Saturn/Uranus Waves}

Much of what follows in this chapter focuses upon how you personally can positively ride the Saturn/Pluto Waves during the Uranus/Pluto Mother-Wave of 2007–2020, by respecting your own and others' boundaries, and thereby contribute to the world itself being more positive too.

Earthly Powers

Saturn is the *ground* we stand upon; Pluto, Lord of the Underworld, is *underground*. When they come into collision during Major Storms, this can manifest as government versus guerrilla/insurgent, or in a literal way as geophysical upheavals – mainly earthquakes. As you will find throughout this book, Major Storms involving any of the planets can stress the actual physical state of planet Earth, but it would seem that Saturn/Pluto, by virtue of what they represent, are particularly 'responsible' for earthquakes and the like.

In an Astro-Quantum sense, the question again arises as to whether and how much human affairs and behaviour affect the physical state of the Earth herself, including her atmosphere and weather. It could be argued that earthquakes and other terrestrial disturbances are the very stuff of the formation of the planet, before we were even here. But the mere fact that it has settled down immeasurably and progressively since man has been present, is an interesting one.

The Astro-Quantum approach of *Understanding The Future* puts forth the idea that everything is *interconnected* in a manner that quantum physics and astrology both bear witness to. In other words, everything – that is *everything* – contributes to the whole, from the flap of a butterfly's wings to the detonation of an atomic bomb. In short, the fewer disturbances and more harmony we create in our individual lives, the fewer disturbances and more harmony there will be in the world, including the actual fabric of the planet itself. Of course, there will still be occurrences like earthquakes, but how damaging and death-dealing they are is 'negotiable'. This point is especially important to grasp, and give actuality to, during Saturn/Pluto Waves, simply because they can be so damaging and death-dealing.

Dateline 2007: Previously, and So Far

Your Planet-Wave surfing can be greatly helped by knowing what happened during previous Saturn/Pluto Waves. If you want to look right away at the Saturn/Pluto Major Storms occurring during the Uranus/Pluto Mother Wave 2007–20 {<19} then go to page 96. This includes the Storm of 2008–11 which is responsible, along with the Saturn/Uranus Major Storm 2007–12 {>188}, for getting the Uranus/Pluto Mother-Wave off to such a pokey start.

The following historical record speaks only too loudly for itself as a testament to how we as a species and a planet respond to and express the difficult and death-dealing energy of Saturn/Pluto Major Storms. This record is in no way exhaustive, as it could fill an entire book! However, if you would like to see a thorough historical account and scholarly investigation into Saturn/Pluto Waves and several other planetary cycles, I strongly recommend *Cosmos and Psyche* by Richard Tarnas.

Our review of the 20th century opens with the first Saturn/Pluto Major Storm of 1906–09, which was representative of that one type of *violent event* that Saturn/Pluto is noted for: earthquakes. The later Storms include most of the 13 largest earthquakes occurring between 1900 and 2007, and those which have had the greatest number of fatalities. By focusing mainly on the times when the Storms are peaking – for technically this is the most powerful part of a Wave – we continue with that other violent event which is unfortunately only too typical an example of Saturn/Pluto Major Storms: *war*!

Saturn/Pluto Major Storm 1906–09 (peaking 1907/08)

January 31 1906	Earthquake off the coast of Ecuador, killing 1000 (at 8.8M one of the 13 largest since 1900).
March 16 1906	Earthquake (6.8M) in Taiwan, killing 1250.
April 18 1906	Great San Francisco Earthquake (7.8M), killing 3000.

August 17 1906	Earthquake (8.2M) in Valparaiso, Chile, killing 20,000.
October 21 1907	Earthquake (8.0M) in Tajikistan, killing 12,000.
December 28 1908	Earthquake (7.2) in Messina, Italy, killing 70,000.
January 23 1909	Earthquake (7.3M) in Iran, killing 6000.

Saturn/Pluto Major Storm 1913–16
(New Cycle, peaking 1914/15)

A new Saturn/Pluto Storm Cycle began in classic 'style' at the very beginning of its peak period in June 1914, when the Serbs assassinated the heir to the Austro-Hungarian throne, leading to the outbreak of the First World War in August. September saw Germany defeat Russia and October found Turkey joining the War. The end of 1914 and beginning of 1915 saw the very nature and rules of war change forever with the use of aircraft and the attacking of neutral shipping. In April of that year (the end of the peak of this Wave) the Allies fought their way ashore at Gallipoli, with the chaotic leadership and horrific casualties that were so typical of this conflict, and in May Italy added to the whole mess by declaring war on Austria. The rest, as they say, is history – but very much Saturn/Pluto history, as we shall see. But it must be emphasized that it wasn't just this Major Storm that humanity so predictably and negatively succumbed to in the form of armed conflict, but also Saturn/Neptune and Saturn/Uranus Storms, which occurred simultaneously. {⊕ 139 Saturn/Neptune; ⊕ 191 Saturn/Uranus}

Saturn/Pluto Major Storm 1921–23 (peaking 1922)

December 12 1920	Earthquake (7.8M) in China, killing 200,000.
December 6 1921	Southern Ireland becomes an independent state.
24 July 1922	League of Nations Council approves Mandate for Palestine.
September 27 1922	Turkey expels Greece from Asia Minor.
October 30 1922	Mussolini's Fascists march on Rome.
November 11 1922	Earthquake (at 8.5M one of the 13 largest since 1900) on Chile-Argentina Border.
January 25 1923	France occupies Ruhr, Germany.
March 2 1923	Earthquake (at 8.5M one of the 13 largest since 1900) in Kamchatka, Russia.

March 24 1923	Earthquake (7.3M) in China, killing 3,500.
May 25 1923	Earthquake (5.7M) in Iran, killing 2,200.
September 1 1923	Earthquake (7.9M) in Japan, killing 143,000.

Saturn/Pluto Major Storm 1930–33 (peaking 1932)

October 24 1929	'Black Thursday' and the Wall Street Crash. {⏱ 32 Uranus/Pluto}
May 6 1930	Earthquake (7.2M) in Iran, killing 2,500.
July 23 1930	Earthquake (6.5M) in Italy, killing 1,400.
March 31 1931	Earthquake (6.0M) in Nicaragua, killing 2,500.
April 27 1931	Earthquake (5.7M) in Armenia, killing 2,800.
July 1931	German banks close.
August 10 1931	Earthquake (8.0M) in China, killing 10,000.
November 1931	Japan occupies Manchuria – at war with China.
December 28 1931	Britain-India talks collapse.
March 2 1933	Earthquake (8.4M) in Japan, killing 2990.
August 25 1933	Earthquake (7.4M) in China, killing 9,300.

Saturn/Pluto Major Storm 1939–41 (peaking 1939/40)

January 25 1939	Earthquake (7.8M) in Chile, killing 28,000.
March 15 1939	Germans enter Prague.
March 28 1939	Franco takes Madrid.
April 8 1939	Italy invades Albania.
May 22 1939	Germany and Italy sign 'Pact of Steel'.
September 3 1939	Britain declares war on Germany following its invasion of Poland – World War Two begins.
September 30 1939	Germany and Russia divide Poland.
November 30 1939	Russia attacks Finland.
December 26 1939	Earthquake (7.8M) in Turkey, killing 32,700.
April 9 1940	Germany invades Denmark and Norway.
May 10 1940	Netherlands and Belgium fall to Germany.
June 4 1940	Allies evacuated from Dunkirk.
Summer 1940	Battle of Britain.
November 10 1940	Earthquake (7.3M) in Romania, killing 1000.

December 7 1941   Japan attacks Pearl Harbour, bringing America into World War Two.

{regarding all above Earthquakes ⏱ 197 Saturn/Uranus}

Saturn/Pluto Major Storm 1946–48 (New Cycle, peaking 1947)

February 1946   Cold War between United States and Soviet Union symbolically begins with Winston Churchill's naming of the 'Iron Curtain' that the Soviets were erecting against the USA's continuing presence in Europe after World War Two.

December 28 1946   Vietnam at war with France.

February 10 1947   New European borders set.

February 15 1947   Chinese Civil War continues.

April 1947   The term 'Cold War' first used to describe the mounting East–West conflict.

May 23 1947   India to be partitioned.

August 1947   Crisis in Indonesia.

August 15 1947   India and Pakistan win independence.

August 31 1947   End of British rule in Palestine.

January 4 1948   Burma becomes independent state from Britain.

May 14 1948   Arab–Israeli war begins.

October 5 1948   Earthquake (7.3M) in Turkmenistan, killing 110,000.

Saturn/Pluto Major Storm 1954–57 (peaking 1955/56)

May 18 1956   Atrocities of Algerian War.

July 26 1956   Egypt seizes Suez Canal.

October 1956   Suez Crisis – Britain, France, Israel move in.

November 4 1956   Soviet tanks crush Hungarian rebellion.

March 9 1957   Earthquake (one of the 13 largest since 1900 at 8.6M) in Andreanof Islands, Alaska.

July 2 1957   Earthquake (7.1M) in Iran, killing 1,200.

December 13 1957   Earthquake (7.1M) in Iran, killing 1,130.

Saturn/Pluto Major Storm 1964–68 (peaking 1965/66)

March 28 1964	Earthquake (at 9.2M one of the 13 largest since 1900) in Prince William Sound, Alaska. {🕐 33 Uranus/Pluto} {🕐 195 Saturn/Uranus}
November 19 1964	South Vietnam attacks North Vietnam in earnest.
February 4 1965	Earthquake (at 8.7M one of the 13 largest since 1900) in Rat Islands, Alaska. {🕐 33 Uranus/Pluto} {🕐 195 Saturn/Uranus}
February 11 1965	US launches first air strikes on North Vietnam.
May 13 1965	US Forces arrive in Dominican Republic.
August 24 1965	Agreement to end Yemen War.
September 1965	India and Pakistan warring in Kashmir.
November 25 1965	Mobutu takes over in the Congo.
August 31 1968	Earthquake (7.3M) in Iran, killing 12,000.

Saturn/Pluto Major Storm 1973–75 (peaking 1973/74)

June 30 1973	Major offensive begins in Cambodia.
July 17 1973	Bloodless coup in Afghanistan.
September 1973	Pinochet takes over Chile.
October 6 1973	Yom Kippur attack on Israel.
November 25 1973	Military coup in Greece.
March 15 1974	Watergate: Nixon found guilty.
December 5 1974	Military violently suppress anti-government protests in Burma.
May 10 1974	Earthquake (6.8M) in China, killing 20,000.

Saturn/Pluto Major Storm 1980–84
(New Cycle, peaking 1982/83)

October 10 1980	Earthquake (7.7M) in Algeria, killing 5000.
November 23 1980	Earthquake (6.5M) in Italy, killing 3000.
June 11 1981	Earthquake (6.9M) in Iran, killing 3000.
July 28 1981	Earthquake (7.3M) in Iran, killing 1,500.
1981	Severe economic recession in United Kingdom.
1981/82	Severe economic recession in United States.

April 2 1982	Argentina invades Falkland Islands.
May–June 1982	Falklands War.
June 29 1982	Israel invades Lebanon.
July 20 1982	IRA bombs London's Hyde Park and Regents Park, killing eight soldiers.
July 27 1982	Israeli jets annihilate West Beirut.
September 18 1982	Christians slaughter Arabs in West Beirut.
December 13 1982	Earthquake (6.0M) in Yemen, killing 2,800.
February 21 1983	600 Muslims massacred in Indian riots.
April 19 1983	US Embassy in Beirut bombed.

Saturn/Pluto Major Storm 1992–95 (peaking 1993)

February 26 1993	World Trade Center bombed {>Sep 11 2001 below}
February 28 1993	Deadly shootout at Waco.
April 19 1993	Waco siege ends in fire and deaths.
September 29 1993	Earthquake (6.2M) in India, killing 9,748.
October 4 1993	Yeltsin crushes rebellion in Moscow.
November 9 1993	Croatian bombing destroys Stari Most Bridge, symbol of the architectural heritage of Bosnia-Herzegovina.
February 28 1994	Bosnia: NATO's first ever offensive action.
March 28 1994	Zulus and African National Congress battle in Johannesburg.
April 21 1994	Mass slaughter in Rwanda.
January 16 1995	Earthquake (6.9M) in Japan, killing 5,502.

Saturn/Pluto Major Storm 2000–04 (peaking 2001/02)

January 26 2001	Earthquake (7.6M) in India, killing 20,023.
September 11 2001	World Trade Center destroyed and Pentagon damaged by Al Qaeda. {☉ 198 Saturn/Uranus}
October 7 2001	US Launches 'War on Terrorism' in Afghanistan.
January 10 2002	US transport al Qaeda and Taliban prisoners to Camp X-Ray at the US Guantanamo Bay naval base in Cuba.
January 29 2002	President Bush declares that 'the war against terror is only beginning,' singling out Iran, Iraq and North Korea as an 'axis of evil'.

January 21 2003	Earthquake (6.8M) in Algeria, killing 2,266.
March 20 2003	US invasion of Iraq.
December 26 2003	Earthquake (6.6M) in Iran, killing 31,000.
December 26 2004	Earthquake (at 9.1M one of the 13 largest since 1900) in Sumatra-Andaman Islands, and ensuing Tsunami killing 283,106. {🕐 143 Saturn/Neptune}

◆

The Destruction of the World Trade Center

This profound history-making event (September 11 2001 at 8.46 and 9.03 a.m. in New York City) was the focus of a Saturn/Pluto Major Storm that was peaking between mid-2001 and mid-2002. This was Pluto in Sagittarius in opposition to Saturn in Gemini. As can be seen from this graphic of the glyphs for these planets and signs, the attack on the twin towers of the World Trade Center by flying objects was astrologically represented in a frighteningly literal way.

Using established keywords for Saturn and Pluto (and for the Signs they were travelling through and the Opposition aspect) we can see further into the meaning of this.

Pluto is **extremism, fiendishness and destruction** in (qualified by) Sagittarius, which represents **religion, preaching and judgement**.

Opposition is **confrontation** and thereby **increases awareness of two opposing factors**, of each other and themselves. {>239 Planetary Cycles}

Saturn is **structure, materialism and authority** in (qualified by) Gemini, which represents **secularity, commercialism, reason and duality**.

From the impartial viewpoint of astrology (which any astrologer must endeavour to cultivate), Opposition only comes about because of two opposing viewpoints. And of course it goes both ways, with **deep religious convictions** (Pluto in Sagittarius) feeling opposed by the **control of materialism and commercialism** (Saturn in Gemini). Opposition is the demonstration that there are two sides to any whole. The trouble is that in human terms this too often leads to division, as opposed to an appreciation of the fact that differences are integral to making up that whole.

Opposition also raises the issue of projection {<82}, particularly where one party projects their desires and fears on to another, opposing, party. Essentially, this Opposition between Gemini and Sagittarius is the age-old one of the **secular** versus the **religious**. Saturn is also secular in quality, therefore taking that end of the spectrum to its extreme. Pluto being the extreme anyway – which can be seen as Fate itself 'upping the ante' – drastically increases this polarization. Looking purely at the two Planets involved we can look at this polarity as **land** (Saturn) versus **underworld** (Pluto), or **suppressing** versus **destroying** – what feels downtrodden rises up from the depths to destroy the perceived suppresser, while the suppresser tries to bury or keep buried what it does not want to see.

In other words, September 11 was a fated event created by this enormous build-up of Opposition. The questions it poses are: Can we find a way of accepting and balancing out extremes of opinion, lifestyle and status? Can the 'haves' surrender their material control for the good of the whole? Can the 'have nots' take back their envy and resentment that they project upon the 'haves' under the guise of religious self-righteousness?

Astro-Quantum Memo

Every cell in your body is powered by the Sun. This power is vested in you for you to use simply by virtue of your being alive. Power is neither good nor evil. It is how you use it that makes it good or evil.

Astro-Quantum

When all is said and done, these questions can only be answered and resolved in one's own heart and mind {<11 Self-Rule}. If you have an attachment to material control, or envy or resentment towards someone or something, then in effect you are contributing to the collective human problem for the simple reason that this is created by each and every human being. Warmongers must look to their own inner conflict; peace-makers must find their own inner peace.

Astrology shows us how things are. Whenever there is a Saturn/Pluto Major Storm there is a **power struggle** of some kind. But the struggle – as every individual Birth Chart will tell you – is always and ultimately within. Saturn and Pluto are just two lords of two intimately connected realms that, apart from the occasional earthquake and volcano, coexist very well. But then again, using this terrestrial scenario as an analogy, that is in essence what 9/11was: a human earthquake or volcano releasing tensions and hidden, repressed material, with commensurate aftershocks and fall-out, contributing hopefully to an increased awareness that we are all living on the same Planet, Earth, and are carrying around within us our own personal power struggles that will contribute to the global power struggle, with commensurate outcome.

✦

Surf It or Wipe-Out?

So which way are you, are we, going to go? One path, riding
these Waves or acting in the true Spirit of these Times, will take
us into a positive future – the other, giving in to the Devil of
these Times, will take us to a negative future.

The Spirit of These Times

The Constructive Use of Power

Looking at the recent history of Saturn/Pluto Major Storms has given us an all-too-
clear idea of what we humans makes of these Planet-Waves. In fact, 'human' seems
to become 'inhuman' during them! Astrologically, to avoid the worst and get the
best out of a conflicting planetary influence, which any Major Storm is, we have
to take each planet's meaning or vibration to a higher level. Imagine an upward-
pointing triangle with the two planets at each corner of the base: they are distant,
out of tune and in conflict with one another. They finally join at the apex of the triangle: the higher the vibration and expression of each planet is, the more united
and therefore positive becomes the combined effect of the two planets.

The term 'base' is very appropriate here because distance and conflict lead
to base behaviour and the lowest expression of what the planets do to one
another – or rather what *we* do to one another! In the case of Saturn and Pluto it
is at its most base because these two planets are, along with Mars, known as
'malefics' – under their influence more harm and distress can be meted out than
with other planets. The reason is that the principles of 'control' (Saturn), and
'power' (Pluto), can be so easily abused and perverted into, respectively,
repression and cruelty.

So let's see how we can raise the vibration of Saturn and Pluto and create that constructive use of power. On the following pages, we see the triangle as a pyramid or 'ladder' that can be climbed step by step in order to reach the higher vibrations or expressions of each planet, ultimately reaching the top, the highest vibration or expression. Beginning with the Saturn Ladder, start reading it from the bottom and see how each step takes you progressively upwards. Notice that halfway up is the critical fifth step. If you can't pass this one then you are bound to go down a 'snake' to the bottom and start all over again, or just keep stumbling up and down the first four steps – with the fourth being the worst – until you finally reach, and pass, that fifth step.

With Pluto there are two types of ladder – Pluto's Ladder for Victims and Pluto's Ladder for Victimizers – but you may find that both apply, in whole or in part. You will notice how they only differ slightly, but significantly, from one another.

Astro-Quantum

Now, after using the first three ladders, we look at these ladders and various steps that each and every one of us is placed upon as a whole, by using Saturn's Collective Ladder, Pluto's Collective ladder for Victims and Pluto's Collective Ladder for Victimizers. We then get a reading of the Saturn/Pluto 'state of play' globally. Note that mostly I have used the collective term nation for the stake of brevity, but such can refer to any collective body such as creed or race.

Combined Collective Effect

Negatively, suppose all or most of us were on the bottom rung of Saturn's ladder and Pluto's ladders. The world would then inevitably get to that worst collective state of the fourth rung before it sees, if ever, the error of its ways.

- Negative reaction from other nations 'hitting back' cycle of retaliation.
- National habit of giving away its power in mistaken belief that another won't harm it.
- Habitually robbing other nations of power in a vain attempt to keep them powerless.

Saturn's Ladder

9   Firmer position and more stable life; no need to find fault and regard others as a threat.

8   Self-control and self-awareness, creating a more stable and effective personality.

7   Recognition of shortcomings leads to ways of correcting them.

6   Humble acceptance of your faults and weaknesses but without blaming yourself.

5   Recognition that you are only getting back what you put out.

4   Negative reaction from others 'hitting back' cycle of retaliation and bad fortune.

3   Blaming others and the world for the way you are and feel.

2   Self-denial and subsequent ignorance of whole picture.

1   Fear of truth about yourself or your situation.

Pluto's Ladder for Victims

9   Making positive, healing and lasting changes to yourself and the world around you.

8   Influential will and deep insight born of a profound sense of the power of own existence.

7   Having the grit and determination to be purged of fears and regenerate your soul.

6   Taking steps to re-empower yourself through deep healing, self-knowledge and self-love.

5   Realization that not owning or reclaiming your power means that it is used against you.

4   Habitually giving away your power in mistaken belief that then 'they' won't harm you.

3   Driven by compulsions and obsessions and addictions that further disempower you.

2   Attracting people who disrespect, use, ignore or incapacitate you.

1   Fear and loss of power as it was first experienced as death, violence or abuse.

Pluto's Ladder for Victimizers

9   Making positive, healing and lasting changes to yourself and the world around you.

8   Influential will and deep insight born of a profound sense of the power of your own existence.

7   Having the grit and determination to be purged of fears and regenerate your soul.

6   Taking steps to re-empower yourself through deep healing, self-knowledge and self-love.

5   Realization that expressing your power harmfully is really a sign of deep insecurity.

4   Habitually robbing others of power in a vain attempt to regain the power you lost.

3   Driven by compulsions and obsessions and addictions that further disempower you.

2   Feeling hostile towards people whose weaknesses remind you of your own.

1   Loss of and obsession with power as it was first experienced as death, violence or abuse.

Saturn's Collective Ladder

9   Firmer and more stable nation; no need to find fault and regard others as a threat.

8   Collective self-control and self-awareness, creating a more stable and effective nation.

7   Recognition of nation's shortcomings leads to ways of correcting them.

6   Nation's humble acceptance of its faults and weaknesses but without blaming itself.

5   Nation's recognition that it is only getting back what it's putting out.

4   Negative reaction from other nations 'hitting back' cycle of retaliation.

3   Nations blaming each other for the way they each are.

2   Self-denial and subsequent ignorance of whole picture.

1   National fear of truth about itself or its situation.

Pluto's Collective Ladder for Victims

9   Making positive, healing and lasting changes to itself and the rest of the world.

8   Global influence born of nation's profound sense of the power of its own existence.

7   Having the grit and determination to be purged of fears and regenerate national soul.

6   Taking steps to re-empower itself through changes in laws, constitution and government.

5   Realization that not owning its power means it is used against it, from without or within.

4   National habit of giving away power in mistaken belief that another won't harm it.

3   Driven by negative national practises that further disempower it.

2   Other nations who further disrespect, use, ignore or incapacitate that nation.

1   Nation's fear or loss of power which was first experienced as invasion and enslavement.

Pluto's Collective Ladder for Victimizers

9   Making positive, healing and lasting changes to itself and the rest of the world.

8   Global influence born of nation's profound sense of the power of its own existence.

7   Having the grit and determination to be purged of fears and regenerate national soul.

6   Taking steps to re-empower itself through changes in laws, constitution and government.

5   Realization that expressing its power harmfully is really a sign of its insecurity.

4   National habit of robbing other nations of power in a vain attempt to keep them powerless.

3   Driven by negative national practises that attract more fear, hatred and resistance.

2   Nation feels hostile towards other nations whose weaknesses remind it of its own.

1   Nation's obsession with power which was first used to invade and enslave.

It is plain to see what a dire mixture of traits this is, be it for nations, creeds or races – and ultimately the whole world. To some degree it is precisely where we are now – and during a Saturn/Pluto Major Storm it must get better or it will get worse!

Positively, suppose that all or most of us – or a critical number of us – got to that critical fifth step.

- Nation's recognition that it is only getting back what it's putting out.
- Realization that not owning its power means it is used against it, from without or within.
- Nation's realization that expressing its power harmfully is really a sign of its insecurity.

This could eventually lead, through steps 6 to 9, to the best case scenario: a firmer and more stable state with no need to find fault and regard others as a threat. We could make positive, healing and lasting changes to ourselves and the rest of the world.

Bridges instead of Walls

An ironic example of 'raising the vibration' occurs when Saturn/Pluto manifests as a natural disaster like an earthquake. As the earth moves so are certain nations moved to rally to the aid of the stricken one. This is especially so when the victims of an earthquake are poor and poverty-stricken people – as is so often the case – for we are even more ready to help those innocents who are seemingly so undeserving of such 'punishment'. International aid then comes pouring in as that 'constructive use of power': machinery, special instruments, search and recovery experts, food, medicine, transport and accommodation.

The Devil of These Times

The Destructive Use of Power

The Saturn and Pluto ladders, going from negative to positive, have already shown to some extent what the 'destructive use of power' is: **paranoia**. This, the most negative but common of all negative human traits originates from being on the receiving end of some form of abuse of power at some point in the past.

Looked at collectively, and conventionally, this goes back to prehistoric times when we were literally fighting for our most basic survival. And that meant, eventually, fighting each other. The trouble is that such defensive/aggressive behaviour created the original vicious circle. There is always someone or something that is in power and someone or something that is not. It seems that an increase in power invariably results in an increase in paranoia, and the subsequent use of that power to create more paranoia. We are talking here of things like **state** (Saturn), **police** (Pluto) and **propaganda** – **secrecy** (Pluto), **control** (Saturn) – along with the usual repression, abuse of human rights and breaking of international laws. The paranoia it creates in its enemy simply empowers its enemy to take revenge. If the paranoia is within itself, it rots from within until it is weakened and therefore vulnerable to whatever that 'enemy' is.

A classic case of this was the Fall of Rome when, corrupted and ridden with internal power struggles and vices, Rome was sacked by the Empire's old foe, the barbarian Visigoths. And this happened in August 410 AD, precisely at the peak of a Saturn/Pluto Major Storm, which was also the beginning of a New Cycle. It is tempting to draw a parallel between this, the attack by bearded hordes on the most powerful city in the world at that time, with the attack on the World Trade Center in New York on September 11 2001, which was also the peak of a Saturn/Pluto Major Storm {<93}.

> *Giving away your power attracts power that is used against you.*

Conspiracy Theories

A more unconventional, yet increasingly popular explanation of paranoia is that of conspiracy theories, which maintain that there is some secret cabal or group that manipulates us all – whatever race, nation or creed – into being at each other's throats while it gloats and controls from some secret place, keeping us all, from governmental puppet to individual, in fear and in thrall. Whether this, the ultimate Divide and Rule tactic, is true or not doesn't really matter, because it is still making the same Saturn/Pluto mistake.

Astro-Quantum

The sick inclination to find an external 'enemy' rather than look within to find and deal with one's inner demon is a critical point with respect to surfing Saturn/Pluto Waves. Every individual who allows themself to be persuaded that the enemy is 'out there' 'informs' many other individuals that such is the case. And the Saturn/Pluto propaganda machine is only too happy, to oblige in implementing this. It is in the paranoid state's interest to keep its citizens paranoid. But the paranoid state is just a projection of the individual's 'paranoid state'.

> *God and devil are fighting there, and the battlefield is the heart of man.*

Fyodor Dostoevsky, *The Brothers Karamazov*

It can be difficult to understand or accept how projection works. 'Surely,' you might ask, 'some evil regime or my inept government has nothing to do with me, does it?' But the mere fact that one has to 'reclaim one's power' in order to oppose or remove such a regime bears testament to this. In other words, until people are willing to say, 'We are taking responsibility for the situation we find ourselves in, and are now doing something about it!' – that regime will remain in power until it possibly but not inevitably, collapses internally. Synchronistically, such inner collapse seems to coincide with some kind of external realization in the hearts and minds of the people that they must do something.

The Role of Uranus

Whereas Saturn/Pluto describes the timing and nature of the 'destructive use of power', it is actually when Uranus, the planet of Freedom, Rebellion and Reform looms into the planetary picture that people rise up against these repressive regimes. As I write in September 2007, the beginnings of uprisings are occurring in two countries whose governments fit this bill only too well: Burma and Zimbabwe. As the Saturn/Uranus Wave 2007–12 {>188} and the swelling Uranus/Pluto Mother-Wave 2007–20 {<27} continue to do their revolutionary thing, we shall see more and more such uprisings, great and small.

Conflicts, Trends and Possibilities

Socio-Cultural

Two Tribes

These Saturn/Pluto Major Storms lend a sense of the utilitarian to our social and cultural style. A 'make-do-and-mend' attitude starts slowly at first, but as it becomes more obvious that things are getting tighter materially and environmentally, this gathers momentum and even becomes a 'style'. As ever, there is an equal and opposite reaction to, or compensation for it. The wasteful and indulgent members of society become more so, adopting a 'devil-may-care' attitude.

The forming of these two factions or expressions of 'hard times' creates a friction in itself. Society becomes polarized between those who are serious about living a simpler and more ecologically aware life, and those who regard such a life as dull and unnecessary. What would once have been a case of the 'rich getting richer and the poor getting poorer' now morphs into something more akin to the conscientious getting quite religious about their burgeoning awareness of how important it is to be conservationist, while those who want to 'fiddle while Rome burns' become more and more marginalized. Or, and it's a big 'or', the reverse becomes the case with the conservationists being regarded ironically, at least at first, like hippies were looked upon in the 1960s.

Serious Social Splits

And yet there is a dark side to such conservationism too. This is the judgemental and hair-shirt wearing attitude that gets neurotic about or even aggressive towards those who are seen as being wasteful and irresponsible. There arises the dangerous Saturn/Pluto inclination to project on to others shortcomings that have been overlooked in an eagerness to do the 'right thing'. And it works the other way too. Finding someone to blame or brand as a scapegoat, particularly in the religious sphere, can amount to serious splits and antagonisms within society and worldwide.

Astro-Quantum

The old Biblical question, 'Why do you look at the speck of sawdust in your brother's eye and pay no attention to the plank in your own eye?' (Matthew 7: 3) is the simple antidote to projections and judgemental behaviour. It is much needed because these attitudes can actually escalate into a very dysfunctional society, civil unrest and ultimately war.

Health

Sexual Health and a Cleansing of the Hives

Pluto represents any kind of power that gets to one's deepest emotions and desires. It is the planet of intimacy and sexuality. When Saturn is making Waves with Pluto, then all sexual involvement gets tested and its weak or questionable spots are forced to the surface. Significantly, AIDS first appeared during a Saturn/Pluto Major Storm in the early 1980s.

Whatever the origins of this disease and the HIV virus that most likely causes it, astrologically it is a Wave that is carrying something dangerous. It doesn't matter how it was contracted, its message is the same: be careful with anything that enters you deeply that came from someone else, be it sexual penetration, shared needles or a blood transfusion. It is not to do with morality either – at least, not necessarily. It is to do with how the individual is squaring or confusing their love needs with their sexual needs, or how they are abusing someone else's personal power and boundaries or allowing their own to be abused, or – and particularly with seemingly 'innocent' cases – it has something to do with putting one in touch with what really and truly matters, like one's destiny and deeper identity, which is why it also has the spectre of death. To paraphrase Samuel Johnson: 'Nothing concentrates the mind so wonderfully as the prospect of death.'

So all these matters are brought to the fore, in one way or another, during Saturn/Pluto Major Storms. This is especially true during the next two, 2008/11 and 2018/21, firstly because a degree of complacency has developed concerning the condition's dangers, and secondly because they occur during a Uranus/Pluto Mother-Wave which adds Uranian shock to Saturnian pressure. To a lesser extent this applies to any sexually related complaint or sexually transmitted disease, with crisis and alarm being the call of the day. As the saying goes, 'There is no such thing as safe sex!' {<32 Uranus/Pluto Mother-Wave}

This means that it is through people's sexual urges that they seek, usually unconsciously, to make their lives more profound and meaningful, leaving them open to harm psychologically as well as physically. A condom is not the only safety barrier they require! Usually this objective is attained through the intensity of emotion that intimacy (through the mixing of body fluids and more) brings with its rollercoaster ride of the extremes of love and hate, ecstasy and desolation.

At a more unconscious and neurotic level, such extremes are sought through some kind of death wish, a need for martyrdom or to escape from life itself. Such desperation, posing as complacency, explains the intensity and paradoxical disregard for life that the sexual urge, or simply that unconscious need for some kind of catharsis through crisis in a person's life, can bring. The case of a young man being anally penetrated by four older men infected with HIV in order to be 'gifted', as it is called in such circles, darkly and vividly illustrates this point. The fact that they also inserted a butt plug in him afterwards to make sure as much infected semen stayed inside him for maximum effect, goes to show the depth and misery to which the human condition can go. Expanding this to a global issue, we can say that some kind of 'cleansing of the hives' is going on while Saturn/Pluto is obliged to do its timely purging. All in aid of putting us in touch with what we truly are deep down.

Trade and Industry

Powerful Pressures

Nations and global organizations vie for a larger share of the 'cake' – natural and human resources – and so there is bound to be a knock-on effect in the world economy. The degree to which economic states, nation by nation, are truly stable determines the degree to which the power of the underlying realities and hidden faults of Pluto will disrupt them. These economic states are dependent on a great number of factors, from the health of the currency to the psychological climate. But it is Saturn/Pluto's unfortunately favourite manifestation that can create the worst kind of economic disturbance and hardship: **wars**. Worse still, the material powermongers of this world actually create war in order to gain more, like profiting from the sale of armaments.

Cracks and Crashes

Because our world has become overly materialistic to a hideous degree, there has to be a proportionate shock to our material state to make us sit up and take notice. This means having a long hard look at what really creates material stability for the whole world and not just a greedy few. Instability within the human race is reflected in the instability of planet Earth herself, a piece of real estate that no one really owns. In fact, she owns us – and to her we are definitely dispensable, even questionable, assets. If we do not look at the ecology alongside the economy, there will be a crash to end all crashes during either the 2008–11 Saturn/Pluto Major Storm or the 2018–21 one. At the very least, the earlier one will be showing us some undeniable warning cracks.

Astro-Quantum

Saturn governs economy, not least of all in the sense that when it is active it pressures us to *be* economical. Pluto, as is its wont, intensifies the effect of whatever planet is making a Wave with it. So it becomes intensely important to practise economy in a personal sense, for in this way we effect the economy as a whole. This does not mean being stingy and wearing a hair shirt, but it does mean living according to *only what you need* to maintain a standard of living that enables you to continue your life and its essential purpose.

Simply put, if you are living your life in a way that serves an end greater than yourself – that is, a spiritual purpose – then you will be supported. Literally or psychologically, Saturn/Pluto puts us under a 'war-time economy'. The opposite end of this spectrum is greed, or neurotically hanging on to what you don't need. The more of us who practise this true economy, the less likely a 'crash' is. But nothing will stop the cracks showing, for they are the proof of the matter making itself known!

Political

Left or Right, Rift or Light?

Without a doubt, there is a distinct swing towards a conservative philosophy during Saturn/Pluto Major Storms. These two, 2008–11 and 2018–21, are no exception, especially considering the instability and unruliness of the whole Uranus/Pluto Mother-Wave period of 2007–20 that are a reaction to very real inequalities and injustices. A swing to the right is therefore much in evidence with an enforced or encouraged return to traditional and family values. The trouble is that society becomes more heavily policed as the restoring and maintenance of law and order becomes the pressing issue.

As usual, though, political mileage is made by appealing to the 'moral majority' which may wind up confirming people's fears rather than reducing them. If there can be a few political figures who find a balance between creating order with a firm hand yet at the same time granting people, or instilling in them, a sense of responsibility, then this would be an enormous step forward, as well as a breaking free from the right wing/left wing swing that has gone on tiresomely throughout political history. But such leaders would have to be unusually strong, for they would have to be guided by principle rather than party politics, or merely winning votes by appealing to the lowest common denominator of what people have been led to believe they want – something which is in itself a product of the split between right and left. As was emphasized at the very beginning of this book, the time for Balance has come {<2 Introduction}.

Extreme Tension Leading to Crisis

In countries where there is a bitter divide between the rulers and those they rule over, Saturn/Pluto makes that division heavier and more unacceptable, leading to some kind of crisis. Currently (2007), Burma, Darfur and Zimbabwe are such countries {>136 Saturn/Neptune Storms; 188 Saturn/Uranus Major Storms, and below regarding Burma}.

Astro-Quantum

'Every country has the government it deserves,' wrote Joseph de Maistre following the French Revolution. This could be interpreted as meaning that our political leaders are only an expression or reflection of our own biases and balances, our own strengths and weaknesses, and our own ability to think for ourselves or not. So the more we recognize what is just and appropriate by simply governing our individual selves, the more likely we are to have a government that does the same for our country.

We would know what is 'just and appropriate' through simply attuning ourselves to how we would like to be sensibly governed; something which in turn necessitates drawing up in writing our own manifesto, for in this way we can get a clearer and more balanced sense of what that might be, and of how it could not be! {>213 Saturn/Uranus Waves/An Invitation}

Environmental

Geophysical Stress

This heading is also included in the Saturn/Uranus chapter, these two kinds of Major Storm are serious candidates for earthquakes and any other form of geophysical upheaval. We have explored this matter already, both in this chapter and in the chapter on Saturn/Uranus, so suffice to say that Mother Earth is going to be in a 'mood'! She is not happy with the way we are living on her – or rather *off* her. Anything you can do that communes with the Earth, like helping and being in touch with the natural world, including the practise of shamanism and Earth religions, assists in 'spreading the load'. Direct action against anything or anyone that abuses the Earth also helps of course. And all these activities will increase and become more earnest during the Saturn/Pluto Major Storms. Unfortunately, as Saturn/Pluto inclines governments towards material and power considerations, environmental issues are in danger of no longer becoming the priority they need to be.

Scientific

The Best and the Worst

The best and the worst of what 'science' has to offer can manifest during Saturn/Pluto Major Storms. This is because there is a great necessity at these characteristically hard and challenging times to 'come up with the goods'. On the one hand, science produces very real and practical solutions to deal with whatever is assailing us – be it from another nation's perceived aggression, an environmental issue, or a widespread health problem. On the other hand, it is inclined to do as much damage with its left hand as it does good with its right – witness weapons of mass destruction, industrial pollution and the mere suppression of symptoms.

Necessity is the mother of invention, but unless scientists really begin to understand how the Mother works – that is Mother Earth/Mother Nature – then it will continue to dig humanity's grave with its well-meaning but short-sighted intentions. In other words, scientists have to ask themselves what is *really* a necessity, as distinct from doing something simply because they can, or because it makes money, is a quick fix, or finds favour with whoever or whatever has power over them.

Spiritual

Spirit Versus Matter?

Unfortunately, what is spiritual in the sense of doing the greatest possible good for the greatest possible number of living things gets very little airplay when Saturn/Pluto Major Storms are raging, because this combination tends to elicit from humanity a need or greed for material power. And material power perennially has been at the opposite end of the spectrum in the sense that it is the province, in spiritual terms, of the Devil and Mammon. So one might say that the challenge during these times is to connect with something that is spiritual in such a way that it addresses these base or basic human drives. Hardship is actually very good at producing this for, as can be seen historically with two World Wars and 9/11, all of which occurred during Saturn/Pluto Major Storms, it prompts in people a very real sense of what does and what doesn't matter. However, the 'Devil' to avoid is refusing to recognize that the same conditions apply to the 'enemy'. The 'Mammon' to avoid is that if everyone does not have a share in the Earth's bounty, then sooner or later those with too little will assail those who have too much.

The Mood of These Times

On their own, that is without considering or experiencing other Planet-Waves occurring at the same time, Saturn/Pluto Major Storms create a distinctly oppressive atmosphere. As a worst case, it can seem that one is living in a totalitarian state where everyone is spied upon and checked for 'correct' behaviour. Unfortunately, in some countries this is actually true. But to whatever degree this is so, there is quite simply a feeling of heaviness and tyranny.

Big Brother Is Watching You

This phrase was coined by George Orwell in his book *1984*, which was written during the Saturn/Pluto Major Storm of 1946–48, the beginning of a New Cycle, and set during the Major Storm that marked the beginning of the very next cycle in 1981–84. Although some countries have indeed reached the depths of control, torture and repression that Orwell foresaw, most of the world has fortunately not sunk quite so low. I would like to think, in the spirit of Astro-Quantum, that his iconic work affected the global consciousness to a degree that contributed to a resistance, through awareness of how easily repressive a state can become. In any event, by reaction, the Mood of these Times can often spell an increased awareness of, and sensitivity towards, anything or anyone that is abusing or misusing power. In fact, this is a testament to the fact that human nature is essentially about *freedom* and it won't abide anything that gets in the way of that for too long.

Whistle-Blowing

Whether it is a boss who is taking unfair advantage of his employees, a giant organization that is behaving like it is a law unto itself, or the government of the day, the feeling is to draw attention to such actions – personally, politically or through the press. If there are Major Storms involving Uranus or Neptune occurring at the same time as Saturn/Pluto Major Storms, then whistle-blowing and protestation are far more likely. As can be see on the Planet-Wave Weather Chart on page 19, this is happily the case for both Saturn/Pluto Major Storms happening during the Uranus/Pluto Mother-Wave of 2007–20 – with the Mother-Wave itself providing at the very least a constant background hum of touchiness concerning anything even vaguely resembling repression.

Powerlessness against Impersonal Fate or Power

The lone individual, or even a tight and organized group, can still feel hopeless and bereft when pitched against the granite-like edifice of whatever has power over them. As I have already discussed, the roots of these controlling and monolithic institutions run deep. One is caused to wonder where these 'creatures' who wield the political, military and legal might on this planet first sprang from. Was it always this way, and will it always be so? The ongoing groundswell of our human need for freedom keeps our feelings of powerlessness at bay to varying degrees. But now, at this particular juncture in history with its corresponding planetary set-up, where our very existence is possibly under threat as a result of the 'anti-nature' habits and practises that have largely been implemented by these faceless entities, we are asking ourselves, 'Have we not had enough of these beings, whoever they are, running our lives?'

Burma: A Microcosm

The case of Burma serves to sharply exemplify the Mood of these Times. Significantly however, because Burma had, and still has, such a strong spiritual tradition, with a large population of Buddhist monks, two Saturn/Neptune Major Storms (Repression of Spirituality) were hugely influential. Burma was first taken over by the military in 1962, and then martial law was imposed in 1989 {>142 Saturn/Neptune Waves}, following the monks' uprising in 1988 {>196 Saturn/Uranus Waves}. Whatever the outcome of the monks' (and Burmese civilians') demonstrations, and further repression by the State owing to the current Saturn/Neptune Major Storm 2004–08, the real test will come with the Saturn/Pluto Major Storm of 2008–11.

Astro-Quantum

This test, and the following one of 2018–21, will not only apply to every one of us but will also provide opportunities to make progress with respect to diminishing those repressive forces still further. For every time someone identifies and deals with the two key Moods of these Times, it contributes to the energy bank of positive human attitude and behaviour, which in turn leads to the eventual eradication of oppressive power on the planet altogether. The two moods which we must fix firmly in our sights are Prejudice and Paranoia.

Prejudice and Paranoia

Prejudice

This is like a poisonous gas that has been forever circulating on the airwaves. As previously discussed, this is down to a fear of loss and a fear of power. Whenever we feel these fears we have to find someone to blame or distrust, and so we are susceptible to adopting the prejudicial idea that anything or anyone that is 'not with us is against us'. Of course this 'enemy' has also been subject to the same poisonous gas and so a vicious circle is created. This negative phenomenon takes place at a very personal level too – which is where we have to be doubly careful.

Take the following example: an Israeli sees an Arab as the enemy, and vice versa – a long-standing prejudice born of some far off event (and perpetuated by subsequent events born of it) which makes empathy and ensuing discussion and agreement very difficult, if not impossible. But this prejudice itself is made possible by the numbers of *individual* Arabs and Israelis thinking in this prejudicial way. Astro-Quantumwise, this antagonism is supported and furthered by *every individual in the world* who thinks and acts in this way. That is, everyone who has been poisoned by the gas called Prejudice helps to create and spread that gas. Which is pretty much every soul on the planet apart from a very few.

Paranoia

This is simply Prejudice squared or multiplied by itself, escalating by its own pernicious momentum. Prejudice to Paranoia is like a detonator to a bomb. Identify your own prejudices and you defuse the bomb of paranoia.

> ### *Astro-Quantum Memo: War-ning!*
> •
>
> When Saturn/Pluto Major Storms are raging, Prejudice and Paranoia can be greatly increased, and so therefore can the chances of War and Strife.
>
> *Simple Equation: Prejudice^2 = Paranoia = War and Strife*

✦

The Abuse of Occult Power

The leaders and governments of some countries use and have used occult methods such as divination and astrology in order to gain and maintain Plutonian power and Saturnian control. In ancient times this was the rule rather than the exception, but such methods are still used to a degree in the present and in recent history. For example, astrology has been employed for the purposes of timing and decision-making by leaders such as Ronald (and Nancy) Reagan, Charles de Gaulle, Francois Mitterand and Leonid Brezhnev. Further back, we have Hitler, Elizabeth I, Catherine de Medici and the Holy Roman Emperor Rudolph II.

Astrology in itself is neutral, like science or language – it is the ends to which you use it that determine whether it is a good or bad thing. And the word 'occult' is neutral too, for it simply means 'hidden' and does not necessarily mean 'black magic', as is so often believed. Any occult method focuses upon and utilizes information and energies that are not discernable to conventional means of thinking and perception. To what purpose this is done is entirely up to the individual. Science gave us nuclear energy, but this can be used to power homes and industry or to destroy cities full of life.

Whether astrology was used or abused by the above people in power is of course open to question, depending what 'side' you are on. But I think, from the humanitarian standpoint which is firmly and almost automatically adopted by most modern astrologers, we can say that the Nazis at least (mainly through Himmler and Hess) were abusing or misusing astrology. The fact that one of their astrologers, Karl Ernst Krafft, was sent to Buchenwald concentration camp (but died in transit) because he had successfully predicted damaging attacks upon Hitler and the Nazis, gives a grim idea of what it means to be an astrologer on the 'wrong' side. Astrologers are, after all, seeing what is happening or will happen regardless of who likes it or not. We know that we are witnessing the workings of the Divine, and so love, peace and understanding have to be the 'policies' of most astrologers. If you are an astrologer who is advising an obviously tyrannical, cruel and suppressive regime, group or individual, then in effect you are abusing astrology and, so to speak, you are inciting the wrath of the planetary gods – that is, a negative fate. An analogy here is the criminal who gains access to police computers and so manages to keep one step ahead of the law, until one day that very access undoes him as his interference is traced back to his own computer. I wonder what Krafft was seeing in his own chart; could it have been saying he had to be true to his art, no matter what?

In the final analysis, astrology raises the eternal question of what is good and what is evil. *Understanding The Future* goes to great lengths to ensure that Planet-Waves are ridden in a way that puts us in touch with – and that causes us to be motivated by and directed towards - something that is *good* in the most universal sense of the word. In short, that which creates a better world in terms of everyone having a decent quality of life, and that identifies, resists and avoids anything that prevents, undermines or wilfully destroys such a thing.

As a topical and all too potent example of all this, let us look again at the crisis in Burma. I believe that it also serves as a demonstration of what 'good astrology' and Astro-Quantum are, but I'll leave that up to you to judge.

Burma

The demonstrations in this country by Buddhist monks and civilians suing for democracy in the face of the repressive military junta that has been in power since 1962, have been referred to in a number of places in this book. {>144; Saturn/Neptune Waves; >196 Saturn/Uranus Waves} Here we will look at the fact that the military junta uses astrology and other occult means – as have this country's rulers since time immemorial – to further and maintain their power. So far, the military junta has been successful in doing this for themselves, but at the expense of the ordinary Burmese people. The fact that the wedding party and gifts of the leader Than Shwe's daughter cost $50million, while the country itself lives in abject poverty, says it all!

So obviously astrology is being employed here for reasons that are not in aid of the common good. And, true to form, astrologers and clairvoyants who give negative predictions to the Burmese generals are liable to arrest and imprisonment.

Burma broke away from Britain and found independence in 1948. The precise date, time and place (January 4, at 4.20 am in Rangoon) were astrologically chosen as the birth of the 'Union of Burma'. Since then, when 'baby state' finally separated from 'mother colonial power', Burma has had several changes of leadership and political idealogy, most significantly going from democratic government to military dictatorship with a coup d'état in March 1962 {>142 Saturn/Neptune}, and to another leadership of the same martial persuasion in September 1988 {>196 Saturn/Uranus}.

However, I believe that the national horoscope of January 1948 still marks the true birth of this nation, with the traumatic events thereafter being the trials that any entity, be it human individual or nation, would go through. Also, from the following brief interpretation of this chart it can be seen that although the time was picked for astrological reasons by the rulers so that it bestowed power on them, they could not control the real hidden spiritual power within that chart. No-one can override the Planetary Lords themselves for too long!

Most significantly, this birth occurred during a Saturn/Pluto Major Storm which was also the beginning of a New Cycle. Without going into an exhaustive interpretation of its horoscope, suffice to say that it shows a nation at war within itself (a Half-Moon birth). On the one side is the abusive expression of power that has unfortunately been given to Saturn and Pluto (which are conjoined in dictatorial Leo), and on the other is a gentle and spiritual nature (the sensitive Moon being conjoined to transcendental Neptune in harmonious Libra) which best finds focus in a female leader (Venus in the democratic sign of Aquarius Opposing/confronting the powerful but ruthlessly expressed Saturn/Pluto conjunction). That 'gentle and spiritual nature' is embodied in its large population of Buddhist monks, a soft-natured people with a fine cultural tradition, and that woman is Aung

San Suu Kyi, leader of the pro-democracy movement, who has been under house arrest since July 1989.

So Burma could be said to be a microcosm of our world as a whole. The gentle and spiritual nature of humanity is kept down by those who have the political and military power. It is through 'reading the Signs and riding the Waves', as made known to us in planetary cycles, that we can better reach a happy outcome. Successful surfing of the Planetary-Waves of Fate means that one has to tune into, and be true to, the dictates of Fate, rather than forcefully overriding it. In this peaceful and passive way – which paradoxically and most definitely includes having to confront the dangers of a Wave – victory of good over evil is eventually attained. And Burma somehow condenses and encapsulates this dilemma and process. How we individually ride all Waves, and especially Saturn/Pluto Waves, determines their fate in particular and that of our race as a whole.

This is the *positive use* of occult power, the Astro-Quantum.

The Choice is Ours
Easy Surfing

The following chart shows us Positive Responses to Saturn/Pluto Waves
that collectively create Positive Effects. The Negative Responses need
to be avoided in order to prevent the collective Negative Effects. Note
the opposing qualities of the Negatives and Positives, and track back
Negative or Positive Effects to the Responses that created them.

2008–11 and 2018–21
The Collective Effect of Saturn/Pluto Major Storms
The Choice is Ours

Negative Response	Positive Response
Using power in a heavy-handed manner that robs others of their livelihoods, property, human rights and ultimately their lives.	Employing whatever powerful resources are available to make lasting changes and to aid those who are worse off.
Paranoid over-defensiveness and overreaction towards a wrongly perceived or exaggerated threat.	Looking to the state of one's own nation before pointing a finger at the state of any other nation.
Using power with good intentions but with no foresight born of a deep consideration of its possible effects.	Taking the trouble to research and consider what would ultimately be a judicious and therefore beneficial use of power.
Squandering resources on projects that only serve the elite or those who do not deserve it.	Investing resources in projects that thorough research reveals will benefit the masses.

THE USE OF POWER

The State becomes progressively unstable. The people, the main resource, lose hope. Inflation and collapse.	The people try harder and have a greater sense of their worth and so the economy flourishes.
Misapplied power escalates quickly and irresistibly into even greater problems.	Wisely applied power benefiting everyone in an utterly fundamental way.
Self-fulfilling prophecy making an enemy out of whoever you mistakenly perceive as being one.	Only when you have cleaned up your own backyard can you help another clean up theirs.
Strife and destruction contributing to an ongoing vicious cycle of attack-revenge-attack. Hard-boiled power structures.	Reduction of poverty and bad living conditions in needful countries creating better conditions the world over indefinitely.

Negative Effect	Positive Effect

A Saturn/Pluto Favourable Wind August 2006–August 2008

What Kind of Time is This?
A Time of Constructive Use of Power

Energies in Play as we Ride This Wave

The harmonious combining of the positive and essential energy and character of Saturn – that of **authority and stability,** which is **establishing and/or ordering** – with the essential energy and character of Pluto – that of **depth and authenticity**, which is **empowering and/or regenerating** – offers the opportunity to get the best of both these worlds.

This Favourable Wind occurs at a time when it is much needed, at the very beginning of the Uranus/Pluto Mother-Wave 2007–20, the middle and end of a Saturn/Neptune Major Storm 2004–08, and the beginning of a Saturn/Uranus Major Storm 2007–12. So what could potentially be a really rocky time – as described in the chapters covering these Waves – is stabilized and managed fairly well by the powers that be, and you and I. Leaders who have relatively positive attitudes about the use of power and authority are able to help those in need of order and regeneration. However, what with quite the opposite happening during this Wave so far (October 2007) in countries such as Iraq, Afghanistan, Darfur, Zimbabwe and Burma, one could be forgiven for thinking, 'What kind of Favourable Wind is this?' The simple answer is that without it, matters here and in other places would actually be worse. And at the time of writing we are just past the peak of this Wave, the halfway mark, so hopefully there will be a more noticeable 'constructive use of power' for the remainder of it.

Astro-Quantum

Here is the whole point of this book. Through being conscious of a Favourable Wind we can use it consciously as individuals and thereby contribute our energies towards creating a more positive effect overall. But it is important here to repeat what has already been pointed out in 'Surf's Up' (< 17): Favourable Winds are nowhere near as strong as Major Storms, and you have to 'set your sails right' in order to benefit form them. Major Storms sweep you up in their dynamic path whether you are thinking about them or not! This is a fact of astrology and a fact of life. It is easier to fall off a log than it is to climb a tree; it's easier to not make an effort than it is to make one.

The Universe is a dynamic place that demands effort and awareness from all who want to function in it, especially on heavy-gravity planets like the one we are living on – that is, we are mostly obliged to 'climb trees' rather than just 'fall off logs' . The planet that governs gravity is Saturn; this is why most of the Major Storms involve Saturn. They are phenomena born of gravity – weight and pressure and force of circumstances – working against the other planet in question, forcing its energies to manifest in the material world. As we have seen in this chapter, Saturn, when interacting with Pluto – the planet of power, destruction and elimination of the outworn – packs a very uncompromising punch, which is more difficult to handle than any other Planet-Wave. Consequently, even a Favourable Wind made by these two planets requires a certain amount of control and insight to reveal its positive aspects.

Making the Most of This Favourable Wind

If you feel some strong emotion, intention or conviction, then find the discipline and patience to do it justice. This will count far more than if you just acted impulsively without any forethought. Saturn and Pluto help you to achieve results if you show willing. If you are half-hearted or just relying on luck to get the best from anything you want to accomplish, then you will be like a yachtsman who doesn't raise his sails. A Chinese proverb says, 'Raise your sail one foot and you get ten feet of wind.' But if you don't raise it at all you get nothing .

Another quality that Saturn/Pluto favours is selflessness. The better the whole world is, the better it is for the individuals living in it, including you! In fact, Saturn/Pluto lays down the law that says one's own life will only ever be in order when the whole world is. So projects and ideas that benefit your neighbourhood, group, friends or anyone or anything deserving of assistance, all catch this wind and cause the sails to billow!

On the world stage, agreements and statutes that stabilize and benefit any region, people or institution can be expected – although their success will vary according to how well conceived and executed they (and your own projects) are. Examples of both extremes that have already manifested are the Northern Ireland peace deal brokered in May 2007 by the then UK Prime Minister Tony Blair, and the disaster that is Iraq, for which Blair is also responsible, along with George W. Bush, which significantly began during a Saturn/Neptune Major Storm. {☺ > 144 and 148 Saturn/Neptune Waves}.

On a personal level, to see how this Favourable Wind affects you, consult and use the House positions of Saturn and Pluto, as described below on page 127. With a Favourable Wind you can expect the best of these interpretations, and see how the influences of both serve and support one another. Also, you can use the Saturn/Pluto Meditation or Prayer on page 134 to greater effect and with greater ease.

The Unfolding Story

⇉ Merging Waves & ⚲ Jupiter Boosters

In addition to the Uranus/Pluto Mother-Wave that has been taken into account in the interpretations of all three Saturn/Pluto Waves covered in this chapter, there are also other Planet-Waves *merging* with them and affecting them as time goes by. As well as these Merging Waves there are Planet-Waves involving Jupiter that come into the Saturn/Pluto picture, and Jupiter kind of *boosts* whatever is happening, blowing things up so we cannot fail to notice problems or take advantage of opportunities! As can be seen on the Planet-Wave Weather Chart on page 19, Jupiter Waves exist in their own right, and are responsible for Minor Storms and Favourable Breezes, but are not covered in this book for reasons of time and space! Along with the Merging Waves, they increase or modify the effects of the two Saturn/Pluto Major Storms and the Favourable Wind when they are happening at the same time.

The Planet-Wave Chronicles

Taken altogether, these Merging Waves and Jupiter Boosters kind of dramatize and pace the overall course of Saturn/Pluto Waves, rather like a storyteller would do, unfolding its stories.

During the Saturn/Pluto Favourable Wind Aug 2006 to Aug 2008

⇉ Saturn/Neptune Major Storm – Nov 2004 to Aug 2008 {>136}

With regard to typical expressions of this kind of Major Storm – such as political bungling and poor decision-making at a high level, like Iraq and Hurricane Katrina – the error of these ways has, thanks to this Favourable Wind, been clocked and appreciated. Even if the perpetrators of these inefficiencies have not taken it on board themselves, a clearer idea is in the mind of the public, making for more transparent and 'listening' government in future, which in turn makes for a more 'constructive use of power'.

✗ **Jupiter/Pluto Minor Storm – Jan 2007 to Sep 2008 –**
The Power of Belief

✗ **Jupiter/Saturn Favourable Breeze – Feb 2007 to Jan 2009 –**
Benevolent Control

The combination of these Boosters with this Favourable Breeze is particularly positive. The happy, and possibly unexpected, release of the British journalist Allan Johnstone after 16 weeks of imprisonment by Palestinian militants, the Army of Islam, in July 2007 is a good example of this in action. This is especially relevant, considering that it was largely due to the positive belief of 200,000 petitioners in the UK alone and, probably most of all, the persistent and heavy pressure applied by the new government of Gaza, Hamas (albeit for political motives) into whose hands he was actually released. Apart from any other kinds of progress that this triple whammy can bestow on us, it is hoped that it may create a foundation for more harmony and agreement in the Middle East. This could be hindered, or helped further, by the next Major Storm.

⟶ **Saturn/Uranus Major Storm – Sep 2007 to Jul 2012 (>188}**

Our Saturn/Pluto Favourable Wind may indeed soften the disruptive and discordant effects of this Saturn/Uranus Major Storm, but only during its first year of 'brewing'. Considering that the Saturn/Pluto Major Storm of 2008–11 (see below) takes over a few months after the Favourable Wind ends, a great deal of good feeling and diplomacy will need to have been established and applied to make a difference to what threatens to be a rocky ride as these two Major Storms, plus the overarching Uranus/Pluto Mother Storm, peak and intensify between 2008 and 2012.

During the Saturn/Pluto Major Storm Nov 2008 to Aug 2011

↗ **Jupiter/Saturn Favourable Breeze – Feb 2007 to Jan 2009 –**
Benevolent Control

As has just been pointed out, this will go some way to reducing or
dealing with the potentially very negative effects of the Saturn/Pluto
Major Storm, the most notorious of all Planet-Waves.

⇛ **Saturn/Uranus Major Storm – Sep 2007 to Jul 2012 {>188}**

Again, as has just been described, this merging of two Major Storms,
together with the Uranus/Pluto Mother Wave, is potentially very
destructive, and the reason why this book was written in the first place.
Understanding what these three Planet-Waves in particular pose, and
riding them properly, is extremely important, at least for maintaining
stability and preventing disaster – hopefully, by using their energy
skilfully and mindfully, we can even go forward and up.

↗ **Jupiter/Saturn Minor Storm – Mar 2010 to Mar 2012 –**
Growth versus Order

↗ **Jupiter/Pluto Minor Storm – May 2010 to Apr 2011–**
The Power of Belief 2

We need these two Boosters like a poke in the eye with a sharp stick!
But obviously the Planetary Lords have decreed that we need to have
the error of our ways driven home to us in no uncertain terms with
respect to this Saturn/Pluto Major Storm 2008/11. In a nutshell: this
could be our last call to co-operate before it's too late, with the cusp of
2010–11 being the most telling in this respect.

⇛ **Saturn/Neptune Favourable Wind – Dec 2010 to Nov 2013 {>170}**

It would be good if this one could arrive a bit sooner, but again that is
not the way of the Cosmos or the plot of life on Earth. But it could be
arriving just in the nick of time considering what has just been said
regarding the end of 2010 and beginning of 2011! It seems that this
period is critical. We could now pull ourselves out of the fire – politically,

---

Astro-Quantum Memo

. . . .

It is in our power, individually as well as collectively, to turn the Armageddon machine around. It mainly depends on waking up to this, following Planetary Lore and using other mind-power tools to manifest positive change. This book provides you with these tools.

We do have the power to change
but we must change to have the power

---

environmentally, economically and spiritually – or find ourselves being roasted some more! See the Astro-Quantum Memo above.

⚹ Jupiter/Pluto Favourable Breeze – May 2011 to May 2012 – *Regeneration*

This positive Booster is somewhat relative considering that it is occurring in the thick of a crisis. It can be anything from damage limitation to too little too late, or it could even bring something to save us at the 11th hour. Some might say that it'll be Divine Intervention. But let's just say, 'Heaven helps those who help themselves.'

During the Saturn/Pluto Major Storm Jan 2018 to Dec 2021

⇗ Saturn/Uranus Favourable Wind – Nov 2015 to Dec 2018 {>217}

Hopefully we will make the best of this one in terms of human affairs and the resolution of certain difficulties, especially relating to the environment, international accord and technical issues. This would put us in a good position in the face of the usual Saturn/Pluto challenges!

⚡ **Jupiter/Saturn Minor Storm – Dec 2019 to Apr 2021 –**
Growth versus Order 3

⚡ **Jupiter/Pluto Minor Storm – Jan 2020 to Jan 2021 –**
The Power of Belief 5

This could be seen as a case of 'If the right hand doesn't get you then the left hand will', for it is in many ways a repeat of the crisis of 2010/2011 described on page 124. In other words, if we as a 'civilization' failed to cooperate with one another in sufficient numbers back then, we will certainly need to get that message this time. But then, this could be purely academic. This time could mark a completely new beginning following a distinct end – but the success of our cooperative efforts could all depend on how long ago that 'end' occurred.

⇥ **Saturn/Uranus Major Storm – Jan 2020 to Oct 2022 {>188}**

This Major Storm drives in the above proviso right up to the hilt. Let's just say that *Understanding The Future* made its appeal for positive action way back in 2008–12, and I hope that my call will have been heard and acted upon in plenty of time.

Personal Effect

This is how, as an individual, Saturn/Pluto Waves can affect you, and be ridden successfully by you, for their duration.

Surfing with Saturn and Pluto Through the Houses

These effects are based upon the two Houses in your chart through which Saturn and Pluto are passing or 'transiting' while the Uranus/Pluto Mother-Wave is active, but most significantly during the times when Saturn/Pluto Waves are active. As it is a case of a need for Order, Discipline and Effort where Saturn is concerned, and for Empowerment, Elimination and Transformation where Pluto is concerned, knowing these positions will help you to manage the energies of each respective planet in an appropriate way, enabling you to find the right balance and surf successfully!

There are two ways to use this aid.

1 **Off-The-Peg** This is using the Saturn and Pluto positions according to what is known as your Birth-Sign, Sun Sign or Star Sign. This looks at what Solar Houses Saturn and Pluto are transiting through while the Uranus/Pluto Mother-Wave is active. So using the **Planet House Transit Guide** (beginning on page 254), first go to the **Saturn: House Ready-Reckoner** on page 262. Next, look at the left-hand column for the time **Period** you are interested in, then look along the row until you get to the column of your **Birth Sign**. There you will see the number of the House being transited by Saturn – 1st, 2nd, 3rd, etc – and just below it

the number of the page where you can read the description of possible situations and actions you can take. Straight after this, do the same thing for Pluto – that is, go to **Pluto: House Ready-Reckoner** on page 286 and use that table in the same way that you used the Saturn one. Now you can get a feel for how the two planet positions compare. All this can be very useful and accurate, but remember that it is only based on your Sun Sign.

2 **Made-To-Measure** This is using the Saturn and Pluto positions according to your individual birth chart which would have to be calculated correctly from a reliably accurate birth time. So if you do know your birth time and have your birth chart accurately drawn up, then anyone with a basic knowledge of a chart will be able to tell you which Houses in your personal chart are occupied by Saturn and Pluto at any given time between 2007 and 2020, but especially, remember, when a Saturn/Pluto Wave is active. Then simply find and consult the readings for those Houses in the **Planet House Transit Guide** (page 254). For example, if your astrologer or your own astrological calculation told you that Saturn was transiting your Tenth House and Pluto was transiting your Fourth House, then you would find those interpretations on the pages indicated in the Planet House Transit Guide by using the **Index** on the first page of it. So for our example the Index would send you to page 267 for Saturn transiting the Tenth House, and to page 292 for Pluto transiting the Fourth House. Note: you do *not* use the Ready-Reckoner when using Made-To-Measure.

The Saturn/Pluto Wave Effect Upon Relationships

Quite simply, a Saturn/Pluto Wave is asking: How deeply involved are you, or do you want to be? As ever, the Major Storms are demanding answers, rather than just offering you opportunities, as the Favourable Wind can. So during Saturn/Pluto Major Storms the heat and pressure are on to forge a deep and strong bond with someone, or a deeper and stronger one if you are already involved with someone. The thing is that neither Saturn, nor Pluto in particular, take any prisoners. This means that you either get closer and more intimately aware of one another on all levels – physical, emotional, mental and spiritual – or the relationship begins to break down on one or more of these levels, or a relationship never materializes.

The Storm might first show itself as increased friction and argument, but this should be read as a call to break through misunderstandings and be far more honest with one another. If the relationship is strong enough it will weather the Storm and come out a great deal stronger by the end of it. Pretence or superficiality just won't wash with this pincer movement from two heavy Planets. Being prepared to expose your deepest and darkest thoughts and feelings is the key. This naturally involves a substantial degree of trust in your partner – actual or prospective.

You'll need to remember two things here. First, there could well be an initial negative reaction to this more profound expression of your needs and feelings. But it is through persevering, and then very possibly receiving a similar disclosure from your opposite number, that the new and stronger bond begins to be forged. Secondly, be aware that you are dealing with your fear – and your partner's fear – of not being loved and accepted for what you truly are, as distinct from an image each of you has been presenting and living with because of that fear.

If you are not that compatible – the word means 'being able to suffer with' then the relationship will die, unless you are prepared to persevere with an increasingly unsatisfactory 'arrangement' rather than with a real relationship. Quite simply the reward is in proportion to the effort.

During the Favourable Wind such a deepening of the relationship is a lot easier, but not necessarily so profound, and you may not even feel the need for it. But that does not mean to say that need isn't there; you may just be pretending it isn't there precisely for fear of a greater intimacy. When a Major Storm comes, though, you will feel the need.

If you are alone, wanting a partner or not, or wishing to get back with a past or estranged partner, then all the above 'rules' still apply, but success depends on you being and showing willing to be more intimate, with all that such entails.

The Choice is Yours
Easy Surfing

The chart on the next page shows us Positive Responses to Saturn/Pluto Waves that create Positive Effects for you personally and ultimately for everyone. The Negative Responses need to be avoided in order to prevent the Negative Effects in your own life. Note the opposing qualities of the Negatives and Positives, and track back Negative or Positive Effects to the Responses that created them.

2008–11 and 2018–21
The Personal Effect of Saturn/Pluto Major Storms
The Choice is Yours

Negative Response

Entrenching yourself in old and outworn ways and places in the face of obviously changing circumstances that seem threatening.

Positive Response

Recognizing the need for major changes even though it seems that they are very challenging and daunting.

Allowing things to degenerate or worsen because you can't be bothered or because you believe you can't afford to remedy them.

Identifying and seeing any structures or conditions that are in need of repair or replacement, even in spite of scant resources.

Believing you are powerless to overcome a negative fate. Something or someone has given you this false impression.

Awareness that something deep inside you is superior to fate. Sensing you have a destiny means you can muster whatever is needed.

Jumping at superficial or apparently easier explanations for or solutions to problems.

Looking for and at the deeper underlying reasons for any problem or condition.

REGENERATE OR DETERIORATE

Problems turn into crises. Crises turn into disasters. Collapse and ruin.

Sound attitude and lasting solutions to long-standing or deep-seated problems.

Negativity empowered by these Waves becomes something very destructive and depressing. Nothing succeeds like failure.

Strength goes to strength as your sense of personal power finds more and more ways to further empower you and improve your lot.

A false economy is worse than a lack of economy because it reflects a lack of faith in your own resources, with a drop in living standard to match.

You find that that not only do you save money and time through maintaining what requires it, but that you are more efficient and profitable.

What you thought was the world and life you had to preserve at all costs now turns out to be rife with problems that did not exist before.

A substantial improvement in your circumstances and lifestyle, especially when you observe that the 'devil you knew' that you left behind has since become unacceptable

Negative Response

Positive Response

The Saturn/Pluto Balance of Power

The following two pages provides two wonderfully basic ways to ride the Saturn/Pluto Major Storms. For a simple way to surf these Planet-Waves, and ride them to where they want to get to – as shown in 'The Spirit of this Time' – and at the same time bypass The Devil of this Time, use the Saturn/Pluto Balance of Power chart on the next page.

In the upper half of the page, you will see in the left-hand column various symptoms that you could be experiencing if you are leaning too much in the Saturn direction, that is, over-emphasizing caution, convention, the known, defensiveness, territory, etc. The right-hand column then suggests various ways of redressing the balance with Plutonian remedies, which mainly involve getting in touch with and using deeper insights and convictions, and more emotionally genuine qualities.

In the lower half of the page, the left-hand column lists symptoms resulting from overdoing Pluto – with obsessions, dark thoughts, etc – and the right-hand column suggests Saturnian remedies that encourage a more pragmatic, realistic and disciplined approach.

As a rule each numbered item is balanced by the equivalent numbered item in the right column, but not always – there are crossovers.

The second basic way to ride Saturn/Pluto Major Storms is the Meditation on page 134

The Saturn/Pluto Balance of Power

Too Much Saturn and not Enough Pluto

If this is the case, you could be experiencing some of these symptoms.

1. Feeling out of control or fearful of losing control. Fearful of those with power over you or who frighten you.
2. Economic hardship. Feeling that you do not have the wherewithal to meet what is required of you.
3. Bedevilled by stale patterns, habits and standards holding you back.
4. Acting too late in response to the need for change, or resenting it. Falling between two stools.

Too Much Pluto and not Enough Saturn

If this is the case, you could be experiencing some of these symptoms.

1. Feeling that what you are doing or have set in motion has little or no chance of success or resolution.
2. A sign that obsessions are posing as convictions is that you cannot remember anything anyone said to you that disagreed with you. This is a bad sign.
3. Having great problems with those who are in authority, or who have more power than you in some important respect.
4. Your desires preoccupy and frustrate you, or get you into hot water.

Plutonian Remedies

Adopt one or more of these remedies to offset and relieve the symptoms of 'too much Saturn'.

1. Either let go completely or vigorously seize power. Danger lies in dithering between the two.
2. Concentrate on creating the feeling that you attract wealth. Identify and be convinced of your assets.
3. Draw up a list of things in your life you wish to transform, remember you are going to die one day, and do what's on the list!
4. Sense the inevitable and then accept it, and go with it in good spirit. You are surprised and deeply moved by its refreshing and healing effect.

Saturnian Remedies

Adopt one or more of these remedies to offset and relieve the symptoms of 'too much Pluto'.

1. First, check that you are being patient, methodical or disciplined enough. If not, it is better to cut your losses than get in even deeper. It is better to lose face than your well-being and self-respect.
2. Take time out to listen to people you depend on, trust, or who are in the business of assessing the viability of things. Follow their advice.
3. Recognize where you have to conform to certain rules, or go along with someone's wishes, because there will be more trouble if you don't.
4. If seeking to satisfy a desire causes more pain than pleasure, that is a bad desire and you must drop it.

Note: It is quite possible to experience both too much Saturn and too much Pluto at the same time.

Saturn/Pluto Wave Meditation

This is the simplest and the best: a Meditation or Prayer for the
Spirit of these Times. Sit quietly with it and gaze at the symbols,
alone or with others, while inwardly or outwardly uttering the
invocation as many times and for as long as you wish. It is
especially recommended that you perform this ritual during any
Hotspots involving a Saturn/Pluto Wave
(see Appendix page 294).

My fellow beings and I
Identify, admit and take full responsibility for
Our own negative feelings and opinions
And all that they bring into our lives.

In this way we no longer judge ourselves
Or bear prejudice towards others.
In this way we eliminate conflict
And ultimately all wars upon this Earth.
And the Land once more shall be Pure.

CHAPTER 4

Saturn/Neptune Waves
2007–20

What Kind Of Times Are These?
Times of Transcendence of Limitations,
and of Practical Vision

Active Periods	Wave Weather	How To Ride
November 2004– August 2008	Major Storm	Pages 136–69, 172–85
December 2010– November 2013	Favourable Wind	Pages 170–71, 174–75
November 2014– September 2017	Major Storm	Pages 136–69, 172–85

Saturn/Neptune Major Storms
November 2004–August 2008
November 2014–September 2017

What Kind Of Times Are These?
Times of Transcendence of Limitations

Energies in Play as We Ride These Waves

The energies of Saturn are interacting with the energies of Neptune and everyone and everything on planet Earth will be subject to these interactions for the duration of their influence, as well as to the after-effects that follow upon these Planet-Waves. Remember that two planets interacting is rather like two very different and strong-minded people coming into contact and the best and the worst of each is brought out and magnified. But Saturn and Neptune do the same to one another on a cosmic scale, and this affects us all!

ℏ   The character of **Saturn** is **Territory and Stability** and its energy is **Suppressing and/or Ordering**

♆   The character of **Neptune** is **Mass Emotion and Spirituality** and its energy is **Uniting and/or Confusing**

Their combined effect is therefore...
Suppressing and/or Ordering Mass Emotion and Spirituality
Uniting and/or Confusing Territory and Stability

Demoralization – Authorities Let Us Down

Saturn/Neptune Waves are a tricky mix, often manifesting as an atmosphere of not knowing where you stand, of feeling despondent, demoralized or listless. What or who we look to for order and authority now appears to let us down, or keep us down by taxing, cheapening or outlawing our dreams and escape routes. A special and subtle characteristic of these Waves – and the secret to surfing them – is that they'll wear you out and down if you are only out for yourself, or if you only believe in what you can touch, see and prove. So the advice here is frequently to make a point of thinking and acting in a way that ignores immediate personal or material satisfaction in favour of something more spiritual and selfless, something that serves the whole, and to see happiness more as a product of the imagination than of reason.

To stay afloat we need to be buoyed up by a sense of our oneness, interdependence and vision. This is why 'Transcendence of Limitations' is the key phrase for these Waves – limitations set down by national boundaries, race, religion, gender or anything else that can lead to separation, segregation or prejudice. Because we live in an age that has conditioned us to be the very things that Saturn/Neptune Waves oblige us to sacrifice – self-serving and materialistic – this means that we can have a very hard time of it. We could define the selfish and materialistic way as that of 'ego', and that of oneness and imagination as 'spirit'.

Land and Sea

In both a literal and symbolic way, Saturn and Neptune can be seen to interact in much the same way as the land and the sea. The land has natural boundaries such as coastlines and mountain ranges, whereas the sea has no boundaries at all other than those defined by the land. The point is that the sea is continually eroding the land, reshaping it, reminding us that in the end there are no such things as boundaries. And in the end the land, starting with the ice-caps and ice-sheets which lie somewhere between the two, will all return to the sea. So Neptune is forever calling us to transcend the limitations set by our boundaries and differences, for as sure as ocean is ocean, that's what will inevitably happen anyway. When Neptune meets Saturn there is always a **dissolving of boundaries**, a theme you'll witness throughout.

Let Me Entertain You

Something else very much in keeping with the betterment of the whole, that is a very positive expression of Neptune's unifying energy and Saturn's form-giving energy, is new forms of music and art, of dance and media, as you will see.

Dateline 2007: Previously, and So Far

Your Planet-Wave surfing can be greatly helped by knowing what happened during previous Saturn/Neptune Major Storms, as well as looking at what has happened so far with the one which is occurring as I write – the Saturn/Neptune Major Storm 2004–08. We have already touched upon this and other Saturn/Neptune Waves back in the Introduction, so as we revisit some of the issues looked at there, you may think you are experiencing déjà vu – which itself is a very Saturn/Neptune thing! For instance, the 2004–08 Wave has probably ended by the time you read this, but even when the Planet-Wave has disappeared from view, it is still with us, below the surface, until it rises again. In this Saturn/Neptune Storm Cycle it will be between 2014 and 2017. So still riding it right will make a difference *now and in the future*. This is the transcendental nature of *Understanding The Future*, for Time (Saturn) is an Illusion (Neptune).

So if you want to jump right into – or right *back* into – this Wave now, then leap ahead to page 143. But we open our review of Saturn/Neptune Major Storms at the turn of the 20th century, focusing mainly on times when they are peaking, for technically this is the most powerful part of a Wave.

Saturn/Neptune Major Storm 1898–1901 (peaking 1900/01)

The Birth of Cinema in December 1900, making mass viewing possible for the first time.
Prohibition of alcohol kicked off in the United States in 1901, which could be interpreted as authority denying escape from its own repressive structures.

Saturn/Neptune Major Storm 1908–11 (peaking 1909/10)

The Prohibition movement spread in the US during 1909. New art movements: the birth of Art Nouveau in 1909 and parallelism in 1910. The Variety Theater opened in 1910, with Fred Astaire and his sister Adele.

Saturn/Neptune Major Storm 1916–19 (New Cycle, peaking 1917)

This was the beginning of a new Saturn/Neptune Storm Cycle lasting 36 years (see Appendix 2 for an explanation of what a Cycle is). You can see just by the events listed that it meant business! {🕐 191 Saturn/Uranus}

Spanish Flu

Yet another form of boundary dissolution can be seen in the Spanish Influenza Pandemic of 1918 (death toll between 20 and 40 million), which happened during this Saturn/Neptune Wave, with the crossing of country boundaries, immune system boundaries, and species boundaries (as this was reckoned to be originally a bird flu that crossed over to humans). At the time of writing, during the Saturn/Neptune Wave of 2004–08, there is increasing alarm at the possibility of this happening again with the current spread of bird flu. {>156 The Butterfly Effect}

World War One

An equally profound but negative expression of Saturn/Neptune was of course World War One (1914–18), particularly in its latter part with its mud (earth plus water), immovability and mounting senselessness. Also consider the use of poisonous gases such as chlorine and mustard that literally crossed both physical and biological boundaries – and one could say moral and legal ones as well. Of course we were monstrously let down by generals and politicians sending millions of young men to their deaths quite needlessly. Rank futility following general stupidity.

The Russian Revolution

The critical and symbolic point of the Russian Revolution that came with the storming of the Winter Palace in October 1917 was not only a classic expression of authority and boundaries dissolving, but perfectly pre-echoed the revolutionaries' own demise with the coming down of the Berlin Wall in 1989, exactly one whole cycle of Saturn/Neptune Waves later. (See explanation of Planet Wave Cycles on page 239).

Saturn/Neptune Major Storm 1925–27 (peaking 1926)

Entertainment and media smashes: The Jazz and Blues Age began in 1925; also premieres of film classics Battleship Potemkin and The Great Gatsby. In 1927 Fritz Lang's sci-fi classic Metropolis opened, and the Charleston dance craze took off. The birth of television occurred in 1926, along with the New Realism art movement.

There was economic crisis in 1926 with the General Strike in Great Britain. Britain also relinquished total dominion of her Empire.

Saturn/Neptune Major Storm 1935–37 (peaking 1936/37)

During the peak in 1936, Fred Astaire and Ginger Rogers created a new dance form, while Saturnian separatism assailed Neptunian unity as the Spanish Civil War began and race issues reared their head at the Olympic Games in Berlin. Saturnian tradition and authority dissolved with the abdication of King Edward VIII.

Land and water resonated with the devastation of the Mississippi and Ohio floods in 1937.

Saturn/Neptune Major Storm 1943–45 (peaking 1944/45)

Both demoralization and relief were prevalent with the disclosure and liberation of Nazi death camps during 1944/45, and the war worsened and wore on. In 1945 European borders were redefined at Yalta, Hitler committed suicide, and Germany surrendered unconditionally.

Saturn/Neptune Major Storm 1951–54 (New Cycle, peaking 1952/53)

November 4 1952 brought an earthquake (at 9.0M one of the 13 largest since 1900) in Kamchatka, Russia. {☉ 193 Saturn/Uranus}

In 1953 {☉ 193 Saturn/Uranus}, Crick and Watson determined the form of DNA, the invisible and universal (Neptune) building block (Saturn) of life. Rock 'n' Roll was born with Elvis Presley, Little Richard and Bill Haley.

Russian tanks crushed revolt in East Berlin – the cold heart of the Cold War.

Saturn/Neptune Major Storm 1961–64 (peaking 1962/63)

1962 witnessed boundary and race issues with the Cuban Missile Crisis, the Sino-Indian War, and troops being sent to quell black/white conflict in Alabama. In Burma, a beautiful and spiritual people were crushed in a military coup. That same year saw the first global television broadcast, but on the demoralizing side Marilyn Monroe died and President Kennedy was assassinated in 1963, a year which also saw the Profumo scandal in Britain.

Saturn/Neptune Major Storm 1970–73 (peaking 1971/72)

Authority was undermined during this Storm with the use of drugs widespread amongst Vietnam troops and Vietnam veterans throwing away their medals in 1971, and burglars being arrested in the Watergate offices in 1972.

1971 witnessed the very first major benefit concert, for the relief of Bangladesh cyclone victims, and the release of the highly controversial film *A Clockwork Orange*. Also in 1972 'Glam Rock' was born.

Border dissolutions included Britain inauspiciously joining the Common Market in 1971 and North Vietnam invading the South in 1972.

Saturn/Neptune Major Storm 1978–81 (peaking 1979/80)

In 1979 Pol Pot was condemned for genocide in Cambodia. Meanwhile, in the same year, another major benefit concert, 'A Gift of Song: the Music for Unicef' was held. Demoralization and border incursions were witnessed with the US embassy hostage crisis in Tehran, the attack on the Grand Mosque in Mecca, Russians invading Afghanistan – and in 1980 the Tehran embassy hostage rescue disaster.

Mother Earth resonated to all this during these same two peak years with the United States and Caribbean being hit by two hurricanes, and Mount St Helens in Washington erupting numerous times leaving 57 dead or missing.

Saturn/Neptune Major Storm 1987-91 (New Cycle, peaking 1989)

Another classic beginning of a new Saturn/Neptune Storm Cycle. In 1989 we saw again dissolution of boundaries and disillusionment with authority with the coming down of the Berlin Wall and the end of the Soviet Union, and the imposition of martial law in Burma following peaceful demonstrations against the regime by the leader of the pro-democracy movement, Aung San Suu Kyi, and indigenous Buddhist monks the year before. Yet during the same year, boundary-breaking 'accidents' or 'acts of god' occurred such as the Exxon Valdez oil spill off Alaska and a massive earthquake in the San Francisco Bay Area. Other typical and contributory events of this Major Storm:

1988	'Perestroika' or restructuring in what was formerly the USSR leading to the dissolution of this and other communist states over the following few years.
1989	Russians withdrew from Afghanistan, having invaded during the Wave before last in 1979.
1989	Hillsborough football stadium disaster in England.
1989	Rebellion crushed in Tiananmen Square, China.
1989	Mass border crossings from East to West Germany.
1989	Massive earthquake in San Francisco.
1989	Solidarity won Polish elections.
1989	US invaded Panama.
1990	Burmese government held free elections for the first time in almost 30 years, but when beaten refused to step down. {☽196 Saturn/Uranus}

Saturn/Neptune Major Storm 1997–2000 (peaking 1998/99)

This saw the dissolution of Yugoslavia, or the Balkan crisis, with its wars and ethnic cleansing atrocities. Wars and country territories changing obviously fall within the 'invasion/dissolution of boundaries' nature of Saturn/Neptune, whereas ethnic cleansing has to do with mass emotion (Neptune) and old karmic scores (Saturn, who is known as the Lord of Karma – Old Father Time, in fact). See also Saturn/Uranus Wave on page 197.

Saturn/Neptune Major Storm 2004–08

This Wave is something of a *prologue* as it began before the start of the over-arching Uranus/Pluto Mother Wave of 2007–20 – which is the main 'time-focus' of this book – and it colours the first couple of years of it. So it has an important influence as it sets the scene for the great Mother Wave.

So as this Planet-Wave is happening as I write, it will have more or less ebbed away by the time of reading. However, to save confusion by using past, present and future tenses as I set down what this Wave bears, I have written it, as a rule, in the present tense. Again, bear in mind that as Waves come in succession and are all interconnected, it also means that how we relate to a Planet-Wave even when it has ebbed away – like this one does around the end of summer 2008 – makes a difference to how future Waves are experienced, expressed and manifested.

Asian Tsunami and Hurricane Katrina

For example, regarding these two events that dramatically, and quite literally, marked the initial appearance of this Wave in 2004 (December 26 earthquake at 9.1M creating the tsunami – ☽ 93 Saturn/Pluto, and Hurricane Katrina in August 2005), we are still strongly affected by them, are still clearing up after them, and are still pondering why such disasters should ever have happened and if and when they will happen again. The following 'planetary lore' goes some way to answering these very questions, along with others that this Saturn/Neptune Wave raises. First, though, it should also be emphasized that another one of the largest earthquakes since 1900 (at 8.6M) struck on March 28 2005 in Northern Sumatra, Indonesia.

As I discuss how this Wave has shown so far, and what happened during previous Saturn/Neptune Waves, we get some idea of what these Waves are all about. First, let's look at this Wave so far, and with the aid of planetary symbolism become more aware of the whys and wherefores.

Remember that the Neptune 'hand' of the Cosmic Clock indicates energies and influences that have, at one end of its spectrum, to do with **dreams** and **ideals**, and a **sense of spirituality** and **oceanic oneness** – but, at the other end, with illusions and subsequent **disappointment**, and being inundated by something **beyond our control**. And you will remember that Saturn indicates matters concerning quite the opposite, such as **authority**, **material reality**, **order**, **control** and **boundaries**.

So 2004 saw immense public disillusionment with authority, evidenced most particularly in Bush's re-election, but also in disenchantment with politicians and government worldwide, not least of all Blair and his government in Great Britain. This was mainly due to that most critical of Saturn/Neptune issues – boundary incursion – with the occupations of Afghanistan and Iraq, for spurious reasons that blurred the line between true and false. {☿92 Saturn/Pluto Waves} Yet, at the same time, there occurred a dissolution of boundaries as the ocean, in the form of the tsunami, inundated the coastline of several Asian countries.

During the same period, in 2005, we saw the flooding of New Orleans as a result of Hurricane Katrina, along with the scandalously inept handling of this disaster by the authorities. Such ineptitude is also in evidence with Greek authorities' handling of the forest fires that began sweeping their country during August 2007. But this disaster itself was down to the Saturn/Uranus Wave 2007–12 commencing at this time, as too were the fires in California in October of that year. {☿ 198 Saturn/Uranus}

A Warning about all Saturn/Neptune Waves

A negative expression or manifestation of these Waves, the next one being **November 2014–September 2017**, is an increased sense of difference or separation. This could mean, therefore, an aggravated continuation of what has already been set in motion with respect to previous Saturn/Neptune Waves. So there could be more, or a worsening or recurrence of disasters like Iraq,

Afghanistan, the Asian Tsunami and Hurricane Katrina, or pandemics like Spanish Flu (see Saturn/Neptune Major Storm 1916–19 above on page 139) if we do not or cannot read the writing on the wall. How natural disasters have an effect on human behaviour is explained in The Butterfly Effect {>156}.

Positive Notes

In the 'tradition' of Saturn/Neptune Waves a Benefit Concert – Live Earth 2007 – was held on July 7 2007. This time such an event was to raise awareness and funds to combat global warming. This is totally in keeping with Astro-Quantum as it contributes to the overall mass-mind-movement that can save the day. Also, a peace deal was brokered between England and Northern Ireland that looks more promising than any before it.

✦

What Is Real?

Saturn/Neptune Waves can raise the question of what is real and what is not. One can get confused over what matters and what doesn't. Do I try harder or just float downstream? A sad story demonstrates this dilemma in a fatal way – actually it's a Saturn/Neptune story within a Saturn/Neptune story. An engaged couple got trapped on a ledge in a cave owing to sudden floods in Thailand. The woman decided to hang on to the rock (Saturn) but her partner thought he could let go and flow with the current to get help (Neptune). He drowned, she survived.

Saturn/Neptune forces one to ask: Is everything an illusion? Is that idea an illusion too? Do I concentrate on my inner world or the outer world? The stock answer is that one should do more of both, or rather create a balance between the two. Where Saturn and Neptune are concerned, however, the answer is that there are *two* versions of reality. This is neatly summed up by these two definitions of what 'dew' is.

Saturn would say dew is 'Condensation that falls on a solid surface as the ambient air temperature decreases below the saturation point of the water vapour in that air'. Neptune would say dew is 'God's breath upon the earth'.

What kind of reality are you in, what kind of reality do you prefer, or what sense of reality does any particular situation call for?

Surf It or Wipe-Out?

So which way are you, are we, going to go? One path, riding
these Waves or acting in the true Spirit of these Times, will take
us into a positive future – the other, giving in to the Devil of
these Times, will take us to a negative future.

The Spirit of These Times

Swim Together or Sink Alone

Because of the great disparity between these two planets, the track record of
Saturn/Neptune Major Storms tells us of something that is both distinct and
vague, clear but confusing. The point that Neptune is making is that we are all
one, that ultimately there are no boundaries between us, no haves and have-
nots, and that this is the only way that true and effective government can take
place. Wrongdoing and ineptitude must and will be 'flushed out'. Yet from
Saturn's point of view, certain boundaries and limits have to be set in place to
prevent chaos. As with all Planet-Waves, the challenge is to find the correct
balance between, and integration and expression of, the qualities or energies of
the two planets involved. This used to be called *rendering the gods their due*, and
'Acceptance with and of Limitations' could be the ultimate qualification of the
Saturn/Neptune key phrase: Transcendence of Limitations. This is what 'time' it
is on the Cosmic Clock: time to accept how things are and not make biased
judgements on the one hand, but not, on the other hand, to be accepting to the
point of irresponsibility, and not knowing where to draw the line.

Primarily, we need to observe this and attend to it in our own personal
spheres, as described under Self-Rule {<11}. It is a case of cleaning up your own

backyard. The ocean is only as pure, or as impure, as each individual drop in it – and just think of the state of our oceans!

Spiritual Obligation

This purity is essential because Saturn/Neptune puts pressure on us to recognize, remember and restore our spiritual nature – for this part of us is actually our Source, both in the sense of what refreshes us like a spring of water, and what inspires us to attain a higher and better state. This pressure to 'spiritualize' can be experienced as a meaninglessness, pointlessness and weariness which can *only* be properly sorted by reconnecting with this Source, or a Higher Power. The simple and obvious practises that meet this necessity are prayer and meditation, awareness of some spiritual philosophy, and giving actuality to serving the good, true and beautiful in our everyday lives.

Service, compassion and acceptance are the Neptunian bywords here, and Saturn presents us with situations that challenge us to adopt and uphold these virtues. However, it also teaches us to avoid being victim-like drudges who slave for little reward and no result, or too soft for fear of being seen as uncompromising (which is really only having a sense of boundaries), or too accepting in the sense of being apathetic, overly suggestible or addiction-prone.

Astro-Quantum

Looked at scientifically, as logical and practical Saturn requires, Neptune can be seen as what the quantum physicist David Bohm calls The Sea of Implicate Order {<1 Introduction; >236 Astro-Quantum}. This is the place from out of which all waves and subatomic particles unfold into life, the universe, and everything – and eventually disappear back into it again, only to reappear in another form, ad infinitum. So Saturn/Neptune Waves are reminding us of this. Only from this viewpoint can we begin to transcend the differences we cling to out of blind materialism and fear-induced factionalism, and heal the ills of the world that are the result of these two things.

The Devil of These Times
Corruption and Distortion

Unfortunately, Saturn and Neptune can bring out the very worst of what each of these planets stands for. The political and material machinations of Saturn can become more than usually corrupt and distorted by the spin and phoney idealism that is Neptune in the negative. Alternatively, the spiritual yearnings and creative imagination that are the positive end of the Neptunian spectrum get downgraded by Saturnian blindness to the spiritual dimension. This can result in seeking escape and artificial highs through drugs and alcohol, and perpetuate our consumer society's mantra of 'take, make and throw away'.

A History Lesson

The invasion of Iraq took place in March 2003 during the Saturn/Pluto Wave of 2000–04, which suggests an outright bid for power {<92 Saturn/Pluto Waves}. The ongoing 'occupation' of this country has taken place during the 2004–08 Saturn/Neptune Wave and so points to the likelihood that what started out as that bid for power – namely oil and tactical position – has become the very obligation to relieve suffering, 'to heal the ills of the world', that was initially put forward as the reason for the invasion. But more than anything, because of the deceptive justification for it in the first place, the suffering has been made worse than before. This is very much the 'devil' of Saturn/Neptune times.

'It becomes increasingly obvious that many so-called accidents and natural disasters, including pandemics, are directly or indirectly caused by our bad habits and addictions – and that there will be far more of them if we do not kick those habits.'

Astro-Quantum

Such undermining of the truth and twisting of reality can lead to material collapse and natural disasters – be it instantaneously through the non locality of quantum physics {>236} or through the gradual knock-on butterfly effect of conventional physics {< Astro-Quantum Health Warning > vii}. Cynically denying, or simply being unaware of, the idea that each and every one of us contributes to the collective state of affairs – by our very thoughts and feelings, let alone actions – is also very much the Saturn/Neptune devil at work.

However, the great paradox here – the truth standing on its head to attract attention – is that the 'devil' is Satan, that Satan is Saturn, and that Saturn is the Adversary (*HaSatan* in Hebrew). In other words, the devil or Saturn is here specifically as the adversary, to test our moral mettle, to challenge us to practically walk our spiritual talk, to deliver ourselves from 'evil' – and this means through Awareness of Waves. As Henry Ford said, 'Evil is simply ignorance bumping its head in the dark.'

> ❛ *The world is the best of all possible worlds, and everything in it is a necessary evil.* ❜

FH Bradley, *Appearance and Reality*

Conflicts, Trends and Possibilities

Environmental
A False Sense of Security

Much has been said elsewhere in this book about the effect Saturn/Neptune Storms have upon the environment because Saturn governs land and earth, and Neptune governs sea and water – and the two are brought into conflict during these times. During previous storms this was not an issue because our interference in this balance – ecology itself – had not reached critical proportions. Even the word 'ecology' is a comparatively recent one. We just didn't know that there was this delicate balance between the elements, between one system and another. The thing is that now we do, but rather like with a dripping tap or the straw that breaks the camel's back, we might not respond appropriately or quickly enough – we might leave it until the flood or collapse is unavoidable. We have lulled ourselves into a false sense of security. The reality of the Gaia hypothesis hasn't sunk in. Planet Earth is like the hard-pressed mother of a large and unruly family who one day blows her top, and all the kids go, 'What?'

Prediction? Not!

I hope it is now clear that this book is not about prediction, but about reading the writing on the wall – in this case provided by astrology, quantum theory and common sense. This is more the case with the environment than with any other area of human concern. It is impossible to say whether the current Major Storm of 2004–08 will tip the eco-balance into red alert, or whether it will occur during the Storm of 2014–17 – or whether there will be some kind of 'rescue' during the intervening Favourable Wind of 2010–13. Everything depends on getting the message NOW with respect to every aspect of the 'human emergency'.

Trade and Industry
The End of a Dream

Here the balance between Saturn and Neptune is particularly critical. This is because it is between materialism/Saturn on the one side, and spirituality/Neptune on the other. The trouble is that our society is so skewed towards materialism that Neptune takes on its lower vibration of advertisement and spin. This is the promotion of a false consumerist 'heaven' – the ideal body, holiday, food, drink, etc. And so unless this balance is redressed by more responsible advertising, honest dealing, and sensible production, then a collapse of some kind will occur. How does this work? People begin to realize that this 'dream' is just a con, they buy less, the market 'suffers'. There are of course environmental issues (see above) that also create changes in expenditure and travel difficulties.

Hitting Us in More Than Our Pockets

The writing on the wall is quite simply that we have to shift from such a materialistic lifestyle to one that considers the finer and subtler realities of existence. Rather like a virus, just because it is not visible or obvious, it does not mean that it isn't powerful and effective; quite the contrary in fact! If we don't see this one coming it'll hit us where it really hurts. The ultimate wake-up call here is of course a breakdown of physical structures totally undermining the material infrastructures that we have progressively installed in the name of 'civilization' ever since the Industrial Revolution.

Socio-Cultural
Rejoicing in Rejoining

As emphasized above, music and all forms of art and entertainment are a strong and significant expression of Saturn/Neptune Waves. So too are events that stir collective emotions and thereby inspire creativity. During more recent Waves music and other arts have been employed for reasons that are not just for entertainment or emotional release, but for raising funds and awareness for pressing and practical reasons – such as poverty, world peace and environmental concerns. Music and art forms that are solely for amusement and distraction become more and more irrelevant, especially during the 2014–17 Wave when such concerns will be even more acute. However, entertainment that raises the spirits is needed even more, but during these times in a more conscious and deliberate attempt to remind us of how we are better off pulling together when the stark alternative is a feeling of insecurity and isolation. The arts, but music in particular, focus more and more upon bringing people together in the spirit of humanity, as the one race on one world that we actually are.

Mini-Renaissance

In a way this could be seen to usher in a 'mini-renaissance', in the sense of a rebirth of classical ideas and images that engender an awareness that art and music are essentially of a spiritual nature and exist primarily for spiritual reasons. The actual Renaissance that began in 14th-century Italy could have just been nostalgia for these ideas, but now, with so much threatening our very existence, there is a very strong need for something that reconnects us to supposedly better, more inspiring, and even romantic times: a regaining of what puts the 'class' in 'classical', you could say! Again, this is more likely while the 2014–17 Wave is flowing, as Neptune will then be going through its own Sign of Pisces. This means that the purer and more genuine qualities of inspiring and mystical Neptune will be to the fore culturally. And seeing as Saturn will be going through Sagittarius for most of this period, there is a religious element lent to the Neptunian muse. What else this poses is explored below in the 'Spiritual' section – namely the conflict between spirituality and religiosity – something art and society would reflect. This could take the form of quite inspired music and lyrics on the one hand, but of out-and-out evangelical persuasion on the other.

Will Disaster Bring Us Closer Together or Separate Us Further?

On the one hand, the more threatened and uncertain we are made to feel by the climatic irregularities and vague uncertainties that correspond to the influence of Saturn/Neptune Major Storms, the more societies around the world will go on a 'wartime footing'. In other words, there is nothing like a common threat to make us realize our common needs and mutual dependence. But on the other hand, there will be those who entrench themselves in a bid to keep at bay those they regard as alien or antagonistic – or as an actual part of the threat. At its extreme, this latter approach could unfortunately involve the ugliest face that certain sectors of humanity give to Saturn/Neptune, namely ethnic cleansing and perse- cution of anyone seen as against or unlike oneself, be it on a national level or just in your neighbourhood. Living up to the call of all Saturn/Neptune Waves – Transcending Boundaries and Limitations – and recognizing everyone as a fellow human being could become a desperate requirement.

Political

Fakes versus the Rare and Real Thing

As we now know, Saturn/Neptune Major Storms bring disillusionment with politi- cians as their ineffectuality and lack of integrity are forced to the surface in the 'swell'. You could say that there is a 'flushing out' process going on. Certainly President George W Bush and Prime Minster Tony Blair have been subject to this during the 2004–08 Wave, with a sleaze-stained Blair finally leaving office in 2007, and Bush's popularity at an all-time low. In essence, there is a challenge to all those in power and authority to address the most essential and pressing collective issues in a pure and imaginative way. This in turn poses a need for people in power to have their hearts in the right place. This is an example of how difficult it is to find a positive expression of Saturn/Neptune Storms in the political arena!

At the Astro-Quantum level this is saying that we need to meditate/pray /visualize into position a truly inspired and inspiring political figure (like Churchill was to the British people in World War Two), which would also mean eschewing the typical glamorous 'suits' who are just playing to the gallery, and appealing to the biased silent majority who vote for whoever embodies their prejudicial fears rather than their ideals. Also, crassly voting for someone simply for the sake of a change is asking for disappointment. In any event, the normal Saturn/Neptune fodder of boundary changes and incursions will continue as a testament to both our divisiveness and the illusory nature of territory.

Scientific
Proof of Oneness

During these Saturn/Neptune Major Storms the conflict rages between conventional science that sees reality as merely material/mechanical/separate and the more cutting-edge science of quantum physics that can't help but acknowledge something that is unseen, universal and amounts to being mystical. At some point, possibly during the Favourable Wind of 2010–13 {>170}, there could at last be discovered 'official proof' that every living thing is ONE, and that everything is living. This would mark a shift in collective consciousness that would herald the true beginnings of world peace. At the Astro-Quantum level this would also mark a change in the physical conditions of the world, from poverty to climate, from conflict to economy.

Failing this, science would carry on battling against the elements. There would be small successes here, but the elements would win in the end, for they represent the greater part of us that we do not recognize, and therefore resist. As such they will inevitably overwhelm us. This is analogous to an individual's immune system attacking its own tissue, for example with arthritis, because it does not accept the tissue (or what it represents) as being part of its own whole. If you do not understand this point it is because you are still looking at reality in the same way that conventional science and the conventional mindset does: that is, in opposition to Oneness, and part of the problem as opposed to the solution.

Health

Body Invasion

Complaints of the auto-immune system can be more in evidence because Saturn/Neptune Major Storms are all to do with the dissolving of boundaries. From a more conventional standpoint, our physical defences come under stress as a result of pollution and other environmentally destabilizing agents such as chemicals in the food chain, and of course viruses {>156 The Butterfly Effect}. Also, the effects of increased alcohol and drug abuse over previous decades become apparent in alarming health deterioration.

Most Illnesses are Psychosomatic or Environmentally Dependent

Auto-immune complaints that become particularly common are those which are regarded by some as purely psychosomatic, such as ME, or that are so odd as to have no recognized pathology. But the whole point that Saturn/Neptune is making with regard to health is that all diseases originate in the mind. Even being vulnerable to environmental causes is ultimately down to the individual mind-body set-up – otherwise everyone would suffer the same complaints, and be allergic to the same things. It is in this area that possible breakthroughs are made with respect to what actually constitutes health – that it is largely down to an individual's personality, lifestyle and attitude. Obviously, if there is a pandemic raging then it'll be a bit late – that would be a classic case of closing the stable door after the horse had bolted. Bodies, human and otherwise, are designed, within certain parameters, for living in the Earth's atmosphere. Change the atmosphere enough and we have a problem – and we do.

And yet with the sharp rise in the use of alternative health methods – especially visualization techniques and dietary changes – many people are finding ways of 'upgrading' their physical defences. This means that ultimately we could train or mutate our bodies to deal with hazards that would have hitherto killed or incapacitated us.

Spiritual

Religion versus Spirituality; Dogma versus Karma

What we are looking for during these times is a spiritual practise that really does address our most down-to-earth questions and needs – like what on Earth is going on? Pie-in-the-sky or dyed-in-the-wool doctrines are very much seen as being past their sell-by date, but at the opposite end of the spectrum, such dogmas attract more followers as folks get scared of 'God's wrath' while at the same time busily blaming it on someone or something else. The big mistake that can be made when riding Saturn/Neptune Waves is finding some 'formula' for living that is black-and-white, two-dimensional. A basis to spiritual living that gains ever more popularity is the doctrine of karma, which states that we are all utterly responsible for own lives as a result of how we have lived before. Naturally springing from this is the idea that if you clean up your own backyard you contribute to cleaning up the world itself.

Anybody's Guess

It's a lottery when it comes to what will come out on top as we stumble and wade through the Saturn/Neptune Storms. Will it be a biased and bigoted blame culture that tips us into chaos and holy war, or a doctrine of self-responsibility that stands some chance of restoring order and mutual respect? Remember, that you do have your individual 'vote' here, which counts as much as anyone else's.

✦

The Butterfly Effect:
Climate, Health and Addiction

Neptune, being the ruler of fine, subtle and invisible things, also governs what is called the Butterfly Effect – that is, 'Does the flap of a butterfly's wings in Brazil set off a tornado in Texas?' Significantly, this also includes the idea that it is the collective mental and emotional state of humanity, and the behaviour that springs from this, that affects the weather and world health. Indigenous races have always believed this because they have remained in touch with Nature. They knew, and those few that are left still know, that there are certain things you just do not do as they jeopardize the environment, the delicate eco-balance – which in turn affects health and weather.

Of course, global warming and other climate problems themselves are conventionally ascribed to carbon emissions and other atmospheric pollutants – but the point is that we are collectively addicted (Neptune) to the standard of living that is dependent upon the very industries and practises that create and promote them (Saturn). We have to unsubscribe to this standard of living. This cannot be done overnight, which would be a kind of cold turkey that sees us reaching for our 'drug' out of desperation as soon as the pain gets too hard to bear. No, first we have to approach it in a more subtle, Neptunian fashion, and with a sense of Saturnian discipline and necessity.

This need to reduce addictive consumption most obviously applies to drugs and alcohol (Neptune) for the State's (Saturn's) current, blindly moralistic 'war on drugs' will prove to be less and less effective – and consequently, addiction and crime will become more rife if we continue vainly to control and suppress the phenomenon. We should attempt to accept and understand it for what it really is: an urge to escape a reality which is too materialistic and spiritually unaware (Saturn) and/or a need to discover a different way of experiencing reality itself. Interestingly, the first way young children seek to do this – alter their conscious-ness – is to spin round and round and make themselves giddy, a word which comes from the Old English *gidig* and means 'like God'. Now this 'war on drugs' is as ineffective as erecting insufficient seawalls to hold back rising sea levels, rather than discovering and dealing with the reasons behind that increase. Of course, this alludes to that literal land (Saturn)/sea (Neptune) problem created by global warming which, thanks to the 2004–08 and 2014–17 Saturn/Neptune Waves, is in danger of becoming a bigger problem far more quickly than is currently predicted.

Any Alcoholics Anonymous or Narcotics Anonymous member will tell you that the only sure route to be free of addiction is a spiritual one, a cleansing of the psyche through communion with the Divine and living according to spiritual principles. And Neptune governs both spirituality and alcohol/drugs, for the former is a transcending of material reality, whereas the latter is an escape from it, or seeking an artificial boost to function within it – 'material reality' itself, remember, being Saturn. This approach is the positive alternative to that of Prohibition in the United States which progressively unfolded and spread during a succession of Saturn (prohibition)/Neptune (alcohol) Waves during the first part of the 20th century. It is now widely regarded as having created even more ill-health from extremely toxic 'home-brews', and even more crime through the creation of a black market and the transgressing of the Prohibition laws themselves. Just as the 'war on drugs' is doing now.

Most of us know that alcoholism and drug addiction are diseases that require healing. The Saturnian authorities and the Neptunian healers must get together to resolve the problem at root, that is, ultimately to remove the need for 'escape' or 'boost' by altering and spiritualizing the very fabric of society. This will come

– or it'll have to if anything is going to make it through the Uranus/Pluto Mother Wave 2007–20. There will then be no need for criminal dealers and opportunistic purveyors, when all addictive substances are controlled by an enlightened (Neptune) state (Saturn), which is the ultimate objective and ideal of Saturn/Neptune Waves – distant though this may seem to be.

Three other Neptunian factors (because they all deal in images and the creating of the collective mindset) – films, television and advertising – will also be seen to be even more of 'a problem' in some way during Saturn/Neptune Major Storms. So Saturnian censorship and restriction is likely to become more stringent and widespread. The trouble is that, like 'prohibition', this misses the subtle Neptunian point again. People have a need to experience something darker or higher than is provided by the staple of their everyday existence. The media currently meets this need in a typically Saturnian or low-grade Neptunian fashion through showing sex and violence (either real or fictional) and fantasy, in greater and greater amounts, rather than looking at the subtleties of human nature that lie behind this need.

Saturn doesn't 'do' subtle as it is solely focused on the obvious, physical, logical and mechanical. Neptune, on the other hand, specializes in the obscure, psychological, empathetic and mythical – and it is in these areas that we see that human nature and behaviour spring from an archetypal realm of monsters and angels, unicorns and dragons, demons and gods/goddesses. Unless there is created a more widespread awareness of this supremely significant, mythological side of human nature, then society will continue to reach for and be fed with the 'junk-food' and 'brain-candy' that fills our media channels, debasing, fattening and debilitating its members in the process.

This poem, 'The World Is Too Much With Us', written by William Wordsworth 200 years ago in 1807, right at the beginning of a Saturn/Neptune Major Storm, sums up the phenomenon of too much negative Saturn and not enough positive Neptune:

> The world is too much with us; late and soon,
>
> Getting and spending, we lay waste our powers;
>
> Little we see in Nature that is ours;
>
> We have given our hearts away, a sordid boon!

This Sea that bares her bosom to the moon,
The winds that will be howling at all hours,
And are up-gathered now like sleeping flowers,
For this, for everything, we are out of tune;
It moves us not. Great God! I'd rather be
A Pagan suckled in a creed outworn;
So might I, standing on this pleasant lea
Have glimpses that would make me less forlorn;
Have sight of Proteus rising from the sea;
Or hear old Triton blow his wreathed horn.

Apart from this more emotional and spiritual dimension, in a practical and everyday sense, a Saturn/Neptune Wave is there to force us as individuals, on the one hand, to know our limitations, and, on the other, to transcend them. This can and will occur on very personal and seemingly trivial levels. For example, a situation could arise that on the face of it suggests that, as mentioned elsewhere, you will be 'hung if you do and hung if you don't'. This could come in the form of having to take a firm stand but exercise compassion at the same time – a challenging dilemma that is reminiscent of the 'tough love' (a perfect example of Saturn/Neptune balance) prescribed as a means of handling addicts and alcoholics, or anyone with behavioural problems. Or it could be a case of finding a difficult, and seemingly mutually exclusive, balance between an orthodox health treatment and a complementary or psycho-spiritual one. The list of Saturn/Neptune possibilities is fairly endless, but hopefully you get the picture. Basically, a Saturn/Neptune Wave poses a challenge to balance and satisfy two disparate requirements. When this balance is not achieved it takes the form of an increasing number of people who are casualties of the Saturn/Neptune imbalance. *Understanding The Future* is expressly intended to aid us in creating and maintaining a healthy balance.

A Healthy Plague?

In terms of world health, a disaster that has been looming during the 2004–08 Saturn/Neptune Wave – and possibly during the next one in 2014–17 – is Avian or Bird Flu, with its crossing of the species barrier to humans, and of country boundaries too. Bacteria and viruses are Neptune-ruled because they are invisible to the naked or ordinary eye (Neptune is mythically called Lord of the Unseen Realms), and like the sea which this planet also governs, they are able to transcend boundaries, which are ruled by Saturn. As stated earlier, the greatest pandemic of all known history, the Spanish flu of 1918/19, actually began during a particularly powerful Saturn/Neptune Wave occurring between 1916 and 1919, one that brought the Russian Revolution, the murder of the Russian Royal Family, and a worsening of the First World War, which began with an equally powerful Saturn/Pluto Wave between 1913 and 1916 (< 88).

In 1918 children would skip to the rhyme:

> I had a little bird,
> Its name was Enza.
> I opened the window,
> And in-flu-enza.

This bird flu pandemic, or any other worldwide disaster if it materializes, is actually Nature's way of doing a spot of 'cleansing' Herself. As was seen with the Tsunami of 2004 and Hurricane Katrina of 2005, these 'natural' causes of suffering elicited compassion and a sense of oneness amongst us all. Being the planet of universality and collective feelings, this is something that is very much on Neptune's agenda. Neptune has a lot to do with suffering and sacrifice, and is actually known as the 'Christ Planet'. This oneness and compassion can be what saves us, if it leads us to accept that there is little or no sense of difference between one life form or one human being and another. There is simply nothing to defend against, for immune systems to react to. However, if we are unable to accept all fellow creatures and organisms as having a place on the Earth, then events will occur that cause us to sit up and realize that, in the words of Martin Luther King, 'We must learn to live together as brothers or perish together as fools.'

Saturn and Neptune may well be attempting to provide us with a 'healthy plague', or some such disaster, to remind us of the real value of life, to level us in more ways than one. From a personal or emotional perspective this may sound heartless and cruel, but Nature and the Cosmos act with a corrective and automatic response to, or reflection of, whatever we are up to on a human level. As above, so below – as within, so without. It appears to be a mystery why certain people suffer or die, but that does not mean to say there is no rhyme or reason to it beyond our ordinary perception. Fate or God's will is, after all, 'the love that moves the Sun and other stars', as Dante puts it in his *Divine Comedy*.

Yet, as much as oneness and compassion do to avert any such disaster that Saturn and Neptune might mete out, it is not as simple as us all being one glorious species, living together under one Sun. This is the grand intention, but it won't occur for a while yet. In the meantime, Saturn, the Lord of Boundaries, is the planet of balance and limitation which means that we must also know how and where to draw the line, to not be *too* accepting (a Neptunian tendency). In Britain in particular, but in other prosperous countries as well, this raises the issue of porous borders and lack of sufficient immigration control becoming even more critical – even though it could be interpreted as 'colonial guilt' with certain states, consciously or unconsciously, letting other nationalities walk into their country as karmic reparation for having once walked into theirs. As far as health is concerned, porous borders, along with a more mobile, air-travelling population greatly increases the risk of diseases spreading, and pollution too. (See Saturn/Uranus Waves/Environmental on page 206 for more about issues concerning air travel).

In any event, though, a Saturn/Neptune Major Storm tells us that the dam will burst if we do not get our finger out, or put it in, as the case may be. But that 'we' is not just some anonymous body, because Neptune is to do with mass emotion, which is itself comprised of how every individual is thinking, feeling, acting and interacting. So it poses the question: What can you as one person do to help avert disaster, in whatever form, personally – and therefore globally? The answer is, quite simply, that each one of us is like a little drop in the River of Life, each making our minute but significant contribution to its state and direction. Some such drops could be like diseased or alien cells in the bloodstream, doing their share of damage to the whole as they spread exponentially. When, however, your 'cell' is clean and bright, aligned and balanced in the way that is suggested by this planetary lore, then the exponential spread will help heal and regenerate our world.

Much depends on how a Saturn/Neptune Wave influences your personal birth chart, for knowing this will guide you towards a precise awareness of where in your life and personality that critical balance needs to be found – where to accept things and go with the flow, and where to contend, make an effort or draw the line. In so doing, the health and equilibrium of your 'butterfly' will make that vital contribution towards averting collective or so-called natural disaster, as well as a personal one. Letting someone or something into your space when you are supposed to, while resisting the same when you are not supposed to, would be making a small contribution towards letting something good come flying through our 'window' – and stopping something very bad from flying in. The one is the many, and the many are the one.

✦

The Wave, the Wave the Dolphin rides –
Of Sirens' sad alluring lays
We lost Sailors dream
In our deep Womb of green –
The Dolphin sighs –
And plies his way.

The Mood of These Times

It has been seen that Saturn is a very 'earthy' planet of reason and order, while Neptune is a very 'watery' one of imagination, sensitivity, otherworldliness and oneness. So while these two planets are interacting, things can get like muddy water! It is hard to be clear about what you think and how you feel. Issues in the outer world will manifest this muddiness as deadlocks and difficulties in getting matters to reach resolution or realization. And like mud, this time makes things sticky, in that it is hard to deal with things cleanly and easily, and affairs get bogged down with convolutions and weird agendas. It is hard to see where anything is coming from or going to – or if they are going anywhere at all. Consequently, it is easy to get disheartened, frustrated and overwhelmed by feelings of pointlessness, helplessness or inertia.

The Importance of Surrender

Remember that the trick with muddy water is not to stir it up in a vain attempt to get through, round or beyond it quicker than is possible, because it'll just make it even muddier. In other words, resist the temptation to resolve or explain anything that is plainly resisting your attempts to do just this. *Relax, surrender, withdraw.* Give things time to settle and try again. If it is still muddy, then relax, surrender and withdraw again. Leave it a bit longer this time. Meditate upon or attune to what the situation is really calling for rather than jumping to conclusions or acting impulsively and making matters worse. Time passing and time limits can be very illusory during this period, so don't feel pressured unless it is absolutely obvious that you are 'against the clock'.

More Force, Less Effect

You may notice that confusion in the outer world is down to people not doing just this; that is, they make things worse by trying to force issues. In the words of Blaise

Pascal, 'All mankind's troubles are caused by one single thing, which is their inability to sit quietly in a room.' Unfortunately, this 'muddying of the waters' can actually be deliberate as certain people seek to capitalize on unclear lines of demarcation, something which is the hallmark of Saturn/Neptune interactions.

A classic example of this took place in March 2007, when Iran took captive fifteen British marines and sailors who had supposedly strayed out of Iraq waters into Iranian ones. From a 'planetary lore' perspective, the appropriate response from Britain would have been to simply surrender to this, and apologise for making a 'mistake'. But trying to force or fudge the issue – that is, wavering between being firm (Saturn) or acquiescent (Neptune) just made matters worse with a loss of face on Britain's part. A case of misjudgement – which to be fair is all too easy under Saturn/Neptune – that was compounded by allowing the sailors to sell their stories to the media. Interestingly, though, the instinct of the marines on board was to surrender in the first place, leading to criticism by government and pundits later, which was wrong from a planetary standpoint. It doesn't take much imagination to see that the sailors opening fire would have had disastrous consequences.

The big secret with Saturn and Neptune is to realize that you gain the higher moral ground by *not* taking issue, or at least, by agreeing to differ. Maybe this is what finally happened between negotiators in the days before the release of the fifteen on April 4 – aided, I must say, by a brief but Favourable Breeze from a Jupiter/Saturn Wave (see page 123)! It is worth pointing out that Saturn/Neptune also brings up issues concerning illusions (Neptune) about what is appropriate (Saturn).

Acceptance with and of Limitations

Saturn/Neptune Planet-Waves are times for 'Acceptance with and of Limitations', and so the Mood of These Times can be characterized by a sense of resignation to the fact that things will work themselves out if one does not struggle too much with them, recognizing how Time (Saturn) and Flow (Neptune) are subtly intertwined. However, to accept things too readily by taking everything lying down can earn one the reputation of being a soft touch or a pushover. Conversely, to dig in one's heels would simply get one bogged down. Finding the balance here is very difficult, which is why a Saturn/Neptune Wave is hard to ride – and why you might require personal assistance in riding it. Generally speaking though, the Balance of Power Chart on page 182 is invaluable as an ongoing aid here.

Times to Transcend

A Saturn/Neptune Wave is, in the end, all about transcending boundaries. This can mean a number of things, but ultimately it is about taking to a higher level what we regard as reality itself. What we think matters may very well not matter; it is just that we have been led to believe that it does. This blurring of the line between 'real' and 'not real' can make the Mood of These Times feel quite unreal, even to the point of feeling that the world has gone mad – or madder than usual. The old question arises of whether the inmates are running the asylum. The fact is that the demarcation between what is real or unreal, acceptable or unacceptable, sane or insane, is all in the confines of your own mind – and wherever that might begin and end! Quantum physics suggests that you make your own reality {>236 Astro-Quantum/Observer Created Reality} and a Saturn/Neptune Wave drives this point home, leaving you high and dry or totally at sea, depending on what reality you are choosing, consciously or unconsciously.

The Dangers of Exclusion

Another classic, but less obvious, example of how a Saturn/Neptune Wave can make itself felt was in the Virginia Tech massacre of April 2007. This has to do with that demarcation between what is real or unreal, sane and insane. In a conventional, Saturnian sense, the killer Cho Seung-Hui was decidedly insane – insanity belonging astrologically to the province of otherworldly Neptune. Saturn equals normality and consensus reality, while Neptune does not recognize such limited concepts and can either be inspired and inspiring or plain mad, with typical voices in the head. The point here is that these two worlds of so-called normality and abnormality, of order and chaos, come into collision during a Saturn/Neptune Wave. Cho Seung-Hui definitely fell beyond the pale of Saturn's normality, and he wanted to get back at that normality for locking him out, for not accepting him. His strangeness attracted scorn from other students, who laughed at his peculiar deep voice and jeered, 'Go back to China!' (he actually came from South Korea).

None of this is aimed at excusing Cho of his horrific deeds, but symbolically it makes the point that where there is a dangerous rift or gap between the normal world of inclusion and acceptance by one's peers on the one hand, and the comparatively strange netherworld of the misfit on the other, then expect the latter to react against the former when a Saturn/Neptune Wave is rolling in. Cho declared in his video about the killings, 'You forced me into a corner and gave me only one option. The decision was yours. Now you have blood on your hands that will never wash off.'

To dismiss this and the rest of his 'rantings', and say that it was wrong to broadcast them, is to miss the point that this Saturn/Neptune event is making. This Wave is saying – screaming – that we cannot afford to be complacent because we reside within the confines of Saturn's conformity and normality. The Saturnian 'dam' can only hold back the Neptunian 'water' for so long. And so the 'message in a bottle' that this Saturn/Neptune Wave is carrying is this: We have to let some of that water through – we have to identify, acknowledge, accept and understand the Chos of this world, because when they want to hit back at feelings of exclusion they won't play by any rules. Rules belong to the very domain they are assailing. And they are rules which are designed to keep 'us' in and the likes of 'him' out. The 'likes of him' resemble the melting icecaps which are that other more obvious expression of this boundary-dissolving Wave. Ice doesn't need holding back or containing; water does – or rather, it must somehow be channelled usefully or harmlessly in a particular direction.

Murderers are often Mortally Wounded Children

Cho's individual birth chart reveals someone with a sensitive and fantasy-prone mentality. But it also shows someone with a score to settle, and an uncompromis- ing urge to attain power and use it against whatever that mentality sees as offending it. In a world where one such as him was recognized, such a mind and urge could have been schooled towards creative and healing ends. In other words, his potential was that of a sensitive mind and a powerful will, but its reality became one of a paranoid mind and a vengeful will. One of the causes of terrorism and criminality in general can be said to be this kind of exclusion or lack of 'respect' for a certain personality type: many a bomber or mugger is hitting back at a system or society that represents everything that he wants but is not allowed to have or be a part of – while doing so in the guise of gaining status in the group to which they have attached themselves, whether it belongs to a religious or drugs/drink culture.

Inclusion or Delusion

The Mood of the Time that is created by such an event as the Virginia Tech massacre can give rise to a wakening up to what is wrong with our world and doing something about it, individually and collectively – starting with just a critical change in our attitude. Such an attitude could be summed up by our Saturn/Neptune key phrase, 'Acceptance with and of Limitations'.

Yet another contributing factor is disclosed by a Saturn/Neptune Wave. This is the glamorous, escapist and fantasy-ridden world of advertisement, film or religious fervour – all negative expressions of the Neptunian archetype – as they run into the brick wall of reality provided by Saturn. In other words, the deluding influence of these Neptunian negatives upon impressionable minds reaches critical mass. What is needed, therefore, is the practise and installation of positive Neptunian expressions such as gentle and compassionate spirituality, prayer and meditation, creative use of the imagination, and the acceptance of what is different as being enriching rather than threatening.

To sum up, the Mood of These Times is, from Saturn's pragmatic, separative and needful-of-order standpoint, one of **uncertainty** – which in the case of the present Wave is very apt considering this Wave is the prologue to the great Uranus/Pluto Mother Wave of profound change 2007–20. The image springs to mind of a lookout on an inadequate seawall espying an approaching tsunami. From Neptune's diametrically opposite, all-inclusive and metaphysical viewpoint, the Mood of These Times is that of **certainty** – that what needs to be cleansed or laid bare will be, and that a spiritual understanding and acceptance of all life being sacred and equally worthwhile, **and subtly and profoundly interconnected**, is the only way forward.

The Choice is Ours
Easy Surfing

The following chart shows us Positive Responses to Saturn/Neptune Waves that collectively create Positive Effects. The Negative Responses need to be avoided in order to prevent the collective Negative Effects. Note the opposing qualities of the Negatives and Positives, and track back Negative or Positive Effects to the Responses that created them.

2004–08 and 2014–17
The Collective Effect of Saturn/Neptune Major Storms
The Choice is Ours

Negative Response	Positive Response
Denying any responsibility for everything and everyone being interconnected; thinking that a little pollution here and there won't matter. Failing to see how subtlety matters.	Dawning awareness that the 'Butterfly Effect' is a profound aspect of our reality, e.g. how we affect the climate {<156}, and of how 'natives' are attuned to environment.
Feeling powerless and hopeless as an individual in the face of seemingly insurmountable world problems, and so giving up the ghost.	Recognition that one's life – its quality and how it is lived – has a direct or indirect effect upon the whole. The ocean is made up of individual drops.
Apathy and uncertainty, inertia and world-weariness in the face of what seems the demoralizing end of a dream. Nothing rhymes.	Seeing disillusionment and deception as a challenge to distinguish the true from the false, and then follow and promote that truth.
Attitude that those who have different beliefs to one's own must be converted or destroyed.	Growing awareness of 'common divinity', and of how it actually helps us all to live together, find a way.

SOCIAL OBLIGATION

Negative Response	Positive Response
Holy wars waged by those who fail to see that 'live and let live' is the best basic creed of humanity.	Promotion of and movement towards a 'world belief' which is simply a profound sense of humanness.
Ignoring our own dreams and continuing to be misled and manipulated by the consumerist/post-modern propaganda machine.	A firmer sense of what and who has real value in a world full of hype and spin. Finding a balance between being practical and spiritual.
A self-fulfilling prophecy of the deterioration of global conditions following upon the expectation of the inevitability of just that. The epitaph of ignorance.	Individuals becoming genuine 'citizens of planet Earth' and the exponential effect that this has upon the general welfare. Strength goes to strength.
Environmental conditions worsen in direct proportion to our ignorance of what creates them in both obvious and indirect ways. Dams burst as a fitting symbol of our damnation.	Increasing awareness of our impact on the environment leads to timely and correctivemeasures, including the use of subtle or spiritual practises.
Negative Response	**Positive Response**

A Saturn/Neptune Favourable Wind December 2010–November 2013

What Kind of Time is This?
A Time of Practical Vision

Energies in Play as we Ride This Wave

The harmonious combining of the positive and essential energy and character of Saturn – that of **territory and stability,** which is **establishing and/or ordering** – with the essential energy and character of Neptune – that of **mass emotion and spirituality,** which is **uniting and/or accepting** – offers the opportunity to get the best of both these worlds. This means that we are able to bring together whatever and whoever is needed to bring unity in a practical and organized way, to bring order where there is confusion, to officially accommodate our higher hopes and finer feelings, and to bring material aid where it is needed. At the same time we are aware of where this cannot sensibly be done.

So there is the strong possibility of greater social, economic and political stability, along with a mutual understanding and acceptance of our differences. It is quite likely that leaders will appear who have a more spiritual sense of what their roles entail giving rise to planning and forward vision based upon and inspired by ideals and aspirations that hitherto have been considered fanciful or suspect. But this is no spin, it is a very real attempt to realize a true *civil*-ization.

The End of the Mayan Calendar

This 'event', which we explore in Appendix 4, coincides with this Favourable Wind. It is tempting to believe that something truly wonderful and out of this world will occur then, as is prophesied, giving form (Saturn) to the miraculous (Neptune).

Astro-Quantum

In synchrony with the above, the physical state of the planet shows signs of improvement or at least stabilization. The degree to which there has been established harmony and agreement between the various peoples of the Earth determines how the environment is behaving. In conventional terms, such could be seen, for example, as a greater mutual understanding bringing a greater possibility of overcoming any threat.

Making the Most of This Favourable Wind

Any project or activity that needs both organization and vision, and is both practical and inspiring – everything from making a film to bringing together different races in the spirit of humanity, from creating a manifesto for a better society to solving environmental problems – is very well-starred now. Not only does every little effort count, but it is now *seen* to count.

On a personal level, consult and use the House positions of Saturn and Neptune, as described below on page 177. With a Favourable Wind you can expect the most favourable of these interpretations, and see how the influences of both serve and support one another. Also, you can use the Saturn/Neptune Meditation or Prayer on page 185 to greater effect and with greater ease.

The Unfolding Story

⇥ Merging Waves & ⟋ Jupiter Boosters

In addition to the Uranus/Pluto Mother-Wave that has been taken into account in the interpretations of all the Saturn/Neptune Waves covered in this chapter, there are also other Planet-Waves *merging* with them and affecting them as time goes by. As well as these Merging Waves there are Planet-Waves involving Jupiter that come into the Saturn/Neptune picture, and Jupiter kind of *boosts* whatever is happening, blowing things up so we cannot fail to notice problems or take advantage of opportunities! As can be seen on the Planet-Wave Weather Chart on page 19, Jupiter Waves exist in their own right, and are responsible for Minor Storms and Favourable Breezes, but are not covered in this book for reasons of time and space! Along with the Merging Waves, they increase or modify the effects of the two Saturn/Neptune Major Storms and the Favourable Wind when they are happening at the same time and are involved with either Saturn or Neptune.

The Planet-Wave Chronicles

Taken altogether, these Merging Waves ⇥ and Jupiter Boosters ⟋ kind of dramatize and pace the overall course of Saturn/Neptune Waves, rather like a storyteller would do, unfolding its stories.

During the Saturn/Neptune Major Storm Nov 2004 to Aug 2008

⇥ **Saturn/Pluto Favourable Wind – Aug 2006 to Aug 2008 {<119}**

> If it wasn't for this very powerfully constructive influence, the negative effects of the concurrent Saturn/Neptune Major Storm would be far more damaging, especially in areas that have to do with the use and application of agencies that are concerned with environmental

disruption such as floods, a common physical effect of Saturn/Neptune. This Favourable Wind enables us to push together in the same direction, recognize our combined strengths through our shared concerns, and so reconstruct and regenerate where necessary – which could be very considerable! This may take a while to get going, though, with 2008 seeing much needed advances in speed and efficiency in dealing with whatever assails us.

↗ **Jupiter/Saturn Favourable Breeze – Feb 2007 to Jan 2009 –**
Benevolent Control

The combination of this Booster with the above Favourable Wind is really important, for not only does it get us to see the writing on the wall, it helps us to respond with some degree of positivity, awareness and practicality – increasingly so during 2008/09. Agreements between various factions and nations are a strong aspect of this, such as the Northern Ireland peace deal made in May 2007, and the early release of British marines and sailors taken prisoner by Iran in April of that year. Very much a case of needs must, considering the next merging Wave.

⇾ **Saturn/Uranus Major Storm – Sep 2007 to Jul 2012 {>188}**

This Wave catches the last year of the 2004/08 Saturn/Neptune Major Storm. It marks a time when the effects of the Uranus/Pluto Mother-Wave really start to kick in, exacerbating the disruption it has the potential to create. Put this together with Saturn/Neptune, and 2008 could present events that leave us in no doubt that we have something going on that is bigger and more pressing than we had predicted – especially where global warming and economy are concerned.

↗ **Jupiter/Neptune Minor Storm – Feb 2009 to Mar2010 –**
Spiritual Vision/Pie in the Sky

This Booster does not actually occur during the Saturn/Neptune Major Storm of 2004/08, but follows closely enough on its heels to prolong it, to give it a sting in its tail, so to speak. Well, not so much a sting, more of

a hangover of numbness and confusion created by the Major
Storm itself!

During the Saturn/Neptune Favourable Wind Dec 2010 to Nov 2013

⇥ **Saturn/Uranus Major Storm – Sep 2007 to Jul 2012 {>188}**

A great deal depends on how we have handled the first three years of
this Major Storm before the Saturn/Neptune Favourable Wind of
2010/12 blows in. If we have employed control where there has been
too much licence, and granted freedom where there has been too much
restriction – a positive response to any Saturn/Uranus Wave – then the
Favourable Wind could 'reward' us with relief, release and reprieve. If,
however, Saturn/Uranus has merely prompted us to break more than
bend or mend, then the Favourable Wind will see us having our work cut
out mopping up and exercising real compassion where such would be
very sorely needed.

⇥ **Saturn/Pluto Major Storm – Nov 2008 to Aug 2011 {<124}**

This looks like a case of the much needed practical vision of the
Saturn/Neptune Favourable Wind bringing aid, recovery and
reconciliation following the international conflicts that are the usual
sad expression we give to Saturn/Pluto Major Storms, if past history is
anything to go by. This Major Storm, or rather the territorial and greedy
side of human nature, does its best to scotch efforts to promote peace
and sane behaviour in the face of universal threats from Nature
herself – threats that are only a reflection of our own foolish and
childish egocentricity.

⚡ Jupiter/Saturn Minor Storm – Mar 2010 to Mar 2012 –
Growth versus Order

⚡ Jupiter/Neptune Minor Storm – May to Aug 2012 –
Spiritual Vision/Pie in the Sky 2

We should really brace ourselves for these two Boosters occurring one after the other, for they demand a great deal from the practical vision bestowed by the Saturn/Neptune Favourable Wind. These challenges take the form of conflicts between typically opposed factions such as hawks and doves, radicals and conservatives, religious and secular, etc, making heavy weather out of what is stormy enough already. Human folly, especially of the political and morally self-righteous variety, rears its head more than usual. Seeing above and beyond what such short-sightedness insists upon is the only way forward.

⚡ Jupiter/Saturn Favourable Breeze – Jun 2013 to Jun 2014 –
Benevolent Control 2

⚡ Jupiter/Neptune Favourable Breeze – Jun to Aug 2013 –
Spiritual Growth

Heaven be praised! Something – from a few good men and women to help from on high – appears now to help save the day, to provide a plan and direction just when they are needed. These Boosters occur at the end of an extremely trying time, and at the perilous peak of the Uranus/Pluto Mother Wave itself, 2013/14.

During the Saturn/Neptune Major Storm Nov 2014 to Sep 2017

⚡ Jupiter/Saturn Minor Storm – Jun 2015 to Jul 2016 –
Growth versus Order 2

⚡ Jupiter/Neptune Minor Storm – Jul 2015 to Aug 2016 –
Spiritual Vision/Pie in the Sky 3

This is dangerous! Religious factions present the greatest threat as they embody that element of humanity which is overcompensating for another element not being religious enough {<41 The Death and Rebirth of God}. This time marks a peak of such opposition and friction and as such needs to be offset by an extra effort to control self-righteous impulses and to look for areas of common concern and reach agreements because of them. Failing this, such a rocky time may well take the form of natural disasters in addition to the collision of those opposing factions. However, there is, too, some hope on the horizon.

➣ **Saturn/Uranus Favourable Wind Nov 2015 to Dec 2018 {>170}**
Here's the cavalry coming to the rescue! What form this takes in meeting the chaos-creating potential of this Saturn/Neptune Major Storm – occurring as it does following the peak of the Uranus/Pluto Mother-Wave and buzzed by the above Boosters – is anyone's guess. So, too, is the matter of whether or not the cavalry will be a bit too late. Assuming that it isn't, technological innovation, unusually concerted group effort, or maybe something entirely out of the blue, could aid us in what promises to be an all-too-real hour of need.

➶ **Jupiter/Neptune Favourable Breeze – Oct 2017 to Oct 2018 –**
Spiritual Growth 2
➶ **Jupiter/Neptune Minor Storm – Nov 2018 to Nov 2019 –**
Spiritual Vision/Pie in the Sky 4
These two Neptunian Jupiter Boosters do not technically fall within the range of the Saturn/Neptune Major Storm of 2014/17, but are close enough to lend the end of it a tricky coda. This aftermath could leave us with a sense of hope (provided by the Favourable Breeze) that causes us to drop our guard, only to find that something dark and ominous is there to take advantage of it. This is the 'wolf' that is the Saturn/Pluto Major Storm of 2018/22 {<125 } dressed up in the 'sheep's clothing' of the Jupiter/Neptune Minor Storm of 2018/19, tempting us, as it does, to rely on promises that are not delivered unless there are some very real spiritual values and awareness forthcoming. So much depends on what has transpired and been learnt during the preceding years of the Uranus/Pluto Mother-Wave!

Personal Effect

This is how, as an individual, Saturn/Neptune Waves can affect you, and be ridden successfully by you, for their duration.

Surfing with Saturn and Neptune Through the Houses

These effects are based upon the two Houses in your chart through which Saturn and Neptune are passing or 'transiting' while the Uranus/Pluto Mother-Wave is active, but most significantly during the times when Saturn/Neptune Waves are active. As it is a case of a need for Order, Discipline and Effort where Saturn is concerned, and for Refinement, Surrender and Attunement to the Spiritual where Neptune is concerned, knowing these positions will help you to manage the energies of each respective planet in an appropriate way, enabling you to find the right balance and surf successfully!

There are two ways to use this aid.

  1 **Off-The-Peg** This is using the Saturn and Neptune positions according to what is known as your Birth-Sign, Sun-Sign or Star-Sign. This looks at what Solar Houses Saturn and Neptune are transiting through while the Uranus/Pluto Mother-Wave is active. So using the **Planet House Transit Guide** (beginning on page 254), first go to the **Saturn: House Ready-Reckoner** on page 262. Next, look for the time **Period** you are interested in, then look along the row until you get to

the column of your **Birth Sign**. There you will see the number of the House being transited by Saturn – 1st, 2nd, 3rd, etc – and just below it the number of the page where you can read the description of possible situations and actions you can take. Straight after this, do the same thing for Neptune – that is, go to **Neptune: House Ready-Reckoner** on page 277 and use that table in the same way that you used the Saturn one. Now you can get a feel for how the two planet positions compare. All this can be very useful and accurate, but remember that it is only based on your Sun Sign.

2 **Made-To-Measure** This is using the Saturn and Neptune positions according to your individual birth chart which would have to be calculated correctly from a reliably accurate birth time. So if you do know your birth time and have your birth chart accurately drawn up, then anyone with a basic knowledge of a chart will be able to tell you which Houses in your personal chart are occupied by Saturn and Neptune at any given time between 2007 and 2020, but especially, remember, when a Saturn/Neptune Wave is active. Then simply find and consult the readings for those Houses in the **Planet House Transit Guide** (page 254). For example, if your astrologer or your own astrological calculation told you that Saturn was transiting your Tenth House and Neptune was transiting your Fourth House, then you would find these interpretations on the pages indicated in the Planet House Transit Guide by using the **Index** on the first page of it. So for our example the Index would send you to page 267 for Saturn transiting the Tenth House, and to page 279 for Neptune transiting the Fourth House. Note: you do *not* use the Ready-Reckoner when using Made-To-Measure.

The Saturn/Neptune Wave Effect Upon Relationships

Reality Checks and Love's Illusions

While Saturn demands that we 'get real' with respect to our relationships and socializing generally, Neptune seduces us into idealizing them or looking for some kind of emotional high. So, on one side, where we have been putting a partner on a pedestal or simply overlooking their shortcomings in the name of 'love', it becomes increasingly obvious that we have been setting ourselves up for being taken for granted or disappointed, or both. On the other side, if we have been enjoying this kind of illusion-inspired indulgence from our partner, then we should not be surprised when they suddenly give us a reality check and send us plummeting from our pedestal. This could take the form of them being anything but indulgent, like withdrawing their attention and affection. They may even just walk out with a cry of, 'I can't give any more!'

But as ever with Saturn's 'earth' and Neptune's 'water', there is just as likely to be a muddy area. This is when the one with the grievance, the 'plaintiff', is compromised by a fear of losing their partner or of getting an evasive or possibly violent reaction from them if they read the riot act. One answer here is to use passive resistance by withdrawing emotionally while at the same time maintaining a diplomatic civility. In this way the 'defendant' may eventually get the message.

If you happen to be the 'defendant', and if you truly value and care for your 'plaintiff' partner, then it is time you realized that a healthy relationship is all about balance, equality and sharing. If a relationship is one-sided in any way, then it is only a matter of time before it lists so badly that it capsizes. And during a Saturn/Neptune Major Storm, it most certainly will! However, a particularly muddy area here is where the defendant and the plaintiff are both guilty of some transgression. Commonly, this can occur when the plaintiff is projecting a lack of self-worth and feelings of being unappreciated on to their opposite number, and expecting more back than they can possibly give.

The great but uncomfortable truth that is borne on a Saturn/Neptune Wave is that both people have to look at their own blind spots – with these romantic illusions or psychological projections being the most likely culprits.

If you are alone and wanting a relationship, then the same rules apply: if you are expecting too much, or giving too much, then any relationship will either be one-sided and doomed to failure, or simply never materialize.

Saturn and Neptune punch home the necessity of applying the oldest rule of all where relating is concerned: Create and maintain a balance of give and take – and communicate!

The Choice is Yours
Easy Surfing

The chart on the next page shows us Positive Responses to Saturn/Neptune Waves that create Positive Effects for you personally and ultimately for everyone. The Negative Responses need to be avoided in order to prevent the Negative Effects in your own life. Note the opposing qualities of the Negatives and Positives, and track back Negative or Positive Effects to the Responses that created them.

2004–08 and 2014–17
The Personal Effect of Saturn/Neptune Major Storms
The Choice is Yours

Negative Response	Positive Response
Confronted with difficult choices you feel you have to come down decisively on one side or the other. But they're not about either/or, but about judgement and balance.	Confronted with such choices as god or science? empathetic or objective? assertive or easy-going? – you realize that a balance between each needs to be found.
Misusing imagination merely to gain more and more material things, or being fantasy-prone, or expecting the worst and ultimately getting it.	Finding that meditation, imagination and visualization are the best means of finding out what you need, and then of manifesting it.
Stress and vexation caused by striving for what you thought you wanted as opposed to finding out what you really needed.	Seeing your choice as simply being either 'worry or pray'. And so you pray for whatever will surely bring you peace and security.
Falling heroes and celebrities make you feel despondent and without hope or meaning.	Disheartening events are seen as lessons in being true to yourself. You see yourself as your own star.

PRACTICAL IDEALISM

False gods will always disappoint you. Your only true hero in the end is you!	Unexpectedly positive life transformations happen as if by magic. All's well that ends well.
What you feared comes upon you. Only now do you appreciate how careful you must be regarding what you wish for.	A simple but satisfying life. Getting and feeling more attuned to spirit brings happiness and contentment.
Disillusionment as what you crave is never attained or when it is you find it to be hollow and disappointing. Or what you feared comes upon you.	Substantial and subtle improvements in the quality of your life and of those around you.
Falling between two stools as you make the wrong choices. Getting the worst of both worlds when you are supposed to find a way of getting the best of both.	Able to tell the real from the unreal, vision from pipe-dream, and to balance and blend difficult extremes, you make dreams come true and stand as an example to others.

Negative Response	Positive Response

The Saturn/Neptune Balance of Power

The following pages provide two wonderfully basic ways to ride the Saturn/Neptune Storms. For a simple way to surf these Planet-Waves, and ride them to where they want to get to – as shown in 'The Spirit of This Time' – and at the same time bypass the Devil of This Time, use the Saturn/Neptune Balance of Power chart on the next two pages.

On the first page, you will see in the left-hand column various symptoms that you could be experiencing if you are leaning too much in the Saturn direction, that is, over-emphasizing caution, convention, the known, defensiveness, territory, etc. The right-hand column then suggests various ways of redressing the balance with Neptunian remedies, which mainly involve getting in touch with and using more spiritual, metaphysical, subtle and accepting qualities.

On the second page, the left-hand column lists symptoms resulting from overdoing Neptune – with escapism, fantasy, victimhood, pie-in-the-sky attitude, etc – and the right-hand column suggests Saturnian remedies that encourage a more pragmatic, realistic and disciplined approach.

As a rule each numbered item is balanced by the equivalent numbered item in the right column, but not always – there are crossovers.

The second basic way to ride Saturn/Neptune Major Storms is the Meditation on page 185.

The Saturn/Neptune Balance of Power

Too Much Saturn and Not Enough Neptune

If this is the case, you could be experiencing some of these symptoms.

1. Feeling sluggish and/or depressed.

2. Feeling intimidated by life, the world and others. A sense of hopelessness. Feeling dull, pointless, unmotivated.

3. Fearfulness. Worry and anxiety, especially concerning material needs or physical fears.

4. Working too much/too hard and getting nowhere. Trying to find a logical solution to everything and just finding more problems in doing so.

5. Being preoccupied with status, with being 'useful', wanting/needing material rewards or objects, being a slave to commercialism and consumerism.

6. Feeling guilty, conscience-stricken.

7. Trying to control matters or others too much, giving rise to increased stress and ill-health.

8. Health problems that do not respond to or benefit from conventional medicine.

Neptunian Remedies

Adopt one or more of these remedies to offset and relieve the symptoms of 'too much Saturn'.

1. Practise hatha yoga, tai chi, or some activity that interacts with forces of Nature such as swimming, surfing, paragliding, walking, etc.

2. Look for inspiration through art, music, the mystical, and Nature – especially the sea and bodies of water.

3. Investigate Guardian Angels; get to know more about angels generally and how they can figure in your life. Visualize and/or pray for what you need.

4. Meditate, tune in to your Inner Voice. Record and listen to your dreams. Realize the importance of divinity and spirituality in your life. 'Life is a mystery to be experienced, not a problem to be solved.' (Einstein)

5. Try automatic painting and/or writing. See what comes through you without keeping to an agenda of having to be practically useful or materially profitable. Use your imagination, express yourself creatively and/or dramatically. Then see what happens!

6. Take a break. Break the spell of feeling guilty when doing nothing. Have a nice hot bath. Sit back and enjoy a good movie.

7. Accept things as they are without trying to 'put them right' – go with the flow. Allow yourself to be what you are feeling without any judgement, and the feelings will change.

8. Visualize a healthy aura to protect you from any kind of invasion. Visualize as healthy any afflicted part of your body.

Note: It is quite possible to experience both too much Saturn and too much Neptune at the same time.

The Saturn-Neptune Balance of Power

Too Much Neptune and Not Enough Saturn

If this is the case, you could be experiencing some of these symptoms.

1. Feeling spaced-out, unearthed, out of touch with reality.

2. Giving in to weaknesses and addictions. Feeling feckless and frustrated by wanting things you cannot realistically or safely have.

3. Giving up too easily because your goals turn out to be harder to attain than you imagined. Suffering illusions, being deceived, or being in denial.

4. Being too prone to fantasy and/or paranoia. Overreacting, being oversensitive.

5. Feeling disinclined to get down to boring necessities which left undone would attract bigger problems. Trouble with officialdom and authorities, bureaucracy and form-filling.

6. Compassion fatigue. Trying to look after everyone else while being neglectful of yourself in the name of being 'selfless' or because you think you have no choice.

7. Being or feeling a victim. Being prone to infection and allergies or feeling invaded in some way.

Saturnian Remedies

Adopt one or more of these remedies to offset and relieve the symptoms of 'too much Neptune'.

1. Practise earthy pursuits such as gardening, pottery, sculpture, building, carpentry, etc. or any hard physical work.

2. Consult someone you trust to put you in touch with reality, or a professional who can furnish you with the facts and methods that enable you to deal with the matters that concern you.

3. Face up to reality, it'll make you stronger. Be an adult. Cultivate 'stickability'.

4. Limit feelings that weaken you or make you feel bad. If you cannot, then make sincere reparation for it in some way. Forgive yourself when that is all you can do.

5. Get down to performing practical tasks with the strong motivation that once done they will allow you to relax and enjoy yourself, and to do 'better things'.

6. Recognize that others have a responsibility to look after themselves and their own affairs. People are often as weak as you expect them to be. Ask yourself what it is that makes you think certain others cannot take care of themselves – like poor parenting in your own childhood, for example. Don't be too soft.

7. Determine and set your boundaries by recognizing that your body and being has its own boundary that nothing and no-one can cross without your permission. This is your most basic right; do not in any event compromise it or let it be compromised.

Note: It is quite possible to experience both too much Saturn and too much Neptune at the same time.

Saturn/Neptune Wave Meditation

This is the simplest and the best: a Meditation or Prayer for the Spirit of these Times. Sit quietly with it and gaze at the symbols, alone or with others, while inwardly or outwardly uttering the invocation as many times and for as long as you wish. It is especially recommended that you perform this ritual during any Hotspots involving a Saturn/Neptune Wave (see page 294)

ħ

My fellow beings and I
See through the illusions of separateness
That we have laboured under.
And so we discover
A real and practical spirituality
That is inspired by our great oneness,
And we build a peace on Earth.

CHAPTER 5

Saturn/Uranus Waves
2007–22

What Kind Of Times Are These?
Times of the Old versus the New,
and of Old Blending with the New

Active Periods	Wave Weather	How To Ride
September 2007–July 2012	Major Storm	Pages 188–216, 219–30
November 2015–December 2018	Favourable Wind	Pages 217–18, 221–22
January 2020–October 2022	Major Storm	Pages 188–216, 219–30

Saturn/Uranus Major Storms
September 2007–July 2012
January 2020–October 2022

What Kind Of Times Are These?
Times of the Old Versus the New

Energies in Play as we Ride These Waves

The energies of Saturn are interacting with the energies of Uranus, and everyone and everything on planet Earth will be subject to these interactions for the duration of their influence, as well as to the after-effects that follow upon these Planet-Waves. Remember that two planets interacting is rather like two very different and strong-minded people coming into contact and the best and the worst of each is brought out and magnified. But Saturn and Uranus do the same to one another on a cosmic scale, and this affects us all!

♄   The character of Saturn is **Authority and Stability** and its energy is **Suppressing and/or Ordering**

♅   The character of Uranus is **Freedom and Innovation** and its energy is **Awakening and/or Disrupting**

Their combined effect is therefore ...
Suppressing and/or Ordering Freedom and Innovation
Awakening and/or Disrupting Authority and Stability

Riot or Reform, Breakdown or Breakthrough

As energies, Saturn and Uranus are starkly opposing. Saturn stands for order, limitation and convention, while Uranus is random, free and outside the box. So a lot of the time, as will be seen, they literally come into collision. This will be either when authority in the form of the state or ruling body is assailed by the minority, 'workers', underdog or whoever is pressing for the change, a fair deal and the new, or when the former decides to put down or resist whatever the latter is up to. Consequently, riot, revolution, radicalism and reform are the order, or initially disorder, of the day.

On a more constructive level, and often as a result of the protest and agitation of those suing for freedom and rights, laws are passed and organizations are formed that uphold them. The sample succession of Saturn/Uranus Waves described below can be seen very much as the process of social and political evolution itself, as standards of the old and the forces of the new thrash it out.

Eureka!

Another positive is the inventiveness and urge to break new ground as the forward vision of Uranus encounters the problems and crystallizing resistance of the old world of Saturn, for as this happens such vision takes form – as innovations, breakthroughs and discoveries – and often comes to answer what had seemed previously insoluble problems. These in turn can amount to 'firsts' or records in various fields of human endeavour.

Astro-Quantum

When these collisions between the Saturnian old and the Uranian new are not recognized, expressed or resolved – out of lack of awareness, apathy, or simply a refusal to bend and meet one another halfway – then these energies break out in some other way that appears to be totally disproportionate, unrelated or random and unaccountable. This is when Saturn/Uranus manifests as shock, accident or the totally unexpected – which may be more simply because someone or something is breaking a rule or convention of some sort. Something has to give, or make itself known, so it finds a way that comes out of the blue or seems like an extreme over-reaction. 'Out of the blue' can be quite literal, for such events often take place in the sky – e.g. involve aircraft – for Uranus governs anything to do with sky, from aviation to astrology itself, or space debris like meteorites, like that strange, sickness-inducing one that landed in Peru in September 2007! In retrospect, sometimes the causes of accidents are found to be down to a glitch or human error, as Uranus also governs all electrical activity, be it in a computer or the human brain.

> *‘ Long-standing tensions can break out*
> *as natural disasters. ’*

When such tensions are longstanding and have found little or no resolution or expression, they build up and can break out as so-called natural disasters, like earthquakes. This effect can occur with any Major Storm, as they all create tension for their own particular reasons; for example, Saturn/Pluto Major Storms were active during nearly all of the biggest earthquakes since 1900 {<87}.

This is not to say that such geophysical events are only down to 'human error', for obviously this planet was experiencing them long before humans even appeared. In fact, such was, and still is, the very way in which planet Earth can be seen to be progressing and evolving herself. Earthquakes are after all the result of tectonic plates pressing against one another along the fault-lines on the planet's surface. The point here, though, is that the existence and state of humanity has 'added to the mix'. Our moods and activities affect the whole, much as a stone cast into a lake would send out ripples that interact with existing ones. We are talking waves again!

Dateline 2007: Previously, and So Far

Your Planet-Wave surfing can be greatly helped by knowing what happened during previous Saturn/Uranus Major Storms.

If you want to look at the Saturn/Uranus Major Storms occurring during the Uranus/Pluto Mother Wave 2007–2020 then go to page 198. This includes the Major Storm of 2007–2012, which is responsible for getting the Uranus/Pluto Mother-Wave off to such a pokey start. Then there is the Major Storm that closes the Mother-Wave with a bang in 2020 and crashes on through to 2022.

We open our review a few years into the 20th century, focusing mainly on times when they are peaking, for this is the most powerful part of a Wave.

Saturn/Uranus Major Storm 1908–11 (peaking 1909/10)

Blows against authority for freedom and rights, or suppression of same

June 1 1909	Negro Rights Committee formed.
August 22 1909	Violent steel strike in the US.
October 26 1909	Prince Ito of Japan assassinated.
January 12 1910	Landmark Mann Act was passed against 'white slavery'.
January 1910	Rebels in control in Nicaragua.

Firsts, records, innovations and discoveries

July 25 1909	Bleriot flies the English Channel.
January 8 1910	New altitude record set in the US.
February 27 1910	X-ray machine first used in surgery.
August 27 1910	Edison's first demonstration of 'speaking pictures'.

Saturn/Uranus Major Storm 1917–21 (peaking 1918/20)

Blows against authority for freedom and rights, or suppression of same

July 16 1918	Russian royal family executed. {🕐 140 Saturn/ Neptune} {🕐 248 Aquarian Age}
November 1918	Riot, rout and revolution in Germany.
July 30 1919	Race riots in Chicago.
October 1919	Red Army gaining supremacy over White Army.
November 1919	Hindenburg statue, symbol of German right wing, taken down.
February 24 1920	Hitler outlines Reactionary Policy.
May 1920	Revolution in Mexico continues with the assassination of the President.

Firsts, records, innovations and discoveries

July 1918	Birth control discussed openly for first time. (Also Blows against authority)
November 30 1918	The new face of Europe following end of World War One.
February 14 1919	Birth of League of Nations. (Also Blows against authority)
November 1919	First woman in parliament: Lady Astor. (Also Blows against authority)
August 26 1920	American women win right to vote. (Also Blows against authority)

Shock, outrage and accident

Shell-shock, trauma, mayhem and after-shock of World War One.

Saturn/Uranus Major Storm 1928–33 (peaking 1929/32)

Blows against authority for freedom and rights, or suppression of same

March 12 1930	Gandhi's symbolic defiance of British rule in India.
April 1930	Rebellion in China.
January 8 1931	Pope denounces sexual freedoms.
April 14 1931	Spain becomes a republic – king flees.
September 30 1931	Unemployed riot in London.

Firsts, records, innovations and discoveries

February 18 1930	Discovery of Pluto – key to irregularities of Uranus.
August 1930	Chrysler Building completed – the tallest structure in the world.
August 7 1930	Unemployment in UK more than two million.
December 31 1930	Unemployment in US more than four million.
January 20 1931	Unemployment in Europe at all time high.
May 1 1931	Empire State Building completed, becoming the tallest structure ever.
May 1931	Highest manned balloon flight.
July 22 1931	Record round-the-world flight.
September 4 1931	Record coast-to-coast flight.

Shock, outrage and accident

September 14 1930	Hitler shock election results.
October 5 1930	R101 airship explodes.

Saturn/Uranus Major Storm 1940–43 (New Cycle, peaking 1941/42)

In addition to the obvious and many disruptions to the status quo, along with commensurate shock and horror, that characterized the height of World War Two, which included the most famous air conflict ever – the Battle of Britain:

Firsts, records, innovations and discoveries

May 30 1942	Thousand-bomber raid on Cologne. (Also Shock, outrage and accident)
June 7 1942	World's greatest naval battle.

Shock, outrage and accident

December 7 1941	Japanese attack Pearl Harbour. {🕐 90 Saturn/Pluto}
March 1942	Heavy bombardment of German cities.

Saturn/Uranus Major Storm 1950–54 (peaking 1951/53)

Blows against authority for freedom and rights, or suppression of same

March 10	Coup in Cuba: Batista regains power.
October 1952	British take action against Mau-Mau rampage in Kenya.

Firsts, records, innovations and discoveries

June 1952	First atomic submarine built.
October 1952	Le Corbusier's Unite d'Habituation completed – a revolutionary design of 'free-flowing space'.
December 1952	First sex-change made public. (Also Shock, outrage and accident)
March 1953	Crick and Watson determine the form of DNA.

Shock, outrage and accident

August 15 1950	Earthquake (at 8.5M one of the 13 largest since 1900) in Tibet.
October 8 1952	Threefold train crash in London.
November 4 1952	Earthquake (at 9.0M one of the 13 largest since 1900) in Kamchatka, Russia {🕐 141 Saturn/Neptune}.

Saturn/Uranus Major Storm 1963–68 (peaking 1964/67)

As can be seen from this sample of events, this Wave was particularly powerful as it merged with the Uranus/Pluto Mother-Wave of 1960–72, as do the two Saturn/Uranus Major Storms described in this chapter merge with the current Mother-Wave of 2007–20!

Blows against authority for freedom and rights, or suppression of same

February 25 1964	Khan ousted in South Vietnam.
March 28 1964	Martin Luther King leads protest march.
February 10 1965	Blacks protest against segregation in US.
August 6 1965	US Voting Rights Bill made law.
August 15 1965	Race riots in Watts, Los Angeles.
November 11 1965	Rhodesia declares its independence from Britain.
November 25 1965	Mobutu takes over in Congo.
November 1965	Two Americans set fire to themselves in protest against Vietnam War.
January 14 1966	Thousand-strong protest in US against expulsion of black legislator.
April 1966	Chairman Mao launches 'cultural revolution' in China.
May 1966	Anti-Vietnam war protests continue to grow.
February 11 1967	Chinese army maintains 'revolutionary order' (Uranus/Saturn).

Firsts, records, innovations and discoveries

March 18 1964	Soviet cosmonaut first man to leave orbiting spacecraft.

September 1965	Confirmation that Vikings discovered America first disrupts Columbus Day.
November 9 1965	Worst power failure in history in US.
December 15 1965	First rendezvous in space.

Shock, outrage and accident

October 13 1963	Earthquake (at 8.6M one of the 13 largest since 1900) in Kuril Islands {and earthquakes below ☉ 33 Uranus/Pluto }.
March 28 1964	Earthquake (at 9.2M one of the 13 largest since 1900) in Prince William Sound, Alaska {and below ☉ 91 Saturn/Pluto}.
February 4 1965	Earthquake (at 8.7M one of the 13 largest since 1900) in Rat Islands, Alaska.
January 17 1966	US lose H-bomb over Spain.
January 27 1967	Three astronauts killed in Apollo 1 fire.

Saturn/Uranus Major Storm 1974–78 (peaking 1975/77)
Blows against authority for freedom and rights, or suppression of same

December 5 1974	Military violently suppress anti-government protests in Burma.
May 21 1975	Baader-Meinhof terrorist group on trial.
August 1 1975	Signing of Helsinki agreement affirming human rights, inviolability of frontiers, etc.
September 1975	Civil war destroying Beirut.
November 11 1975	Civil war erupts in Angola, Africa.
December 30 1975	Bomb kills 14 at La Guardia airport, New York.
June 19 1976	Most violent protest in 15 years hits South Africa.
July 4 1976	Israelis free hostages at Entebbe, Uganda.
September 13 1976	'Right-to-die' made law in California.
October 6 1976	Chaos in Thailand culminates in coup.
July 5 1977	Bhutto ousted in coup in Pakistan.

Firsts, records, innovations and discoveries

July 19 1975	US and USSR spacecraft join up in space.
October 1976	First soft landing on Mars.

Shock, outrage and accident

July 27 1976	Earthquake kills 255,000 in China, prior to Mao dying on September 18.
September 13 1976	Ozone layer under threat – controls suggested on aerosols, etc.
March 28 1977	Worst airplane disaster in history kills 574 in Tenerife.
August 16 1977	Elvis Presley dies.

Saturn/Uranus Major Storm 1985–90
(New Cycle, peaking 1987/88)

Blows against authority for freedom and rights, or suppression of same

March 1988	Sandinistas and Contras end civil war in Nicaragua.
May 16 1988	Russians pull out of Afghanistan, defeated by Mujahideen.
July 1988	Iran–Iraq war ends after eight years.
September 1988	Soviet troops move into Armenia to end unrest.
September 1988	Pro-democracy demonstrations against military junta in Burma, 3000 civilians killed.
November 14 1988	Arafat establishes state of Palestine, recognizes Israel, and rejects terrorism.
May 1990	Burmese government hold free elections for the first time in almost 30 years butrefuse to step down when beaten.

Firsts, records, innovations and discoveries

December 10 1987	US and USSR sign Nuclear Arms Reduction Treaty. (Also Blows against authority)
April 20 1988	Stealth bomber officially displayed.
April 23 1988	Pedal-powered craft, the Daedalus, flies 74 miles in Greece.

December 7 1988	US assist Russians for first time since WW2 with Armenia earthquake. (See Shock, outrage and accident)
December 18 1988	US and PLO meet for first time. (Also Blows against authority)
December 1988	Worst fires in Yellowstone Park this century. (Also Shock, outrage and accident)

Shock, outrage and accident

April 26 1986	Chernobyl nuclear reactor blows up. (Also a First)
March 6 1988	British shoot IRA trio in Gibraltar. (Also Blows against authority)
July 8 1988	US ship shoots down Iranian passenger jet, killing 290.
August 28 1988	Three jets collide at German air show, killing 46.
September 1988	Gilbert, strongest hurricane this century, hits Caribbean. (Also a First)
December 7 1988	Mighty earthquake hits Armenia.
December 22 1988	Lockerbie air crash kills 259.
January 4 1989	US jets shoot down two Libyan jets.

Saturn/Uranus Major Storm 1998–2001 (peaking 1999/2000)

There was outrage and uprising throughout this period, especially with the Balkans conflict, but here only a small but cruel sample is given that occurred while a Saturn/Neptune Wave {<143} merged, peaked and patterned at the same time in the Spring of 1999.

Blows against authority for freedom and rights, or suppression of same

March/April 1999	Serbs kill or drive out Albanians from Kosovo. NATO planes attack Serbs.
April 1999	Rebellion and civil unrest in Balkans, Uganda, Chechnya, Sri Lanka and Sierra Leone.
April 1999	48 people injured by a nail bomb in London, the first of three bombs to explode in the capital within a two-week period.
May 1999	NATO troops arrive in Kosovo.
May 1999	Rebel strongholds bombed in Congo by government.

Firsts, records, innovations and discoveries

May 11 1999	The solar wind from the Sun dies away almost completely for 24 hours and allows the Earth's magnetic field to stretch out to the Moon.

Shock, outrage and accident

April 1999	In Littleton, Colorado, two Columbine High School students kill 12 other students and one teacher before killing themselves.
April 1999	In Colombia, Marxist rebels and right-wing death squads kill at least 371 civilians in three months.
April 1999	In Iraq US fighter planes bomb anti-aircraft sites in the northern no-fly zone.
April 1999	Earthquake (5.5M) hits Belgrade.
May 1999	In Sumatra soldiers open fire on villagers; over 30 people are killed and thousands flee the town following the massacre.
May 1999	Tornadoes kill and injure many on US Plains.
May 1999	The bodies of 1500 ethnic Albanians are burned in a blast furnace just before NATO troops arrive in Kosovo.
September 11 2001	World Trade Center destroyed and Pentagon damaged by Al Quaeda. (Also Blows against authority) {☺93 Saturn/Pluto}

Saturn/Uranus Major Storm 2007–12

This Major Storm, and the very beginning of the next one in 2020, is akin to the one that occurred between 1963 and 1968 {<194}. This is because they all coincide with a Uranus/Pluto Mother Wave. Concerning Freedom (Uranus) from Repression (Saturn) this is already showing strong signs of manifesting with, for openers, the protest, unrest and near crisis in Burma {<196, 1988} and Zimbabwe.

Regarding earthquakes, three out of the thirteen biggest quakes from 1900 to 2007 all occurred during this previous period, the sixties. Admittedly, one equally strong contender for earthquakes, a Saturn/Pluto Major Storm, was also involved at that time. But then, these Major Storms will also be occurring during the current Uranus/Pluto Mother-Wave of 2007–20, and again Saturn/Uranus and Saturn/Pluto Waves merge closely in 2009–10 (*see* Weather Chart on page 19). Could this (particularly during Hotspots >294) mean...

EARTHQUAKE ALERT 2009–12!

Earthquakes and other natural disasters, plus freedom from repression, repression of freedom and terrorist acts are all likely to intensify during this period.

'THE KING OF TERROR SHALL COME FROM THE SKY'

It was for July 1999 that Nostradamus made the above prediction. He was only a few months out if you can consider, without too much difficulty, that many of the above events for that year amounted to such an occurence. However, during the same Storm there occurred an event far more fitting of such a prediction. This was when a peaking Saturn/Pluto Wave merged with the tail-end of this 1998–2001 Saturn/Uranus Storm, and the 9/11 disaster struck from the sky, quite literally. This led the United States into war with Al-Quaeda in (supposedly) Iraq and Afghanistan.

A very similar event to 9/11, and noted as such at the time, was the Japanese attack on Pearl Harbour in December 1941. This was astrologically the exact reverse, as it was at the peak of a Saturn/Uranus Wave and at the tail-end of a Saturn/Pluto Storm. But in both cases it was very much an 'out-of-the-blue' act of aggression which again led the US into a state of war, this time with Japan, and then all the Axis powers.

In the light of these facts, this and other predictions of Nostradamus appear somewhat questionable. This is one reason why this book frowns upon such so-called predictions. They are hit-and-miss affairs that have no purpose other than to entertain and mildly intrigue, when the way of our current world demands far more than that from us. We need to know not just when any terror might come at us from any direction and in any form, but what we can do about it. Astro-Quantum holds that the future is in our hands, not those of some dubious king of terror.

Rumblings: A Preview

In August 2007, just before its actual beginning in September, this Saturn/Uranus Wave introduced itself very dramatically as a national disaster in Greece. Terrible forest fires destroyed hundreds of square miles of country, killing dozens of people, and even threatening one of the most famous symbols of Ancient Greece, the Parthenon. And they were set by arsonists – so this is a classic act of terrorism, probably out of greed for land in order to develop it for property. Rumour tells us that it is so hard for property developers to obtain land through the notorious Greek bureaucracy that they resort to destroying the forest, so that the land is no longer protected against development.

Whatever the truth, this is still terrorism as there is no doubt in anyone's mind that the fires were deliberately set. Another dimension to all this has been the alleged inefficiency and slowness of Greek officialdom in coming to the aid of those who were threatened or actually afflicted by the fires.

In October 2007, fires also raged in California destroying thousands of homes belonging to rich and poor alike. The poor planning in California and the laxness of Greek authorities are actually expressions of the Saturn/Neptune Wave occurring 2004–08. {⊕ 136 Saturn/Neptune}

The Difference Between Freedom and Licence

All this brings to mind one of the most difficult issues raised by Saturn/Uranus Waves, particularly when they are empowered by merging with a Uranus/Pluto Mother-Wave – as already mentioned, the 2007–12 and the beginning of the 2020–22 Saturn/Uranus Waves are both examples of this. This difficulty comes when the healthy traditions and restraints of Saturn – as distinct from the repressive ones – are overrun by the desires for freedom and the 'new' that are Uranus. But freedom in excess or using any means to get what you want is just another term for 'licence', which gives rise to an absence of structure or sense of limitation. At first, such 'freedom' can appear liberating and progressive, but it actually winds up being the opposite. This merging of Saturn, Uranus and Pluto Waves also occurred between 1963 and 1969 and the liberalism of that time has, according to many social pundits, come home to roost in the form of feckless and feral youth with no sense of boundaries or morality. One could say that this applies to the Western world as a whole.

Such licence has also been fed by Uranian technology outstripping the natural rhythms and emotional qualities of life that give rise to human empathy. Hi-tech has replaced 'hi-touch'. Children are addicted to computer games, stunting those human 'skills' even further. What is worse, children fill themselves with chemically corrupted junk food as a substitute for a good wholesome diet. Consequently, obesity, hyperactivity, allergic reactions and plain bad behaviour are increasingly common in the young. It could also be said that other eating disorders, like anorexia and bulimia, which have arisen since the sixties, are a Uranian protest against being fed what isn't good for you. More commonly, these disorders are psychologically ascribed to being the only means of control that the sufferer feels is available to them. Control is Saturnian thing, so one can see how they are trying vainly to redress the balance by offsetting the excess of Uranus.

These problems tend to occur in countries that have little or no religious ethos to act as a Saturnian 'brake' to Uranian licence. For example, Britain is currently beset by a distinct youth problem with knife and gun crime – and crime generally – escalating. This raises a significant point with respect to the Saturn/Uranus effect: the manner and efficiency of government determines what kind of rebellion or licence it attracts. We will look at this in detail on page 212 with 'What's Your Beef?'

Astro-Quantum

None of this needs necessarily be so. Acts of terrorism and war, earthquakes and other natural disasters, and mistaking licence for freedom are all connected. Surfing the Planet-Waves through simply absorbing the information and using the aids given here will subtly but powerful make a difference. Finding the balance between Saturn and Uranus, between discipline and freedom, and

---

Astro-Quantum Memo

Order + Freedom = Civilization

---

knowing what's fine to keep as it is and what needs changing, all contribute towards creating a balance of these energies globally. The more positively attuned and properly balanced our collective consciousness is, the more difficult it is for negative expressions to manifest. Very simple ways of striking this balance and becoming so attuned are given later in this chapter.

Just Around The Corner: Anarchy

During Saturn/Uranus Waves, anarchy is always just around the corner, but particularly as it occurs against the intensifying and extreme-producing backdrop of a Uranus/Pluto Mother-Wave. Uranus-ruled anarchy, by definition, is 'the failure of law and government' and some might say that is what it takes to wake us up to the ills of society. But this, from Saturn's cautious and objective side of the equation, is a 'kill-or-cure' remedy which might look good in a film or on a news bulletin, but probably not in the street where you live.

Astro-Quantum

Exercise discipline in your own life, while balancing it with allowing yourself and others the space to be human. Looking for this balance in leaders rather than creating it within yourself is asking to be misled. That is how Hitler got a whole country behind him and led them to destruction and defeat.

Surf It or Wipe-Out?

So which way are you, are we, going to go? One path, riding
these Waves or acting in the true Spirit of These Times, will take
us into a positive future – the other, giving in to the Devil of
These Times, will take us to a negative future.

The Spirit of These Times
The Best of the Old and the Best of the New

Looking at the recent history of Saturn/Uranus Major Storms has given us a
strong idea and sense of what they are about. Like tectonic plates causing earthquakes, a central theme is that of forces of the new grating against forces of the
old, or revolution against preservation – irresistible force meeting immovable
object. But as they rub together the friction creates something which is either a
blend of both, or a product of one side winning outright. It is usually difficult, if
not impossible, to see how things will pan out as anything with Uranus in the mix
is inherently unpredictable. One example occurred during the Saturn/Uranus
Major Storm in World War Two, when the Nazis believed their victory would
mark the beginning of their thousand year empire, the Third Reich – the New
Order as they dubbed it. As it turned out, it was the Europe they tried to conquer
that became the New Order.

In any event, we seem to make headway on these Waves even though it is
often with two steps forward and one step back. A start-stop-start, jerky
movement often characterizes the process. These are times of cautious reform,
and of old things resurfacing, being used or looked at in a new way. Overall, we
can simply dub the Spirit of These Times: progress.

The Devil of These Times
The Worst of the Old and the Worst of the New

As implied above, the two greatest dangers in surfing Saturn/Uranus Waves are either ignoring and suppressing a genuine need for change, or affecting changes merely for the sake of it. The first danger leads first to stagnation and dissatisfaction, then to strikes, civil disturbance and unforeseen negative effects resulting from not making necessary changes, especially with respect to fairness and equal rights. Terrorism and bloody revolution can also be a consequence, but in a more long-term and complex way. These in turn result in a breakdown of society and the fabric of civilization, and also deterioration in health as tension and stress build up.

Then there are changes that are just cosmetic, or plain ineffective. Most dangerous of all, though, is the 'baby out with the bathwater' syndrome where something extremely useful and valuable is lost for ever. A rueful example of this took place in Britain with the 'Beeching Cuts' to her national rail network. This began at the very start of the Saturn/Uranus Major Storm in 1963 and was pretty well done with by the end of it in 1968. As recently opined by Paul F Withrington, Director of Transport-Watch, UK, 'It is not the cuts themselves that were the tragedy ... but the loss of 9,000 miles of superbly engineered right of way.' Britain now has a disastrously crowded and overworked road system with pollution and fuel consumption to match, while rural areas which were previously supplied by the rail system still have inadequate public transport. That 'right of way' is just what is now needed.

Finally, there are those that promise freedom and rights, only to be revealed as no better or worse than the regime they replaced. As the saying goes, 'Today's radicals become tomorrow's conservatives'.

> *‘ They that drink of the old wine have no place*
> *for the new. ’*

Proverb

Conflicts, Trends and Possibilities

Health

Tensions and Solutions

As has we have seen, Saturn-Uranus creates a high degree of tension as the new presses to be acknowledged and realized, while the old digs in its heels. The human psychological and physical systems naturally register this tension. On a psychological level, according to the individual, such tension can manifest as more self-awareness and self-control – both of which are key, collectively and personally, in positively managing Saturn/Uranus Storms. The ability to be present and aware is an evolving human quality that allows us to understand what is truly happening at any given moment and place. This in turn means that highly intuitive and practical responses give rise to quite miraculous solutions regarding not just health but all manner of human problems.

Accidents and Conflicting Paradigms

In terms of physical health, skeletomuscular complaints increase, with back trouble especially being even more of a problem, both personally and economically, owing to the cost of absenteeism. All essential physiological and chemical balances become more critical, with a resultant increase in related complaints. Also, erratic behaviour and tension internally make physical accidents more numerous. Self-awareness and self-control are key to preventing these physical manifestations. As a consequence of all this, yoga and other psycho-physical methods of creating and maintaining health should become far more widespread, leading ultimately to better health at a holistic level. However, the old guard, religious or medical, oppose this trend in equal proportion.

Trade and Industry

Disruption Brings Change

Strikes and the economic instability and repercussions that they bring are a common manifestation of Saturn/Uranus Major Storms. Changes in work patterns and practises are now more affected by technology and the internet than ever before. But this also presents problems as old forms and systems are scrapped and new ones fail to deliver what was expected. Terrorism and natural disasters are bound to have a profound effect upon business and money. Personal freedoms, mostly indulged in as a respite from the mounting stresses or dissatisfaction of modern life, increasingly interfere with or sabotage the running of business, transport, etc. Early signs of this are employees spending unacceptably long periods surfing the net or emailing friends. (See also Scientific/Internet Overload page 210.)

All of these 'disturbances' demand radical rethinks regarding what 'working life' actually means, and regarding the whole economic philosophy upon which business and industry are based. Also, simple measures like making spare parts to products available indefinitely rather than having to dump them and buy a new one, for the sake of, say, a refrigerator shelf being broken. Failure to address and deal with these issues during the 2007–12 Major Storm contribute to serious global breakdowns in the state of economy and industry during the 2020–22 Storm, not to mention compounding environmental problems.

Astro-Quantum

To address all of the above, the way we think in economic terms has to change as we realize more and more that not only is one country's wealth another's poverty, but also that this inequality destabilizes the whole. {>209 Equality and Restriction: Food}

Environmental

Geophysical Stress

As we have seen, Saturn/Uranus seriously affects any geophysical stresses already in existence. Areas prone to earthquakes, typhoons and tornadoes are gravely at risk. Concerning the climate, more stringent and well-enforced laws, worldwide, will follow upon flagrant acts of pollution by certain countries. Also, there are restrictions and problems concerning electrical power supply and various technological methods. People and industry object to new rulings, but eventually some kind of agreement and method is thrashed out, as is typical of the Saturn/Uranus process – just because sooner or later it *has* to be.

Technophobia

'Environmental discipline' has to be more vigorously enforced owing to critical environmental conditions, despite the apparent infringement of civil and individual liberties. A steep rise in accidents, especially in the air, makes restriction of air travel absolutely essential, after much prevarication previously. There is, overall, a peaking in awareness of, and subsequent objection to, the ills created by technology.

Socio-Cultural

Rebellion and Disorder

Mounting discontent and disillusionment with the State and anyone in authority become rebellious stirrings, mounting to outright dissent with street demonstrations and the like. Young people become more than usually vociferous and violent as they hit out at what they see as restriction. Restructuring and reform in some areas follows upon this, but so too does more repression in other areas. Right-wing groups and vigilantism gain favour where existing official bodies continue in their failure to deliver.

Pervading the 2007–12 Major Storm is a strong 'start-stop-start-stop' mode as something new makes itself felt, only to be halted or stymied by doubts, conservative elements and recalcitrant attitudes; followed by renewed urges for change, then more resistance to it, etc, etc.

If Youth Knew; If Age Could

Older people are now more liable to become entrenched in their ways, exacerbating the differences and conflict between themselves and the young. The old will have to work out what actually commands respect from youth, rather than just expecting or demanding it. The licence given to the young progressively since the sixties when a Saturn/Uranus Major Storm occurred at the same time as a Uranus/Pluto Mother-Wave and a Saturn/Pluto Major Storm (and which is happening in 2008–11 too, <19 Planet-Wave Weather Chart) gets to be a greater problem during the 2007–12 Storm. The 'respect' that the young demand, often quite violently, is ironically really a call for the structure and order that they haven't had since Sixties liberalism. This is the Awakening to Order that Saturn/Uranus Waves are about, just as much as they are a Rebellion against the wrong sort of Order – i.e. repression.

New Art Forms

There is a surge in art forms that are expressed in a more and more shocking way. Fashion also comes up with some very outlandish, disturbing and absurd styles. Scientific discoveries concerning the very nature of reality (see 'Scientific' below) create a sea-change in the way people look at life in an every day sense, with lasting effects, and this is reflected in the arts.

Political

Possible Flashpoints

Those troublesome or 'rebel states' will commit some destructive act. Countries such as Iran and North Korea, who threatened problems with nuclear weapons back in 2006, could now very well make such threats real during the 2007–12 Storm. But this is more likely, or made worse, when a Saturn/Pluto Major Storm joins this one in 2009–11 (see Merging Waves below). Repressive regimes get more and more backlash and rebellion from the people or opposing factions. There also occur many scandals and 'outings' concerning disreputable and con-spiratorial goings on in corridors of power.

Party Lines Become Fuzzy

With respect to democratic government, it becomes confusing for the voter as ostensibly opposing parties seem to become more interchangeable and not so clearly defined. This is because Saturn/Uranus is revealing the basic absurdity of a two- or three-party system or rather of any political party trying to toe their own line too literally. In other words, there is a political revolution going on in the sense that politicians are having to be both more pragmatic in meeting the needs of the people and changing world conditions, and more idealistic or radical at the same time in order to gain any respect at all. If a sudden change or U-turn is required then so be it, because this is precisely what Saturn/Uranus Major Storms demand, especially as the 2007–12 one merges with the Saturn/Pluto Storm of 2008–11 during 2009–11.

Spiritual

Spirit Gets Scientific

A stronger sense of the differences between various religions gives rise to even more frictions and acts of aggression towards one another on the one hand, but paradoxically to a reconciliation of those differences on the other, mainly because of similarities being noticed. The (scientific) discovery of other dimensions described below has something to do with this realization. This effect also occurs between the secular world and the religious world, with those subscribing to the one getting more intolerant of the other, or a more pragmatic approach being adopted by the religious, and the recognition that the spiritual realm has some important points with respect to management and containment of anti-social elements in society. During these times, the idea that the moral behaviour

---

EQUALITY AND RESTRICTION: FOOD

As you have probably noticed, during Saturn/Uranus Waves there is a strong emphasis on equality (Uranus) and restriction (Saturn), but not necessarily paired together. Usually it would be Uranian freedom that opposes Saturnian restriction, or Saturnian status that is at odds with Uranian equality. But if we oppose Saturn and Uranus with equality versus restriction, we can ride and use the Waves to serve both ourselves and others with respect to food supply.

Most Westerners consume too much food and drink, are overweight and commensurately unhealthy, or disgracefully they throw away uneaten food. In any event, they sap world resources in the process. By cutting down on our food intake we get in better shape, physically and financially, decrease that drain on supply and shift the whole economy and lifestyle of the West and then the world.

---

of human beings actually affects the weather and geophysical state of affairs becomes more of a factor in spiritual philosophies, simply because of such phenomena becoming more alarming. This will be in addition to, or rather seen as the cause of, man's abuse of the environment.

Scientific

Shocks and Surprises

There is a strong chance of Industrial accidents, especially of a nuclear variety. On the positive side, certain discoveries and innovations now make a significant difference to efforts to reduce pollution and global warming, and to find renewable energy sources. Conventional schools of scientific thought become more polarized with the more radical ones. Breakthroughs are likely to occur in our understanding of what 'reality' actually is, with some surprising realizations that the supposedly more off-the-wall approaches, such as astrology and reincarnation, are based in fact after all. However, such breakthroughs give rise to aggressive or unequivocal stances being taken by either side. Issues regarding UFOs are likely to again come to the fore. This has something to do with the discovery that there are indeed other dimensions existing parallel to our own. A main focus of interest then becomes the question of who or what dwells therein, and what have it/they have to do with us, or want from us.

Internet Overload

The Saturn/Uranus Major Storms of 2007–12 and 2020–22, occuring as they do during the Uranus/Pluto Mother-Wave, are likely to bring about severe problems with the Worldwide Web as technology, facilities and servers are stretched to breaking point, yet the Favourable Wind of 2015–18 is liable to see solutions that resolve or prevent damage. For more regarding this important dilemma, see page 53.

Astro-Quantum

In turn, this will have the effect of redistributing wealth so that poor and poverty stricken countries have an equal slice of the collective cake. All this also helps to offset the likelihood of food shortages worldwide.

The Mood of These Times

A combination of feeling both stuck and rebellious creates an atmosphere of tension. Also there is a crackle of the unexpected in the air, as if something is going to go off – with a bang! Essentially, there is a sense that something's got to give. It is apparent that one has to struggle through doubts, difficult decisions and upset plans as it is revealed what can and must change and what cannot and must not. The overall national or global state of affairs seems to mirror this atmosphere, or to actually create or contribute to it. But of course, in astro-quantum terms, one is creating the other simultaneously.

A War Footing

Remember such times of Saturn/Uranus Major Storms as World War Two and the 1960s when the new and old order battled it out? It could be a good idea to see life during these times as being on a 'war footing' in the sense that risks have to be taken and changes made, sometimes daily, in order to get through to the desired outcome. Resistance to, or fear of, change blocks the intuition that helps you see your way to freedom from whatever is confining you. It is well to realize that the old saying, 'Better the devil you know than the devil you don't,' is misleading or actually false. The opposite of the devil you know is actually the *god you don't know*.

Saturn is Satan, the devil, and he is trying to keep you from finding a more evolved and free state by insinuating that there is nothing better than what you already have. We must challenge the old values and practises along with the outer authorities or inner fears that keep them in place. If they can then prove that they are worth keeping, that they are wise authorities that have our interests at heart, and healthy or real fears that keep us from harm, then well and good. But otherwise we have to sue for change.

The Grey Area

At the same time the Mood of These Times has a distinct grey area that should be respected, otherwise things could become impossible to resolve or just plain unreal. For example, no one can be totally 'right wing' or 'left wing', 'pro' or 'con', etc. If we are to be honest, we all have a bit of us in both camps. The whole secret to riding a Saturn/Uranus Wave is to maintain a balance between being liberal and authoritarian, between permissiveness and resistance, between sticking with tradition and striking out for the new. In both political and personal terms, the advice to be democratic in spirit and autocratic in method is valid, especially when having to hold fast against unwelcome change and at the same time hold fast to a programme of reform.

Earlier, I pointed out that the effect of Saturn/Uranus Waves is often felt or noticed more in the state of one's own country as well as, if not more than, in the world at large. But to this extent, it also means that it is your own personal polit-ical views that become more than usually sharpened between Saturn's stone and Uranus's blade. I myself am not as a rule a particularly 'political' person, and I have *not* voted a lot more than I have. But the current state of my own country and the way that it is run is beginning to make my blood boil. This is because the main Mood of These Times could be summed up in the following chart.

WHAT'S YOUR BEEF?

- What's been keeping you penned in, been making you snort with rage and frustration?

- Has the State been pushing you around or letting you down?

- Who do you wish would shut up, wake up and grow up?

- Who ought to quit moaning and free-loading and get down to some hard work and take responsibility for themselves?

Astro-Quantum

The Universe is very Saturn/Uranus because it too is, as mentioned above, 'democratic in spirit and autocratic in method'. Every little bit of energy – which includes you – contributes to make up the whole; it has its vote. The more coherent and justified your own thoughts and opinions, which means the more keen your *consciousness* is, then the more it'll contribute to and influence the whole. If you see your consciousness as being like a radio station: the more powerful and constant its signal, then the more its broadcast is heard. But where you are conflicted or unsure or just non-committal, then the signal is commensurately weakened. Democratically, we all get our vote, but we each have to cast it like we are a king or a queen and act as if we are running our little corner of the Universe if we wish to affect the whole.

An Invitation

And so you are invited, or actually constrained, to come out and make clear what it is that you wish to see change in your life/country/world. Here, as a citizen of the United Kingdom, is a draft of my 'Saturn/Uranus Manifesto', compiled for my own benefit, but also to encourage you to do your own. You may or may not agree with some or even all of it – but that is the whole Saturn/Uranus Wave point: expressing your opinion!

Lyn's Saturn/Uranus Manifesto for the UK

- Zero tolerance of anti-social behaviour, especially violence, like the US used so successfully in cities like New York and Chicago.
- Drug and alcohol abuse to be treated as a symptom of a spiritual void that needs to be filled with spiritual philosophies and practises such as prayer and meditation. This is particularly needed in prisons. Total legalization and state dispensation of all drugs with subsequent removal of black market and crime.
- Punishment to fit the crime, but with an emphasis on rehabilitation.
- Programmes and incentives to help and encourage the nation's youth to direct their energies in a socially profitable direction. This would have to involve non-denominational spiritual education – such as

astrology and mythology – and a hands-on involvement with the
natural world.

- An end to the dumbing down of entertainment and education. Setting
  higher goals and a greater emphasis on the arts, especially music,
  classics, nature and mythology.
- A withdrawal of the application of politically correct thinking at an
  official level, and the recognition that everyone has equal rights in
  direct proportion to how much they respect the rights of others.
- In the health sector, reinstallation of traditional caring methods – such
  as bedside manner and rigorous cleanliness rather than emphasis
  being placed upon technology, academic achievement and government
  targets and bureaucracy. Hi-tech must be matched by 'hi-touch'.
- Heavy restriction on the use of gratuitous violence and sex as a means
  to make money – especially out of the young – in both advertising
  and product Placement.

I could go on, but this is merely an example of focusing one's opinion of what
would make a better world. In making such a list, it is surprising how one's
Saturnian tendencies of order and control jostle with one's Uranian tendencies of
liberalism and the unconventional. Saturn/Uranus Waves seem unerringly to
present one with the paradox that life is. Instanced here is the point that Uranian
technology can improve life on the one hand, but degrade it on the other by
putting the impersonal in places where the human touch should hold sway.
And possibly most significant, how disorder invariably has to precede a better
kind of order.

The Choice is Ours
Easy Surfing

The following chart shows us Positive Responses to
Saturn/Uranus Waves that collectively create Positive
Effects. The Negative Responses need to be avoided in
order to prevent the collective Negative Effects. Note the
opposing qualities of the Negatives and Positives, and
track back Negative or Positive Effects to the Responses
that created them.

2007–12 and 2020–22
The Collective Effect of Saturn/Uranus Major Storms
The Choice is Ours

Negative Response

Positive Response

Ignorance of, or resistance to, the need for change and those that need help and understanding. Suppression of agents and voices for change.

Openness to, and awareness of, the need for constructive change and discussion, and flexibility and innovation in applying it. Carefully considered reform.

Thinking that technology can solve all problems. Approaching issues in a linear rather than intuitive fashion. Hi-tech overriding hi-touch.

Implementing changes for practical and popular reasons. Using natural, humanitarian, hands-on methods. Reinstalling or updating traditional practises.

Increasing commercialization/ industrialization. The short-sighted thinking and greed behind it. The drug of consumerism that it creates.

Creative enforcement of recycling and reduction of pollution. Seeking clean technological, spiritual and aesthetic solutions.

Allowing systems that have patently failed the requirements of people and Nature to still hold sway.

Breaking with traditions and authorities that do not have the common interest at heart.

TIME TO CHANGE

The continuance of civil and moral decline, creating a soulless, Big-Brother type of society.

Creation of a more informed and spiritually aware society, where self-responsibility is seen as the priority.

Ill-health and the burden this puts upon everyone; the 'have-nots' resorting to more crime in order to get what the 'haves' possess.

Healthier environment, healthier populace, more efficiency, and a sense of pride in our surroundings. Reduction in crime.

Inventions and installations that go against Nature and offend human sensitivities, giving rise to health and environmental problems, eyesores and white elephants.

Improvement in healthcare and all service industries. Revivification of inner city and run-down areas. Involvement with Nature as standard in education.

Violent uprising and revolution. Social and civil unrest. Destruction of property. Terrorism. Strikes. A grave absence of any sense of what 'humanity' actually means.

Old practises and structures appropriately overhauled, reformed, or replaced with new ones. A real sense of what 'humanity' actually means.

Negative Response

Positive Response

A Saturn/Uranus Favourable Wind November 2015 – December 2018

What Kind of Time is This?
A Time of Old Blending with New

Energies in Play as we Ride This Wave

The harmonious combining of the positive and essential energy and character of Saturn – that of **authority and stability**, which is **establishing and/or ordering** – with the essential energy and character of Uranus – that of **freedom and innovation**, which is **awakening and/or advancing** – offers the opportunity to get the best of both these worlds.

So this time holds the promise of resolving many problems and issues that have been dogging us in the past. At the same time, old methods are comfortably applied to meet new problems. Some advances, especially in the technological and research fields, are truly astounding, with links being made between the logical and metaphysical, between science and spirituality. This has the effect of progressively altering humanity as a whole's perception on reality. Of course, all of this is strictly dependent on what has transpired in the seven or eight years leading up to this time.

Looking on the bright side, assuming we have ridden the very difficult Wave combinations of 2007–12, then this Wave marks a time of extraordinary leaps in human development and understanding of life generally. In many ways, this Favourable Wind could be the main indicator of the beginning of that 'new time' predicted by many New Age movements during the preceding decades.

Making the Most of This Favourable Wind

In many respects, this Wave is what *Understanding The Future* is all about, in that it marks a time when ideals and new ways of seeing and living life become a reality, or at least it is far easier to make them so. So for those activities or attitudes that aim to make an almost science-fiction vision real, now is the hour!

On a personal level, consult and use the House positions of Saturn and Uranus, as described below on page 224. With a Favourable Wind you can expect the positive aspects of these interpretations, and see how the influences of both serve and support one another. Also, you can use the Saturn/Uranus Meditation or Prayer on page 230 to greater effect and with greater ease.

Feel the Wave
Know the Wave
Ride the Wave
Change the World

The Unfolding Story

⇉ Merging Waves & ⤯ Jupiter Boosters

In addition to the Uranus/Pluto Mother-Wave that has been taken into account in the interpretations of all three Saturn/Uranus Waves covered in this chapter, there are also other Planet-Waves *merging* with them and affecting them as time goes by. As well as these Merging Waves there are Planet-Waves involving Jupiter that come into the Saturn/Uranus picture, and Jupiter kind of *boosts* whatever is happening, blowing things up so we cannot fail to notice problems or take advantage of opportunities. As can be seen on the Planet-Wave Weather Chart on page 19, Jupiter Waves exist in their own right, and are responsible for Minor Storms and Favourable Breezes, but are not covered in this book for reasons of time and space! Along with the Merging Waves, they increase or modify the effects of the two Saturn/Uranus Major Storms and the Favourable Wind when they are happening at the same time.

The Planet-Wave Chronicles

Taken altogether, these Merging Waves and Jupiter Boosters kind of dramatize and pace the overall course of Saturn/Uranus Waves, rather like a storyteller would do, unfolding its stories.

During the Saturn/Uranus Major Storm Sep 2007 to Jul 2012

⇉ Saturn/Neptune Major Storm – Nov 2004 to Aug 2008 {<143}

 As stated in the Saturn/Neptune chapter, the end of this Wave catches the first year of this Saturn/Uranus Major Storm. It also marks a time when the effects of the Uranus/Pluto Mother-Wave really start to kick in, exacerbating the disruption it has the potential to create. Taken all together, 2008 could present events that leave us in no doubt that we have something going on that is bigger and sooner than we had predicted – again especially where global warming and economy are concerned – but also something which was totally unexpected.

⤳ Saturn/Pluto Favourable Wind – Aug 2006 to Aug 2008 {<119}

This one, a 'Constructive Use of Power', really holds off the heavier destabilizing effects of the Saturn/Uranus Storm, but only until summer 2008. So it could amount to a 'calm before the storm'.

⤳ Jupiter/Uranus Minor Storm – Dec 2006 to Nov 2007 – *Awakening Faith*

This one has whipped up the first stirrings of the Saturn/Uranus Major Storm, making it appear to begin sooner than 'scheduled' for September 2007. The mood for change, justice and equal rights has quickened, as too has an awareness of the times of great change that lie ahead of us all.

⤋ Jupiter/Saturn Favourable Breeze – Feb 2007 to Jan 2009 – *Benevolent Control*

The combination of this Booster with the above Favourable Wind is really important in a helpful and productive way as positive pro-grammes and progressive policies make provision for the impact of the following Major Storm as it merges.

⤳ Saturn/Pluto Major Storm – Nov 2008 to Aug 2011 {<82}

Taking into account the Uranus/Pluto Mother-Wave, here is a merging of three swelling Waves, all carrying Major Storms, which amounts to a 'wall of water', metaphorically if not literally. The effects of the Saturn/Uranus Storm described above now become compounded and intensified as Pluto enters the scene. What was worrying becomes dangerous; what was a mere confrontation becomes an out-and-out conflict; what were signs of global warming become something far more unequivocal. The last time that Saturn, Uranus and Pluto teamed up together in a similar fashion was in the mid-1960s, the Sixties Revolution no less. Effectively then, this too is a Revolution – focussing on 2009–12 – but with added 21st-century environmental spice!

↗ **Jupiter/Saturn Minor Storm – Mar 2010 to Mar 2012 –**
Growth versus Order
↗ **Jupiter/Uranus Minor Storm – Mar 2010 to Apr 2011 –**
Awakening Faith 2
These Boosters tweak the peak of the Saturn/Uranus and Saturn/Pluto Major Storms, giving Uranus a particularly unmitigated magnification. The temptation, in the face of sudden and radical change and shock, could be to tie ourselves to something immovable. But the better course of action is to be alive to what this immense wind of change is telling us, and to respond appropriately. Positively, this could act as some kind of release and impetus to take radical action. Very much a breakthrough or breakdown!

⇥ **Saturn/Neptune Favourable Wind – Dec 2010 to Nov 2013 {<170}**
This constructive influence could show us the way to handle disturb-ances that are by now besetting us with some force. People with both vision and practical ideas introduce timely means and attitudes to help us see what we must do and how we must meet and deal with our dilemmas and follies. A viable plan of recovery?

During the Saturn/Uranus Favourable Wind Nov 2015 to Dec 2018

⇥ **Saturn/Neptune Major Storm – Nov 2014 to Sep 2017 {<136}**
So much depends on how much damage this Storm has already done with respect to what this enormously useful, constructive and inventive Saturn/Uranus Wave can do for us, or rather what we can do with it. Considering the Jupiter Major Storms below also joining in the mêlée, then it's probably a case of making as much of it as we possibly can –

because we really have to. Our backs could be against the wall. Or perhaps it is a case of rebuilding walls and bridges – both literally and, in the case of the latter, metaphorically too. Something is bringing us all closer together. It all comes down to a combination of needs must and seeing the light.

Jupiter/Saturn Minor Storm – Jun 2015 to Jul 2016 – *Growth versus Order 2*

Unfortunately there are still opposing factions complicating matters, in spite of there obviously being a common enemy. But human ingenuity and diplomacy should resolve this idiocy.

Jupiter/Uranus Minor Storm – Oct 2016 to Jan 2018 – *Awakening Faith 4*

As mentioned above, this really lets us know that there is something at hand that we ought to respect, and thereby take a radically new path out of present dangers.

Saturn/Pluto Major Storm – Jan 2018 to Dec 2021 {<82}

These are the most severe type of Storm where human divisiveness and lack of cooperation are concerned. Coming as it does at the end of the Saturn/Uranus Favourable Wind, hopefully we have enough sanity and ingenuity in place to minimize its effects. If not, it could be delivering a *coup de grâce.*

During the Saturn/Uranus Major Storm Jan 2020 to Oct 2022

Saturn/Pluto Major Storm – Jan 2018 to Dec 2021 {<82}

By 2020 this very heavy Major Storm is past its peak but the Saturn/Uranus Wave gives it a new lease of life – unfortunately. But this time does mark a major break with all that has gone before, and the 'breakaway' energy of Saturn/Uranus is a necessary part of this process. Pretty choppy though, as all aboard planet Earth get slung into a very different era.

✦ **Jupiter/Saturn Minor Storm – Dec 2019 to Apr 2021 –**
Growth versus Order 3

Not surprising that this is here too, as the cosmic all-change is declared at this momentous time. A tug-of-war between the past and the future, no less.

Personal Effect

This is how, as an individual, Saturn/Uranus Waves can affect you, and be ridden successfully by you, for their duration.

Surfing with Saturn and Uranus Through the Houses

These effects are based upon the two Houses in your chart through which Saturn and Uranus are passing or 'transiting' while the Uranus/Pluto Mother-Wave is active, but most significantly during the times when Saturn/Uranus Waves are active. As it is a case of a need for Order, Discipline and Effort where Saturn is concerned, and for Change, Disruption and Innovation where Uranus is concerned, knowing these positions will help you to manage the energies of each respective planet in an appropriate way, enabling you to find the right balance and surf successfully!

There are two ways to use this surfing aid.

1 **Off-The-Peg** This is using the Saturn and Uranus positions according to your Birth Sign, Sun Sign or Star Sign. This looks at what Solar Houses Saturn and Uranus are transiting through while the Uranus/Pluto Mother-Wave is active. So using the **Planet House Transit Guide** (beginning on page 254) first go to **Saturn: House Ready-Reckoner** on page 262. Next, look for the time **Period** you are interested in, then look along the row until you get to the column of your **Birth Sign.** There you will see the number of the House being transited by Saturn – 1st, 2nd, 3rd, etc – and just below it the number of

the page where you can read the description of possible situations and actions you can take. Then, do the same thing for Uranus – go to **Uranus: House Ready-Reckoner** on page 270 and repeat the process. Now you can get a feel for how the two planet positions compare. All this can be very useful and accurate, but remember that it is only based on your Sun Sign.

2 **Made-To-Measure**This is using the Saturn and Uranus positions according to your individual birth chart which would have to be calculated correctly from a reliably accurate birth time. So if you do know your birth time and have your birth chart accurately drawn up, then anyone with a basic knowledge of a chart will be able to tell you which Houses in your personal chart are occupied by Saturn and Uranus at any given time between 2007 and 2020, but especially, remember, when a Saturn/Uranus Wave is active. Then simply find and consult the readings for those Houses in the **Planet House Transit Guide** (page 254). So, if Saturn was transiting your Tenth House and Uranus was transiting your Fourth House, then you would find these interpretations on the pages indicated in the Planet House Transit Guide by using the **Index** . For our example you would go to page 267 for Saturn transiting the Tenth House, and to page 271 for Uranus transiting the Fourth House. Note: you do *not* use the Ready-Reckoner when using Made-To-Measure.

The Saturn/Uranus Wave Effect Upon Relationships

The combination punch of Saturn/Uranus Major Storms is quite tough on relationships as it accentuates the perennial conflict – commitment versus freedom. So, at times there is a great degree of tension as one part of you wants to hang on to a partnership, while another part of you just wants out or to 'play away'. The thing to bear in mind is what Saturn/Uranus have been saying all along: this is a process of evolution and progress and it will first feel stuck, then free up and look clear, then get stuck again, and so on. The trick is to not take any particular stage as a final judgement or reading of where you, your partner or the relationship should be. It gets a lot more choppy and changeable as you reach the peak of a Wave (<Planet-Wave Weather Chart, page 19). Things will gradually start to calm down and either you will settle into a new 'version' of your relationship, or it will already have broken up as it proved unable to take the Saturn/Uranus buffeting. Always bear in mind that this testing is very good for a relationship that has staying power and an openness to change and experimentation because it takes it to a new level that is both more stimulating and more stable.

If you are on your own, Saturn/Uranus can bring you a relationship out of the blue providing you are open to the possibility and are not too fearful of commitment, because it'll try you on that too. Remember that it will have a start-stop-start pattern that determines whether the relationship has got some mileage or is just a flash in the pan (which in itself can have a freeing effect).

Whether in a new relationship or a longstanding one, the key is to be open to what it brings and not to presume you know where it's going. Be prepared to be surprised. At the same time, stick with this process and use time as your instrument for getting from one state to another.

The Choice is Yours Easy Surfing

The chart on the next page shows us Positive Responses to
Saturn/Uranus Waves that create Positive Effects for you
personally and ultimately for everyone. The Negative Responses
need to be avoided in order to prevent the Negative Effects in
your own life. Note the opposing qualities of the Negatives and
Positives, and track back Negative or Positive Effects to the
Responses that created them.

2007–12 and 2020–22
The Personal Effect of Saturn/Uranus Waves
The Choice is Yours

Negative Response	Positive Response
Discomfort and tension as a result of being stuck in the Valley of Decision. Wanting to have your cake and eat it. An unwillingness to make an agreeable compromise.	Honestly confronting any unacceptable situation while being open to the idea that it is very likely the result of conflicting values within yourself. Being willing to bend.
Believing the 'devil you know is better than the devil you don't' when the strain and bad feeling from staying with the former are (close to) unbearable.	Realizing that the opposite to the 'devil you know' is actually the 'god that you don't know'. In other words, making a change will be for the better.
See-sawing between doing what you feel others expect of you, and not listening to anyone and insisting on your own way.	Consciously creating a balance between your conventional traits and behaviour and your more unusual or radical ones.
Going blindly into new ventures out of impatience, restlessness or insecurity.	Researching the pros and cons of your field of interest before making any changes or commitments.

CONSTRUCTIVE CHANGE

Negative Response	Positive Response
Things go pear-shaped. Falling between two stools. Bad choices make for bad situations.	A sound and informed idea of what you are getting into attracts a sound and informed situation.
Erratic behaviour attracts unstable and unpredictable situations and people, with relationships to match. Trouble!	Feeling balanced and stable within yourself, giving rise to a better state of affairs regarding health, money and relationships.
Situations that go from bad to worse, from the merely inconvenient to the downright destructive. Things start to snap, be they minds or bones.	Finding the 'god you did not know' was in fact the unexpected. What you feared did not happen, and you are happily surprised at the results of trusting that 'god'.
Changes occurring that you have no control over or choice in, because you sat on the fence too long. Baby being thrown out with bathwater as you lose out on both or all fronts.	Constructive and beneficial changes made as a result of finding precisely what needed changing – probably beginning with your own attitude.
Negative Response	Positive Response

227

The Saturn/Uranus Balance of Power

The following pages provide two wonderfully basic ways to ride the Saturn/Uranus Major Storms. For a simple way to surf these Planet-Waves, and ride them to where they want to get to – as shown in 'The Spirit of This Time' – and at the same time bypass the Devil of This Time, use the Saturn/Uranus Balance of Power Chart on the next page.

In the upper half of the page, you will see in the left-hand column various symptoms that you could be experiencing if you are leaning too much in the Saturn direction, that is, over-emphasizing caution, convention, the known, defensiveness, territory, etc. The right-hand column then suggests various ways of redressing the balance with Uranian remedies, which mainly encourage ways of taking a step back, chilling out, or seeing things from a higher, more open, perspective.

In the lower half of the page, the left-hand column lists symptoms resulting from overdoing Uranus – over-emphasizing ideas, theories, principles, liberties, etc – and the right-hand column suggests Saturnian remedies that encourage a more pragmatic, realistic and disciplined approach.

As a rule each numbered item is balanced by the equivalent numbered item in the right column, but not always – there are crossovers.

The second basic way to ride the Saturn /UranusMajor Storms is the meditation on page 230.

The Saturn/Uranus Balance of Power

Too Much Saturn and Not Enough Uranus
If this is the case, you could be experiencing some of these symptoms.

1. Feeling stuck, stiff and/or stale.

2. Feeling tense and restless.

3. You have status and finances in a secure position, but you are by no means happy.

4. Blowing your top and hitting out at people and things because you feel limited and held back, but not necessarily by them. This compounds your feeling of being trapped, and you may pay an unacceptable price for your outburst.

Too Much Uranus and Not Enough Saturn
If this is the case, you could be experiencing some of these symptoms.

1. Colliding with people and things.

2. Rebelling against people and things that have more authority than you have, with the consequence that you wind up even less free than you were.

3. Mistaking a theory, plan or idea for the real thing, only to find it doesn't stand up – maybe too late.

4. Causing more disruption and distress than is worth it to those close to you as a result of you 'doing your own thing'.

Uranian Remedies
Adopt one or more of these remedies to offset and relieve the symptoms of 'too much Saturn'.

1. Make some changes, either small or great. Take a (not too) calculated risk.

2. Just do anything different, or something that you've always wanted to do but were afraid to.

3. At a certain point it becomes necessary to adopt an alternative or spiritual view of life that will change your values – then you find what has real value for you.

4. Such outbursts are the release of tension and frustration resulting from 'behaving yourself' for too long. That's okay as long as you now make a point of truly freeing yourself from whatever inhibits or intimidates you.

Saturnian Remedies
Adopt one or more of these remedies to offset and relieve the symptoms of 'too much Uranus'

1. Your sense of timing is out. Slow down before you break down.

2. Take time out to research whatever or whoever it is that you intend to take issue with, get around, or make use of.

3. Write down ideas to see if they still stand up, always finding examples of what you mean. Then present them to practical people who will give you their honest opinion.

4. Learn the difference between freedom and licence. Liberating yourself will eventually liberate others too. Just doing what you want to excess (licence) won't liberate anyone, and will find you more alone than free.

Note: It is very possible to experience both too much Saturn and too much Uranus at the same time.

Saturn/Uranus Wave Meditation

This is the simplest and the best: a Meditation or Prayer for the Spirit of these Times. Sit quietly with it and gaze at the symbols, alone or with others, while inwardly or outwardly uttering the invocation as many times and for as long as you wish. It is especially recommended that you perform this ritual during any Hotspots involving a Saturn/Uranus Wave (see page 294).

My fellow beings and I
Loosen any attachments we have
To what is holding us back.
And so we are liberated into the new
While we retain the traditions

That are tried and true.
In this way we go steadily
Onwards and upwards.

CHAPTER 6

Jupiter Waves
Between 2007 and 2020

As can be seen on the Planet Weather Chart on page 19, Jupiter Waves exist in their own right, and are responsible for Minor Storms and Favourable Breezes. Here we see them as responsible for two types of influence: Jupiter Boosters and Personal Effect.

✵ Jupiter Boosters

Whenever a Jupiter Wave occurs at the same time as a larger Wave – the ones involving Pluto, Neptune, Uranus, and Saturn (the Major Storms and Favourable Winds) then Jupiter kind of *boosts* whatever is happening, blowing things up so we cannot fail to notice a problem or miss an opportunity. As such they can increase or modify the effects of the Major Storms and Favourable Winds when they are going on simultaneously. They also kind of dramatize their overall course, rather like a storyteller would do, unfolding the story of the Planet-Wave in question as it swells and rolls through time and our lives.

So the interpretations of the Jupiter Boosters are found in chapters 2 to 5, under The Unfolding Story, showing how they affect each respective Wave.

Personal Effect

Surfing with Jupiter through the Houses

These effects are based upon the Houses in your chart through which Jupiter is passing or 'transiting' between 2007 and 2020. These interpretations will tell you how to boost your own surfing ability, to keep up your head and spirits as you ride them and other Planet-Waves. It will effectively inform you of what is your 'strongest suit' at any given time, where you have faith, confidence and zest. This is particularly helpful when another Planet-Wave is causing you to wobble!

As ever, there are two ways to use this aid.

1 **Off-The-Peg** This is using the Jupiter positions according to your Birth Sign, Sun Sign or Star Sign. This looks at what Solar House Jupiter is transiting through while the Uranus/Pluto Mother-Wave is active. So using the **Planet House Transit Guide** (beginning on page 254) go to **Jupiter: House Ready-Reckoner** on page 255. Next, look for the time **Period** you are interested in, then look along the row until you get to the column of your **Birth Sign.** There you will see the number of the House being transited by Jupiter – 1st, 2nd, 3rd, etc – and just below it the number of the page where you can read the description of possible situations and actions you can take. This can be very useful and accurate, but remember that it is only based on your Sun Sign.

2 **Made-To-Measure** This is using the Jupiter positions according to your individual birth chart which would have to be calculated correctly from a reliably accurate birth time. So if you do know your birth time

and have your birth chart accurately drawn up, then anyone with a basic knowledge of a chart will be able to tell you which Houses in your personal chart are occupied by Jupiter at any given time between 2007 and 2020. Then simply find and consult the readings for those Houses in the **Planet House Transit Guide** (page 254). For example, if your astrologer or your own astrological calculation told you that Jupiter was transiting your First House, then you would find that interpretation on the page indicated in the Planet House Transit Guide by using the **Index** on the first page of it. Note: you do *not* use the Ready-Reckoner when using Made-To-Measure.

APPENDICES

APPENDIX 1

Astro-Quantum

Below we compare the main features of Astrology with those of Quantum Physics. In doing so it can be seen how much the one mirrors the other. At the very least, the two subjects are analogous, and they support each other's theories and findings. Together, they begin to present a profound and sophisticated explanation of how life actually works at its most fundamental level.

Astrology

Inner Reality
Astrology is about the inner reality of life and those that live it. One astrologer cleverly dubbed it the 'algebra of life' in that the planets, signs and houses, etc, symbolize the essential and archetypal energies, qualities and experiences of Earth life. All these things interacting then manifest in the physical, giving us various types of seemingly separate people and events. Yet really they are all just different manifestations of those same basic energies.

The Source
Symbolically, the astrological planets represent, according to their individual qualities, what is stored in potential, rather like a reservoir of different types of water. These 'waters' are constantly flowing out from this 'reservoir' and, as they do so, they manifest as someone or something in our here-and-now reality, the material world. This is why you can identify a Planet-Wave – a moving body of water – and what it poses or has in store for us, according to its 'colour' or planetary makeup.

Quantum Physics

Inner Reality
Quantum physics is about the inner reality of matter. The stuff of quantum mechanics, such as electrons, neutrons and other sub-atomic particles (anything smaller than an atom) and their own components such as quarks, are the most essential units of matter. How all these things interact and behave gives us various types of seemingly solid objects. But they are not really; they are mostly empty space plus all those basic 'ingredients', those sub-atomic particles.

The Source
'The Sea of Implicate Order' is a term coined by the quantum physicist David Bohm. 'Implicate' meaning enfolded, this 'Sea' was hypothesized as the place in which sub-atomic reality is stored until it unfolds into the Explicate Order, that being what is actually seen as existing in the here and now. Eventually this will fold away again, back into the Sea of Implicate Order, to return to the Explicate Order, ad infinitum.

Astrology

Duality and Uncertainty
Until you actually experience the effect of a Planet-Wave, it is only a set of probabilities. As soon as it hits you (catches you unawares) or you start to surf it (engage with it consciously), it is then something of substance, a personal or global event or experience. But the nature of that event or experience is strongly determined by how well prepared you are.

Instant Interconnection
These so-called planetary 'influences' and their 'manifestations' are really two interrelated things happening at exactly the same time, a great distance from one another, rather than the one causing the other. This is the essence of Astro-Quantum in *Understanding The Future*. Doing or thinking something that is related to a planet's 'influence' has an immediate and corresponding effect in other places, near and far, and thereby affects the whole, either negatively or positively, depending on whether you are aligned with the Spirit or Devil of that Time/Wave. This means that we are all co-creators of our reality.

What You See Is What You Get
Our 'fate' as indicated by the planets depends upon how we interpret, or what we make of, the possibilities they pose, or how we ride those Planet-Waves. And all this depends on the nature of the personality doing the interpreting and making the choices of how to live their lives. This is itself 'written in the Waves', that is, written in your Birth Chart.

Reality Is All Yours In The Making
Astrology has it that 'people happen to events and not the other way around'. (Dane Rudhyar) Astrology can tell you what your potential is but not what you've made of it, or are going to make of it.

Quantum Physics

Duality and Uncertainty
Until you measure the position of a moving object, it is only a Wave Function, that is, a set of probabilities. When you measure it, it becomes something in particular – a Particle, in fact. However, the Wave and the Particle exist together at the same time. This has to do with Heisenberg's Uncertainty Principle, best explained here in a joke: Heisenberg was speeding in his car, and got stopped by a traffic cop. 'Do you know what speed you are going at, sir?' 'No, but I know where I am!'

Instant Interconnection
Two sub-atomic particles that are or have been related in some way are able to transmit changes or information to one another instantaneously – that is, faster than the speed of light – across enormous distances. This is called Non Locality. Looked at another way, this is saying a particle can be everywhere at the same time.

What You See Is What You Get
Light starts out as Waves and then, as soon as we look at it, becomes Dots, that is, perceivable reality. But who is doing the encountering and perceiving, and when they are doing it, has everything to do with what that reality happens to be. This is an important point, often overlooked by the 'quantum-opportunists' of the New Age movement. What you visualize or wish for will never happen if you have a stronger background or unconscious fear that is inhibiting the granting of those wishes. This is called Observer Created Reality, or more accurately Observer Influenced Reality – or better still: Consciousness Created Reality. So Super-Mind-Power {<15 and <67} depends heavily and acutely on your level and quality of consciousness. The old maxim 'Man, know thyself' persists.

Reality Is All Yours In The Making
The experimenter will only get what he or she is looking for. And until you look into the box where you are told a 'cat' is, you won't know whether that cat is dead or alive (Schrodinger's Cat).

The above is not supposed to be an exhaustive, least of all scholarly, comparison of these two gigantic subjects, but will, I hope, provoke thought and justify the use of quantum physics as a metaphor for life in *Understanding The Future*, much in the same way that astrology itself is a metaphor. And yet, quantum physics is not just a metaphor, and neither, I believe, is astrology. There are many mysteries concerning both astrology and quantum physics, and more to the point, there are many astrologers and quantum physicists who have conflicting views within their respective disciplines. So the jury's still out – but someone knows who did it, and how, and why!

Astro-Quantum Memo: Resonating With Fate

Planet-Waves can be seen as 'Bringers of Fate'. Riding these Waves is simply what life is. We can fight their power and direction and get into trouble, or attune to them and go with their direction, use their power, like a surfer riding an ordinary wave. Quantum theory states that absolutely everything is fundamentally waves, as light and sound are waves. Our thoughts are waves. Waves can interact with one another in-phase or out-of-phase, harmoniously or discordantly. Think of two people singing in or out of tune, or turbulence where a river meets the sea. So how your thoughts interact with what is happening, or appears to be about to happen, has everything to do with what occurs now or in the future. Through describing Planet-Waves, this book is showing you what is fundamentally happening or possibly about to happen, rather like reading the wind itself instead of the objects that the wind is blowing about. Your mind is thereby given the opportunity to resonate with those Waves at their own level – having your thought-waves harmonize with the Planet-Waves. This produces a positive outcome or fate.

Understanding The Future
shows us how to co-operate with fate

APPENDIX 2

Planetary Cycles

Planet-Waves are generated by the 'engine' that is the interaction between any two planets. This can be seen as the two 'hands' of the Cosmic Clock, and the two planets in question depend on what 'mode' the Clock is in {<4 The Cosmic Clock}. The actual 'dial' of the Clock is the Zodiac which encircles the Earth. So how those two hands are positioned in relation to one another describes their Cycle, from both hands being together – the same spot in a Sign of the Zodiac – until they meet up again at a different spot. Throughout the Cycle there are particular times which are more significant or critical than others. These times are when a Planet-Wave occurs, and the most significant of these are the Major Storms that occur every time the planets in question, or 'hands', are either on the same spot, at right angles to one another, or opposite one another. The Wave lasts for a certain period around each of these times.

The illustration overleaf shows how these Cycles work, using a Saturn/Pluto Cycle as an example. This Cycle, happening between 1982 and 2020 (from the first peak of the 1980/84 Wave to the first and only peak of the 2018/21 Wave in January 2020), began with both planets positioned together, as is the case for the beginning of any planet-to-planet cycle. In this case, Saturn and Pluto were positioned at the very end of the Sign of Libra (1) in November 1982 (that is, when the 1980/84 Wave first peaked). These planets moved on from there until they reached a point where they were at right angles to one another. How long this takes depends upon the speed at which each planet is travelling. In our example, we see that Pluto moves a lot more slowly than Saturn, as it had only got out of Libra and near the end of the following Sign of Scorpio (Pluto 2) by the time Saturn formed a right-angle with it near the end of Aquarius (Saturn 2) in March 1993 (that is, the first peak of the 1992/95 Wave). The next critical point or Major Storm occurred when Saturn reached the middle of Gemini (Saturn 3), directly opposite Pluto, by now in the middle of Sagittarius (Pluto 3) during August 2001 (the first peak of the 2000/04 Wave). The fourth critical stage will be when Saturn gets to the very beginning of Libra (Saturn 4) and Pluto to the very beginning of Capricorn (Pluto 4), this time at right angles to one another in January 2010 at the first peak of the 2008/11 Wave. Finally, the two planets will come back together again, this time in the last third of Capricorn (5) in January 2020 – the first and only peak of this 2018/20 Wave – which is also when they begin an entirely new cycle, again of around 36 years duration.

The simplest, most well-known, and easily observed example of this kind of cycle is the one which takes place with the Sun and Moon, and lasts just one

EXAMPLE OF A PLANET-TO-PLANET CYCLE

(SATURN/PLUTO 1982–2020)

month. A New Moon is when the Sun and Moon are at the same spot, like (1) in the picture if you make Pluto the Sun and Saturn the Moon; the First Quarter when they are at right angles to one another like (2); the Full Moon occurs when they are opposite one another like (3) with the Earth in the middle; the Second Quarter when they are at right angles again, as (4); and another New Moon when they conjoin again, like (5).

So there are planetary pairs, be they the Sun and Moon, Saturn and Pluto, or any other coupling, constantly cycling, generating Waves and Storms of various significance and intensity. There are also the Favourable Winds and Favourable Breezes which occur between points (2) and (3), and (3) and (4) of a Cycle. There are very mild Winds and Breezes too, that occur between points (1) and (2), and (4) and (5), but these are not included here. All of this is what could be called the World's Cosmic Weather, affecting us all, one way or another, until ultimately our Sun goes supernova, gathers all its planets back into itself, and dies.

The following chart shows the planetary pairs or cycles looked at in this book. These have been selected for study because they cover longer, and therefore more historically significant, periods. However, shorter ones such as the Sun/Moon Cycle are shown in Hotspots on page 294, as you will see.

Planetary Storm/Cycle	Duration of Whole Cycle from (1) to (5) approximately	Occurrence of each Major Storm (midpoint to midpoint)
Uranus/Pluto	110 to 144 years*	Every 27 to 36 years*
Saturn/Pluto	36 years	Every 8 to 10 years
Saturn/Neptune	36 years	Every 8 to 10 years
Saturn/Uranus	46 years	Every 9 to 12 years
Jupiter/Pluto	12 to 13 years	Every 3 to 4 years
Jupiter/Neptune	14 years	Every 3 to 4 years
Jupiter/Uranus	14 years	Every 3 to 4 years
Jupiter/Saturn	20 years	Every 5 years

* This varies so much because both planets are very slow-moving and Pluto has a particularly elliptical orbit.

The Internet

There are also two more long Cycles, those of Neptune/Pluto and Uranus/Neptune, but these are longer than any of the above and do not occur during the years 2007–20 covered in this book. However, it is important to note that the Uranus/Neptune Wave of 1985–2001 – the beginning of a 172-year Cycle – saw the birth and proliferation of the Internet. Uranus = Technology/Computers, while Neptune = Unification, and interestingly we *surf* the Net like we do the sea of Neptune and the electronic or wireless waves of Uranus, and the Planet-Waves as described in *Understanding The Future.*

Internet Problems 2007–20

Unless measures are taken early on during this period, certain Planet-Waves will present increasingly critical technical, practical and moral problems on the Internet. {< 53, 60 Uranus/Pluto Mother-Wave; <210 Saturn/Uranus Waves}

Uranus/Pluto Mother-Wave: Historical Record and Major Storm Overview 1900–2019

Historical Record

328–318 BC	Alexander the Great
74–65 BC	Spartacus's rebellion against Rome. Julius Caesar's rise to power
1196–1206	Genghis Khan
1450–61	Fall of Constantinople. Gutenberg's printing press. Leonardo da Vinci born
1489–1507	Columbus rediscovers America
1533–45	The Protestant Reformation peaks. Copernicus's heliocentric hypothesis
1563–70	Shakespeare and Galileo born. World's first modern atlas. First newspaper
1592–1602	Kepler and Galileo confirm Copernicus's hypothesis. Shakespeare's works
1620–27	Mayflower sets sail for America. First submarine. Francis Bacon
1643–54	Puritan Revolution in England. Rebellion in Europe and Asia. Descartes
1674–83	Bunyan's *Pilgrim's Progress*. First leavened bread.
1705–16	Birth of Industrial Revolution with age of steam, coal and iron
1749–65	Goethe, Mozart and William Blake born. Rousseau's statement 'Man was born free and everywhere is in chains'.

1787–98	The French Revolution. Napoleon. Births of automation and mass production, and of modern chemistry (Lavoisier). John Keats born
1816–24	Revolution and insurrection in Latin America and Europe. Byron's and Shelley's poetic masterworks. Karl Marx born
1845–56	Revolution in most European capitals. Rebellion in China, Japan, India and Ottoman Empire. Communist Manifesto published. Anti-slavery and women's rights movements. Proliferation of railroads, sea links, telegraph and highways. Darwin
1873–80	Alexander Graham Bell makes first telephone call. Edison's inventions (gramophone, etc). Carl Jung born
1896–1907	Birth of Socialist and Communist Parties, of Women's Militant Movements, of Black Civil Rights Movements. Worldwide socio-political upheavals. First powered flight by Wright brothers. Freud and Einstein. Quantum physics
1928–37	Atom split: birth of nuclear age. Hitler and Mao. Spanish Civil War
1960–72	The sixties. First man in space; Moon landing. Radical scientific theories.

Major Storm Overview 1900–2019
(start/end times rounded to nearest quarter)

1900s

Planet-Wave	1900	1901	1902	1903	1904	1905	1906	1907	1908	1909
Uranus/Pluto	~	~	~	~	~	~	~	~		
Saturn/Pluto								~	~	~
Saturn/Neptune	~	~							~	~
Saturn/Uranus									~	~

1910s

Planet-Wave	1910	1911	1912	1913	1914	1915	1916	1917	1918	1919
Uranus/Pluto										
Saturn/Pluto					~	~	~	~		
Saturn/Neptune	~	~					~	~	~	~
Saturn/Uranus	~	~							~	~

1920s

Planet-Wave	1920	1921	1922	1923	1924	1925	1926	1927	1928	1929
Uranus/Pluto									~	~
Saturn/Pluto		~	~	~	~					
Saturn/Neptune						~	~	~		
Saturn/Uranus	~	~							~	~

1930s

Planet-Wave	1930	1931	1932	1933	1934	1935	1936	1937	1938	1939
Uranus/Pluto	~	~	~	~	~	~	~	~		
Saturn/Pluto	~	~	~	~	~					~
Saturn/Neptune						~	~	~		
Saturn/Uranus	~	~	~	~	~					

1940s

Planet-Wave	1940	1941	1942	1943	1944	1945	1946	1947	1948	1949
Uranus/Pluto										
Saturn/Pluto	~	~					~	~	~	~
Saturn/Neptune				~	~	~				
Saturn/Uranus		~	~	~	~					

1950s

Planet-Wave	1950	1951	1952	1953	1954	1955	1956	1957	1958	1959
Uranus/Pluto										
Saturn/Pluto					~	~	~	~	~	
Saturn/Neptune		~	~	~	~					
Saturn/Uranus	~	~	~	~	~	~				

1960s

Planet-Wave	1960	1961	1962	1963	1964	1965	1966	1967	1968	1969
Uranus/Pluto	~	~	~	~	~	~	~	~	~	~
Saturn/Pluto						~	~	~	~	
Saturn/Neptune		~	~	~						
Saturn/Uranus				~	~	~	~	~	~	

1970s

Planet-Wave	1970	1971	1972	1973	1974	1975	1976	1977	1978	1979
Uranus/Pluto	~	~	~							
Saturn/Pluto				~	~	~				
Saturn/Neptune	~	~	~	~					~	~
Saturn/Uranus					~	~	~	~	~	

1980s

Planet-Wave	1980	1981	1982	1983	1984	1985	1986	1987	1988	1989
Uranus/Pluto										
Saturn/Pluto	~	~	~	~	~					
Saturn/Neptune	~							~	~	~
Saturn/Uranus						~	~	~	~	~

1990s

Planet-Wave	1990	1991	1992	1993	1994	1995	1996	1997	1998	1999
Uranus/Pluto										
Saturn/Pluto			~	~	~	~				
Saturn/Neptune	~							~	~	~
Saturn/Uranus	~								~	~

2000s

Planet-Wave	2000	2001	2002	2003	2004	2005	2006	2007	2008	2009
Uranus/Pluto								~	~	~
Saturn/Pluto		~	~	~	~					~
Saturn/Neptune	~					~	~	~	~	~
Saturn/Uranus	~	~							~	~

2010s

Planet-Wave	2010	2011	2012	2013	2014	2015	2016	2017	2018	2019
Uranus/Pluto	~	~	~	~	~	~	~	~	~	~
Saturn/Pluto	~	~							~	~
Saturn/Neptune					~	~	~	~		
Saturn/Uranus	~	~	~							

The Beginning of the Aquarian Age and the End of the Mayan Calendar

The Beginning of the Aquarian Age

Astrological Ages are determined by the Earth very slowly wobbling in the opposite direction to which it rotates on its own axis. In effect then the axis of the Earth at the North Pole will track backwards through the Zodiac – and it takes 25,920 years to go through all twelve Signs, what is called the Astrological Great Year.

So it takes on average 2,160 years to pass through one Sign – and that is an Astrological Age, marking a major epoch in human history and development that is characterized by the nature of the Sign being passed through. There is some debate as to when it all began exactly, but the most popular or symbolic idea is that the Age we are now near the end of, the Piscean Age, begun at the time of Jesus Christ. There are some satisfying and literal connotations here; Jesus means 'fish' in Classical Greek (*icthys*) and Jesus was known as the Fisher of Men. He came from his mother, Mary, whose name means 'sea'. And there has to be some significance with regard to the story of 'The Feeding of the Five Thousand' with two fishes and five loaves. The five loaves could well refer to the opposite Sign to Pisces, Virgo, the Sign of the Harvest, for the opposite Sign carries some considerable significance in all this, as we shall see.

And so, with all this in mind, we can say that the Piscean Age ends *around* AD 2160, when the next, or previous Sign (it's wobbling backwards, remember) begins – that of Aquarius. But as an Age is such a long time, its 'cusp' lasts about three hundred years either side of 2160. So as Pisces began to wind down in around 1860, Aquarius appeared on the horizon; and as Aquarius burgeons after 2160, Pisces fades away completely by 2460. Evidence of the presence of this Sign has been around for some time, even before 1860. The Astrological Ages don't go off and on like light switches, but more like sunlight appearing some time before the Sun itself actually rises on the eastern horizon, or disappearing some time after it has set in the west.

Aquarius is the Sign of 'equality, liberty and fraternity' – the call of the French Revolution back at the end of the 1700s, a time when the second of the two planets said to 'rule' Aquarius – Uranus, the Great Awakener and Liberator – was discovered. This was also a time of great upheaval and rebellion worldwide, not least of all America's War of Independence. Personally, I think that the Aquarian Age was 'rising' then, and has been looming larger ever since. Furthermore, Aquarius and its rulers Saturn and Uranus are symbolic of science and technology which had their advent in the 18th century – its key phrase being 'I know', as distinct from the preceding Piscean Age qualities of spiritual belief and emotionality, with the key phrase 'I believe'.

In effect, then, the shift is from an era of blind faith to a more conscious and scientific sense of what reality is. For many now, there has to be a more scientific explanation of God or a Creator. {<41 The Death and Rebirth of God} It also sees the progression away from an overly emotional and fervid knee-jerk reaction, to a realization that our reality is determined by how we think with, all being well, an increasing sense of our powers of mind over matter, and a moral compass that will use such powers in a healthy and collectively beneficial way.

Whereas the birth of the Piscean Age saw Christian martyrs nailed to crosses for their beliefs, the Aquarian Age uncompromisingly sees off anyone or anything opposing its bid for that 'equality, liberty and fraternity'. More recently than the French Revolution – a time which one could definitely regard as a 'preview' of the Aquarian Age – there was Karl Marx's founding of Communism in the mid-19th century along with, before and since, the ongoing destruction of class barriers, liberation of slaves and the implementation of racial and gender equality. This birthing of the Aquarian Age has also seen off much of what is the province of the opposite Sign of Aquarius: Leo. The Lion is all about royalty and privilege –

and starting with the execution/murder of the Russian royal family, monarchy has been in steady decline ever since that July day in 1918.

The 'teething problems' of the Aquarian Age, as with the early days of anything so big, are quite notable. It has ushered in a rather godless society in many parts of the world where everyone simply does whatever they want as long as they can get away with it – what could be called a *false* freedom or just *taking liberties*. Wrapped up in all of this there is that Aquarian 'madness', political correctness, a contradiction in terms where one is not free to think and feel as one wishes to think and feel. Liberal thinking is also a precarious Aquarian animal for it can, in its bid to make us more civilized, encourage very uncivilized behaviour as it is too liberal in its understanding of what 'human rights' mean.

But Aquarius is essentially the Sign of Paradox, for in the process of living up to ideals one is bound to be hypocritical at some level. One cannot arrive at 'equality, liberty and fraternity' overnight, and to an equal degree such ideals have to be enforced by rule of law. This authoritarian side of Aquarius, which seems to be at odds with its liberal aspect, is down to its first and original ruler, Saturn. The interaction of these opposing energies is very notable during Saturn/Uranus Major Storms {<190}.

Essentially, Aquarius is the Water Bearer, which means that it is here to refresh and cleanse humanity with its waters of Truth, and it has – or rather we have – the next 2000 years or so to make that a reality rather than just an idea. It is all in the name of becoming more civilized, of creating a true civilization.

Not surprisingly, Aquarius is also the Sign of the Future, for it is about evolution itself, born of scientific progress, Utopian vision, and plain humanitarianism. As such it is probably making itself felt ahead of time, as indicated by the French Revolution, Marx , etc. On the other hand, the fundamentalism of Piscean beliefs – witness suicide bombers, 'born-again' Christians and other religious cults who 'love-bomb' their prospective recruits – is evidently not going to exit with a mere whimper. As the Piscean Age wanes and the Aquarian Age dawns, *Understanding The Future* is very much an attempt to help ease this difficult passage from one Age to another. In addition to the book's main metaphor of 'waves' being in keeping with the actual glyph of Aquarius, its key planetary focus of the Uranus/Pluto Mother-Wave 2007–20 is very apt because it represents the empowering (Pluto) of what is most forward-looking, mentally evolving, scientifically innovating and freedom-loving about Aquarius, represented by its most recent planetary ruler, Uranus. It shouts 'Sleepers Awake!' – even if it takes the Earth shaking us up with earthquakes and volcanoes, or the shifting of its poles, to make us do so. It is also, as we shall now see, a period that coincides with something else that makes these such 'interesting' times.

The End of the Mayan Calendar

The Mayans of Mesoamerica were great sky-watchers, and their knowledge of celestial cycles, planetary positions and sunspots is impressively accurate considering their lack of astronomical instruments. Consequently, when their Long Count calendar of 5125 years ends on December 21 2012 with the prediction that the world will end then too, a great number of people feel they have to sit up and take notice. Added to this is the fact that several other ancient cultures, like the Egyptians and the Cherokees, also predict this time as being a significant end/beginning, or at least major shift in our reality.

On top of all this is the astronomical fact that this time, or thereabouts, coincides with our Sun aligning with the centre of our galaxy, the Milky Way, something which occurs every 25,920 years, the same length of time as the Astrological Great Year discussed above. The Mayans, and other ancients, knew this, and whether they chose to end their Long Count Calendar then for that reason, or they just happen to coincide, is open to debate. Even the year 2012 itself is not entirely agreed upon, with 2011 and 2020 being just two other alternatives, all of which fall within the time focus of this book.

In fact, with respect to all things Mayan, nearly everything is open to debate, and you only have to enter '2012' into a search engine to find this out to a very confusing degree. So what does it all mean?

From my own research and my position as an astrologer of more than 30 years, I have come to the following conclusions about December 21, the Winter Solstice, 2012.

The Day Itself is Only a Focal Point

I don't think we are going to wake up on December 22 and find everything is gone or magically transformed. Supporting this idea, the Mayan Elders have mooted that 2012 is really just the centre of a 'zone' that is anything up to a **hundred years** long (1962–2062). Astrologically, as *Understanding The Future* has endeavoured to demonstrate, the period of 2007–20 that actually sits around December 21 2012 is also powerfully significant with respect to human and earthly evolution. And just as the cusp of the Astrological Ages lasts around **three hundred years** (1860–2160), it too sits with this period at its centre (see diagram below). Consequently, I think that 2007–20 is possibly the hottest spot in a hot area, so during this period of **fourteen years** we are most likely to get or make the worst and/or the best of what's going down.

```
                 2007>>>UTF>>>2020

            1962>>>>>>2012>>>>>>2062

1860>>>>>>>>>>>>>>>>>>>>>>>>>CUSP OF AGES>>>>>>>>>>>>>>>>>>>>>>>>>>>>>2160
```

The Great Hope of Being Liberated From it All

I am not too convinced that something amazingly cosmic is going to occur at the Winter Solstice 2012, but, as Ringo Starr once said, 'tomorrow never knows'. It is only human to long for something that is going to sweep away all the horror, strife, insecurity and confusion that has dogged us through the ages – particularly right now when we appear to have backed ourselves into a very tight corner. And so 12/12 and all the talk of something great and wonderful happening is very attractive. Here are a few quotes to demonstrate this 'hope' or prediction that run from the New Age fantastic to the classical to the seemingly scientific:

> *The human race will unify as a single circuit. Solar and galactic sound transmissions will inundate the planetary field. A current charging both poles will race across the skies, connecting the polar auroras in a single brilliant flash.*

> Jose Arguelles

... evolutionary quantum leap. Human/ET interface and the arrival of a new species or kingdom on Earth.

Jon King

... translation or dematerialization to another sphere of the Universe.

Teilhard de Chardin

As the Schumann resonance increases to 13Hz, Gaia goes from Alpha to Beta frequency and wakes up. Increasing tryptamine and beta-carboline neuro-chemistry allows us a telepathic communion, as we become used to our light bodies in preparation for the magnetic pole reversal when there will be a mass out-of-body-experience.

Geoff Stray

If any of this is going to happen, I still feel the need to qualify it somewhat.

The Vale of Soul-Making

The above list of possible 12/12 scenarios all point to some kind of dramatic event/transformation. What I would add to this list – by way of summing up what I think this book is saying – is, you are now living on planet Earth at a time when your very reason for being is sharply highlighted, challenged and tested – and hopefully proved. To quote Samuel Johnson again, 'Nothing concentrates the mind so wonderfully as the prospect of being hanged in the morning.' Whether this time means everything or nothing, the prospect of it certainly causes each individual to find some way of squaring up to it or squaring it away, depending on your individual persuasion or world view. In either case, consciously or unconsciously, we have arrived at a time of reckoning.

So rather than saying we are *all* going to be whisked off to a different dimension – whatever that might mean – let's say that some kind of *acid test* of humanity, individually and collectively, is going on. It might take a number of years or appear to happen overnight, but an intensification of what it means to be alive is what is happening. And this means that its effect upon us depends upon the individual. Literally or metaphorically, we are being subjected to some kind of 'scan' that reads our 'vibration', our state of spiritual evolution, our energetic make-up. What that scan is could be anything from just the demands of living in these times of Planet-Waves that challenge you to keep your balance and 'stay on your surfboard', or it could be the arrival or intensification of some unknown energy within the Earth's biosphere; something akin to whatever it is that so mysteriously creates crop circles. The point is that we are born here and will most likely die here, and how we live this mortal Earthly life in between is of the utmost importance. For me personally, if there is any one line that sums up what life is about it is that of the poet John Keats: 'Call the world if you please, "The vale of soul-making".' Earth is a proving ground and so for everyone to be 'beamed up' when the going gets too tough would, it seems to me, be denying the point of it all. So at the risk of putting it too simply, I see three basic readings and outcomes that the 'scan' makes and dictates, but there are bound to be shades in between.

1. It finds your soul to have evolved to a relatively high level of evolution and so you move on to a higher level, but this level may as well be still here on Earth. It is just that it will feel and even look very different.
2. It finds your soul has too much conflict and negativity within it. Consequently, it cannot take the increased intensification and so it seriously dysfunctions, meaning that illness or madness, or both, ensues. From here though it can inevitably only go up or down, to (1) or (3).
3. It finds your soul has so much conflict and negativity that nothing can be done to remedy your mental and physical state this time around, so that death is the only outcome, with whatever might follow upon that.

If none of this is so, and the Aquarian Age and 2012 are just another illusion or a mental construct, then I still think we are in for a literally very trying time, with Earth conditions such as global warming and other climate and geophysical conditions being the obvious, yet also symbolic, signs of this. What you personally make of this 'trying time' is entirely up to you. As for myself, I'm getting my soul in shape and intend to surf those Planet-Waves into the future!

The Planet House Transit Guide

You will have been referred to this section by the Personal Effect/Surfing with the Planets Through the Houses part of a Planet-Wave chapter. Alternatively, you already know what you are looking for! If it's neither then go back to the relevant page and see what this is about.

Index

If you are using 'Off-The-Peg': Go to the House Ready Reckoner for the Planet in question. For example, if you want the Ready-Reckoner for Saturn, the Index will send you to page 262.

If you are using 'Made-To-Measure': Go to the Transiting the Houses section for the Planet in question. For example, if you are looking for Jupiter transiting the Eighth House, the Index will send you to page 259.

Jupiter

House Ready-Reckoner (for 'Off-The-Peg' calculation only) – page 256.

Transiting the Houses (for 'Made-To-Measure' calculation only):

1st	2nd	3rd	4th	5th	6th	7th	8th	9th	10th	11th	12th
p257	p257	p257	p258	p258	p258	p259	p259	p260	p260	p260	p261

Saturn

House Ready-Reckoner (for 'Off-The-Peg' calculation only) – page 262.

Transiting the Houses (for 'Made-To-Measure' calculation only):

1st	2nd	3rd	4th	5th	6th	7th	8th	9th	10th	11th	12th
p263	p263	p264	p264	p265	p265	p266	p266	p267	p267	p268	p268

Uranus

House Ready-Reckoner (for 'Off-The-Peg' calculation only) – page 270.

Transiting the Houses (for 'Made-To-Measure' calculation only):

1st	2nd	3rd	4th	5th	6th	7th	8th	9th	10th	11th	12th
p270	p270	p271	p271	p272	p272	p273	p273	p274	p275	p275	p276

Neptune

House Ready-Reckoner (for 'Off-The-Peg' calculation only) – page 277.

Transiting the Houses (for 'Made-To-Measure' calculation only):

1st	2nd	3rd	4th	5th	6th	7th	8th	9th	10th	11th	12th
p277	p278	p278	p279	p280	p280	p281	p281	p282	p283	p284	p284

Pluto

House Ready-Reckoner (for 'Off-The-Peg' calculation only) – page 286.

Transiting the Houses (for 'Made-To-Measure' calculation only):

1st	2nd	3rd	4th	5th	6th	7th	8th	9th	10th	11th	12th
p286	p287	p287	p288	p288	p289	p290	p290	p291	p292	p292	p293

Jupiter: House Ready-Reckoner (for 'Off-The-Peg' calculation only)

Your Birth Sign ↓ House Transited ↓ Page Number

Period (Sign being transited)	♈ Aries	♉ Taurus	♊ Gemini	♋ Cancer	♌ Leo	♍ Virgo	♎ Libra	♏ Scorpio	♐ Sagittarius	♑ Capricorn	♒ Aquarius	♓ Pisces
Jan 1 2007 to Dec 18 2007 (Sagittarius)	9th	8th	7th	6th	5th	4th	3rd	2nd	1st	12th	11th	10th
	p260	p259	p259	p258	p258	p258	p257	p257	p257	p261	p260	p260
Dec 18 2007 Jan 5 2009 (Capricorn)	10th	9th	8th	7th	6th	5th	4th	3rd	2nd	1st	12th	11th
	p260	p260	p259	p259	p258	p258	p258	p257	p257	p257	p261	p260
Jan 5 2009 to Jan 18 2010 (Aquarius)	11th	10th	9th	8th	7th	6th	5th	4th	3rd	2nd	1st	12th
	p260	p260	p260	p259	p259	p258	p258	p258	p257	p257	p257	p261
Jan 18 2010 to Jun 6 2010 (Pisces)	12th	11th	10th	9th	8th	7th	6th	5th	4th	3rd	2nd	1st
	p261	p260	p260	p260	p259	p259	p258	p258	p258	p257	p257	p257
Jun 6 2010 to Sep 9 2010 (Aries)	1st	12th	11th	10th	9th	8th	7th	6th	5th	4th	3rd	2nd
	p257	p261	p260	p260	p260	p259	p259	p258	p258	p258	p257	p257
Sep 9 2010 to Jan 22 2011 (Pisces)	12th	11th	10th	9th	8th	7th	6th	5th	4th	3rd	2nd	1st
	p261	p260	p260	p260	p259	p259	p258	p258	p258	p257	p257	p257
Jan 22 2011 to Jun 4 2011 (Aries)	1st	12th	11th	10th	9th	8th	7th	6th	5th	4th	3rd	2nd
	p257	p261	p260	p260	p260	p259	p259	p258	p258	p258	p257	p257
Jun 4 2011 to Jun 11 2012 (Taurus)	2nd	1st	12th	11th	10th	9th	8th	7th	6th	5th	4th	3rd
	p257	p257	p261	p260	p260	p260	p259	p259	p258	p258	p258	p257
Jun 11 2012 to Jun 26 2013 (Gemini)	3rd	2nd	1st	12th	11th	10th	9th	8th	7th	6th	5th	4th
	p257	p257	p257	p261	p260	p260	p260	p259	p259	p258	p258	p258
Jun 26 2013 to Jul 16 2014 (Cancer)	4th	3rd	2nd	1st	12th	11th	10th	9th	8th	7th	6th	5th
	p258	p257	p257	p257	p261	p260	p260	p260	p259	p259	p258	p258
Jul 16 2014 to Aug 11 2015 (Leo)	5th	4th	3rd	2nd	1st	12th	11th	10th	9th	8th	7th	6th
	p258	p258	p257	p257	p257	p261	p260	p260	p260	p259	p259	p258
Aug 11 2015 to Sep 9 2016 (Virgo)	6th	5th	4th	3rd	2nd	1st	12th	11th	10th	9th	8th	7th
	p258	p258	p258	p257	p257	p257	p261	p260	p260	p260	p259	p259
Sep 9 2016 to Oct 10 2017 (Libra)	7th	6th	5th	4th	3rd	2nd	1st	12th	11th	10th	9th	8th
	p259	p258	p258	p258	p257	p257	p257	p261	p260	p260	p260	p259
Oct 10 2017 to Nov 8 2018 (Scorpio)	8th	7th	6th	5th	4th	3rd	2nd	1st	12th	11th	10th	9th
	p259	p259	p258	p258	p258	p257	p257	p257	p261	p260	p260	p260
Nov 8 2018 to Dec 2 2019 (Sagittarius)	9th	8th	7th	6th	5th	4th	3rd	2nd	1st	12th	11th	10th
	p260	p259	p259	p258	p258	p258	p257	p257	p257	p261	p260	p260
Dec 2 2019 to Dec 19 2020 (Capricorn)	10th	9th	8th	7th	6th	5th	4th	3rd	2nd	1st	12th	11th
	p260	p260	p259	p259	p258	p258	p258	p257	p257	p257	p261	p260
Dec 19 2020 to May 13 2021 (Aquarius)	11th	10th	9th	8th	7th	6th	5th	4th	3rd	2nd	1st	12th
	p260	p260	p260	p259	p259	p258	p258	p258	p257	p257	p257	p261

| ♈ Aries | ♉ Taurus | ♊ Gemini | ♋ Cancer | ♌ Leo | ♍ Virgo | ♎ Libra | ♏ Scorpio | ♐ Sagittarius | ♑ Capricorn | ♒ Aquarius | ♓ Pisces |

Jupiter Transiting the Houses
Jupiter Transiting your First House

Opportunities and occasions arise that offer or provide furtherance, enjoyment and improvement in matters concerning your image, appearance and what constitutes your sense of presence. Your very identity is more a matter of significance than usual, and generally your interest is drawn to understanding the bigger picture and your place in it. All this can make you feel either self-conscious or, on the other hand, a bit larger than life or even arrogant and holier-than-thou. If your sense of greatness and expansiveness can be tempered with understanding and grace, then this time could make you and the world in which you live far more meaningful and positive.

Jupiter Transiting your Second House

Opportunities and occasions arise that offer or provide furtherance, enjoyment and improvement in matters concerning your finances, possessions, earning power and sense of what has value for you. So applying energy to this end will more likely meet with success than at other times. However, there is also the inclination to overspend or get carried away with the material side of things to the point that either you are setting yourself up for debt later out of a false sense of wealth, or you eventually find that material things do not satisfy in the way that you believed. Taking on board a philosophical or professionally informed point of view with respect to 'what is worth what' is advisable – and may be necessary. Ultimately, this transit is asking you to evaluate your means of evaluation itself.

Jupiter Transiting your Third House

Opportunities and occasions arise that offer or provide furtherance, enjoyment and improvement in matters concerning your everyday affairs and encounters, and your relatives (especially siblings). This could bring a more philosophical or religious element into your day-to-day life and outlook, and those of others too. If you are prone to getting stuck in a rut in terms of your thinking and routine, this influence will help you to 'think globally and act locally', or to introduce the cosmic into the commonplace. You will find that hot debates and clashes of opinion are therefore the stuff of this transit, as they force you to verbalize your beliefs – and then to walk your talk.

Jupiter Transiting your Fourth House

Opportunities and occasions arise that offer or provide furtherance, enjoyment and improvement in matters concerning your home and family, and your sense of security and belonging. House purchasing, moving or redecorating are well-starred now. On an emotional level, seeing the bigger picture and entertaining feelings of largesse will allow you to create or appreciate love and understanding in your most private life, particularly where your parents are concerned. Exploring and discovering your deeper roots and origins is both possible and favourable now. It is also a time of growth in your innermost sense of what and who you are, or at least, experiences tend to emphasize or even exaggerate the need for such. This is a time to find out 'where you live', both literally and psychologically – to feather your nest and put down roots.

Jupiter Transiting your Fifth House

Opportunities and occasions arise that offer or provide furtherance, enjoyment and improvement in matters concerning your manner of creative self-expression – and this includes everything from pastimes to romance, children to drama, and partying to making anything that is a demonstration of your unique personality. You find through letting out what's on the inside that the world, be it personal or professional, responds to you in a way that is fruitful and productive of under-standing and appreciation. There is a slight danger of being a bit over-the-top if you are naturally extrovert, but this is not supposed to be a time for false modesty! Let it all hang out and be the wiser and happier for it.

Jupiter Transiting your Sixth House

Opportunities and occasions arise that offer or provide furtherance, enjoyment and improvement in matters concerning work, co-workers, health and service to others. This is a time when you can appreciate how valuable promotion and development of such pursuits can be. This is also a time for healing, of yourself or others. However, any health problem that has been lying under the surface can make itself felt now. Additionally, bear in mind that growing in a creative and productive way is essential to health, but resisting growth for any reason, such as fear of criticism or being too fussy, can actually give rise to negative growth, like excess weight. Duties and responsibilities may seem to inhibit your freedom now, but actually this is a call to clear out and clean up in any areas of your life and personality that need it. Then the way will be clearer for a more fruitful inter-action with the world and others.

Jupiter Transiting your Seventh House

Opportunities and occasions arise that offer or provide furtherance, enjoyment and improvement in matters concerning relationships, your partner if you have one, and even your manner of relating to others. This could mean a new and adventurous encounter, or introduce something new to an existing partnership. Basically there is a green light for making more of relationships. But if there is anything getting in the way of this, then Jupiter could introduce a 'wild card' that is there to make it apparent that relationships should never be allowed to become complacent or get into a rut. You should increase your understanding and exploration of each other if you are in a relationship, or the exploration of what's 'out there' if you are not. In the first case, though, failing to grasp this can in some cases lead to a 'playing away' situation. In the end, this is a time to get wise to the fact that any relationship is an expression and reflection of your alter ego. Bear this in mind and any and all relationships will become far more fulfilling and intriguing.

Jupiter Transiting your Eighth House

Opportunities and occasions arise that offer or provide furtherance, enjoyment and improvement in matters concerning other's resources and intimate involve-ments, be they emotional or financial. Windfalls or inheritances are a possibility now – but don't bank on this! At a deeper level this transit is saying that change and transformation is the way forwards and upwards, but possibly by first going inwards or even downwards. So this can mean that some form of crisis or intense experience is what precedes a breakthrough. Consequently, resist trying to avoid such when really it is inevitable, for this could create a block to emotional or financial flow. Joint ownership and intimacy are growth areas now, and that growth depends upon knowing where and when to keep a secret on the one hand, and where and when to be totally honest on the other.

Jupiter Transiting your Ninth House

Opportunities and occasions arise that offer or provide furtherance, enjoyment and improvement in matters concerning travelling and seeking, higher education, covering new ground, finding laws and meanings, or generally broadcasting yourself to a wider audience. This is a time when experience is highly important as it is this that prevents knowledge gained from being merely academic, one-sided or self-righteously opinionated. The world can be seen to be your oyster during this period, allowing you to grow and prosper from whatever opportunity or challenge presents itself to you. It may well just be a crusading time, with all the advances, setbacks, friends and enemies that such can attract.

Jupiter Transiting your Tenth House

Opportunities and occasions arise that offer or provide furtherance, enjoyment and improvement in matters concerning your career, status and reputation. Recognition and promotion are more likely during this period than most others, especially if you seize the opportunities and cultivate the connections that are going to come your way now. Travel and people of different cultures may well figure in your professional life. Generally a time of flourishing in the outer, material world, but paradoxically there may, if you are spiritually inclined, be an urge to rise above it all and see your role in life from a more philosophical or philanthropic perspective.

Jupiter Transiting your Eleventh House

Opportunities and occasions arise that offer or provide furtherance, enjoyment and improvement in matters concerning your friendships, group activities and any communal/political interests. The power and opportunities that are provided by a number of individuals rather than just you on your own is what makes things happen now. 'No man is an island' could be your motto for this time. It is the ideals and aspirations of yourself and those who share your social values that occupy your mind more than usual, and which provide a meaning and buoyancy to your life.

Jupiter Transiting your Twelfth House

Opportunities and occasions arise that offer or provide furtherance, enjoyment and improvement in matters concerning 'behind-the-scenes' activities and what is more subtle and less obvious about life and yourself. Somehow or other, through meeting someone or through some form of spiritual search, you encounter a sense that there is more to life than is apparent from an outside or conventional point of view. How you and others are now, in the present, has everything to do with the past, going back as far as the womb – or even before that, for previous lives can become a significant issue now, one way or the other.

Saturn: House Ready-Reckoner (for 'Off-The-Peg' calculation only)

Your Birth Sign ↓ House Transited ↓ Page Number

Period (Sign being transited)	♈ Aries	♉ Taurus	♊ Gemini	♋ Cancer	♌ Leo	♍ Virgo	♎ Libra	♏ Scorpio	♐ Sagittarius	♑ Capricorn	♒ Aquarius	♓ Pisces
Jan 1 2007 to Sep 2 07 (Leo)	5th	4th	3rd	2nd	1st	12th	11th	10th	9th	8th	7th	6th
	p265	p264	p264	p263	p263	p268	p268	p267	p267	p266	p266	p265
Sep 2 2007 to Oct 29 2009 (Virgo)	6th	5th	4th	3rd	2nd	1st	12th	11th	10th	9th	8th	7th
	p265	p265	p264	p264	p263	p263	p268	p268	p267	p267	p266	p266
Oct 29 2009 to Apr 7 2010 (Libra)	7th	6th	5th	4th	3rd	2nd	1st	12th	11th	10th	9th	8th
	p266	p265	p265	p264	p264	p263	p263	p268	p268	p267	p267	p266
Apr 7 2010 to Jul 21 2010 (Virgo)	6th	5th	4th	3rd	2nd	1st	12th	11th	10th	9th	8th	7th
	p265	p265	p264	p264	p263	p263	p268	p268	p267	p267	p266	p266
Jul 21 2010 to Oct 5 2012 (Libra)	7th	6th	5th	4th	3rd	2nd	1st	12th	11th	10th	9th	8th
	p266	p265	p265	p264	p264	p263	p263	p268	p268	p267	p267	p266
Oct 5 2012 to Dec 23 2014 (Scorpio)	8th	7th	6th	5th	4th	3rd	2nd	1st	12th	11th	10th	9th
	p266	p266	p265	p265	p264	p264	p263	p263	p268	p268	p267	p267
Dec 23 2014 to Jun 15 2015 (Sagittarius)	9th	8th	7th	6th	5th	4th	3rd	2nd	1st	12th	11th	10th
	p267	p266	p266	p265	p265	p264	p264	p263	p263	p268	p268	p267
Jun 15 2015 to Sep 18 2015 (Scorpio)	8th	7th	6th	5th	4th	3rd	2nd	1st	12th	11th	10th	9th
	p266	p266	p265	p265	p264	p264	p263	p263	p268	p268	p267	p267
Sep 18 2015 to Dec 20 2017 (Sagittarius)	9th	8th	7th	6th	5th	4th	3rd	2nd	1st	12th	11th	10th
	p267	p266	p266	p265	p265	p264	p264	p263	p263	p268	p268	p267
Dec 20 2017 to Mar 22 2020 (Capricorn)	10th	9th	8th	7th	6th	5th	4th	3rd	2nd	1st	12th	11th
	p267	p267	p266	p266	p265	p265	p264	p264	p263	p263	p268	p268
Mar 22 2020 to Jul 1 2020 (Aquarius)	11th	10th	9th	8th	7th	6th	5th	4th	3rd	2nd	1st	12th
	p268	p267	p267	p266	p266	p265	p265	p264	p264	p263	p263	p268
Jul 1 2020 to Dec 17 2020 (Capricorn)	10th	9th	8th	7th	6th	5th	4th	3rd	2nd	1st	12th	11th
	p267	p267	p266	p266	p265	p265	p264	p264	p263	p263	p268	p268
Dec 17 2020 to Mar 7 2023 (Aquarius)	11th	10th	9th	8th	7th	6th	5th	4th	3rd	2nd	1st	12th
	p268	p267	p267	p266	p266	p265	p265	p264	p264	p263	p263	p268

♈ Aries ♉ Taurus ♊ Gemini ♋ Cancer ♌ Leo ♍ Virgo ♎ Libra ♏ Scorpio ♐ Sagittarius ♑ Capricorn ♒ Aquarius ♓ Pisces

Saturn Transiting the Houses
Saturn Transiting your First House

Circumstances demand or help you to establish, make stable or put into order issues concerning your image, appearance and what constitutes your sense of presence in the world around you. So your actual identity can become a serious matter or question, and the bearing of your responsibilities is of unavoidable and immediate concern. Whereas at other times you could put certain matters on the backburner, you now have to deal with them immediately. The upside to all this is that you get a lot more done than usual, with achievement and success as the eventual results. However, while it appears to be the external world that is making more demands on you than usual, it is actually the question of who you are as an individual that is the real issue. The more you know about how you work as a person, the better and more effective you will work in the outer material world. In turn, this means that you have to manage your time well, assume or respect authority where needed, set boundaries and recognize limitations, and generally act in an increasingly mature and appropriate manner. Any negative events, be they material, physical or psychological, stem from your not measuring up to what circumstances are demanding of you, for those very circumstances are both the substance of and the solution to your problems.

Saturn Transiting your Second House

Circumstances demand or help you to establish, make stable or put into order issues concerning your finances, possessions, earning power, self-worth, and sense of what has value for you. If you experience financial difficulties during this time, then it is because you are either undervaluing yourself or overemphasizing the importance of money compared to matters of more fundamental worth. A more basic reason, however, could be that you have let your financial affairs get out of control. This is a period when economy is the byword, but unnecessary parsimony would only make a possibly lean time bleak as well. As ever with Saturn, you are being squeezed so you might feel what shape you are in – this time with respect to what you feel you and life are worth. Consolidate and affirm your assets, in every respect.

Saturn Transiting your Third House

Circumstances demand or help you to establish, make stable or put into order issues concerning your everyday affairs and encounters, your relatives (especially siblings) and anything relating to communication. Day-to-day interactions and short trips may present you with blocks or delays, but this is just life telling you to stop, slow down or reconsider what you are saying, how you are thinking and where you are going. The firmer your idea of these matters then the more effective you will be with respect to them. Learn to pick your moment, and to see that your attitude of mind has everything to do with how something will turn out. On the other side of all this may loom the necessity that demands you to take things less literally or stop trying to be 'right' all the time and impress others with your knowledge and connections. This will have the 'so what' effect of knowing facts but not actually applying them to the practical issue in hand, or rather not seeing what is truly relevant. This time is all about being pragmatic, not merely clever. Finding the right word or contact, or getting the facts right, has to be a means to an end, not an end in itself.

Saturn Transiting your Fourth House

Circumstances demand or help you to establish, make stable or put into order issues concerning your home and family, and your sense of security and belonging. This mostly boils down to your sense of your roots and connection to your past. If these are healthy then this time will find you more secure than ever, possibly extending your base to benefit others, but with the definite proviso that they use this in an industrious and disciplined way. On a purely physical level, this could mean building onto where you live. But on the other hand, the need for repairs or restructuring could present itself. In both cases it would be symbolic of what is going on deep within you. Your home and home patch are after all an expression of your feelings of security and belonging. Saturn is, one way or the other, drawing your attention to the status of such matters. Another effect of this transit can be that you feel like you have come to a standstill, particularly profes-sionally. This again would be because you are being forced to establish where you are coming from as opposed to where you are trying to get to in the outer world. You are building foundations now, and having to have a closer look at the 'ground' they are built upon. The 'superstructure' will come later – and that will depend upon how stable the foundations are. All this can mean that you have to dig deep emotionally and psychologically.

Saturn Transiting your Fifth House

Circumstances demand or help you to establish, make stable or put into order issues concerning your manner of creative self-expression – and this includes everything from pastimes to romance, children to drama, and partying to making anything that is a demonstration of your unique personality. So there is a definite paradox at work now, for you have to get serious about having fun, to tighten up in order to loosen up, to be disciplined in your artistic expression, to set definite boundaries so that you or others know where they are free to be themselves. Children particularly, your own or others, can become a great responsibility as they force you to connect with the 'adult' in you, that is the one who has authority born of a sound sense of what is and is not permissible – yet at the same contacting the 'child' in you, for this enables you to understand the actual child. Any weakness in this respect will mean having to pay the price – and this won't just concern children. Not recognizing when you or others have crossed the line can attract quite dramatic problems. So this is a time of learning how to enjoy and freely express yourself, while observing certain limitations and rules.

Saturn Transiting your Sixth House

Circumstances demand or help you to establish, make stable or put into order issues concerning work, co-workers, health, technical method and service to others. You have to work hard now and it can seem to be for little reward, but beware of overworking for that could lead to health problems. The reward will come later, after Saturn has left this House and entered the next, the Seventh House and beyond. It is as if you are preparing or training for an appearance or examination. The gardener clears the ground of stones and weeds, fertilizes it and plants the seeds; all hard work with nothing yet to show for it. But come spring, there will be food and flowers! With regard to health this can be a time when you can or must adopt a disciplined regimen to improve your physical and/or psychological state. In many respects this time can be regarded as an apprenticeship or an exercise in devotion – to whatever you regard as worthy of your efforts, which should certainly include your health, and possibly that of others too.

Saturn Transiting your Seventh House

Circumstances demand or help you to establish, make stable or put into order issues concerning relationships, your partner if you have one, and your actual manner of relating. On the face of it, this usually means a challenging period in your close partnerships and dealings with others generally for the simple reason that such matters are nearly always subject to difficultly – that is unless you are fortunate enough to have a very stable relationship and attitude. In other words, if there are any cracks, they'll show up now. Where Saturn is concerned, the reason behind any problems is that you or the other person, or both, are not living up to responsibilities or making and sticking to commitments – which could also be the reason for not being in a relationship at all. The secret is to accept that there are always limitations and lessons factored into close relationships, and that fears and shortcomings regarding getting involved will ensure that no one is there for you – or a certain someone is not there for you. On the positive side, you could well feel stable enough to make a firmer commitment, with marriage being a likelihood if such has been a possibility. In terms of what or who you attract at this time, older or more mature people are likely to signify in your life, and learning or serious relationships – or the need to be serious about relationships – are the call of the day rather than more frivolous or flirtatious encounters, even though that is what might appear to be the case at first.

Saturn Transiting your Eighth House

Circumstances demand or help you to establish, make stable or put into order issues concerning others' resources and intimate involvements, be they emotional or financial. Disagreements, disappointments or delays over what you need to acquire from others can be an issue, the resolution of which may mean having to cut your losses, meet someone halfway, or be very respectful and aware of how the other party operates. Also, avoid acrimonious situations for that will only draw matters out longer than necessary – quite unbearably in some cases. The Eighth House is also the area of your chart that has to do with 'death and taxes' – those two things that it has been said no one can avoid. If and when it comes down to it, surrendering to the inevitable might be your only course of action. With respect to intimate relationships, fears and shortcomings with respect to getting closer to someone – or allowing them closer to you – could reach critical mass. In other words, it could be a case of either the death of resisting intimacy, or the death of an intimate relationship itself.

Saturn Transiting your Ninth House

Circumstances demand or help you to establish, make stable or put into order issues concerning travelling and seeking, higher education, covering new ground, finding laws and meanings, or generally broadcasting yourself to a wider audience. When all is said and done, success in these areas is dependent upon having a firm idea of what is and is not allowed and accepted. Being in a foreign country involves knowing and respecting its customs; seeking higher meaning invariably entails following some kind of moral code; academia has its established ways of doing things; reaching the masses means being cognizant of the mores of the segment of society you are aiming at. So, whatever area of endeavour you are involved in, knowing and following the 'rules' is essential. Failure to do so will lead to setbacks and difficulties. Adventure has to have purpose or a journey can become more an endurance test than fun; expansiveness has to be aware of limitations if overextending yourself is to be avoided. However, by observing and abiding by the rules of whatever game you are involved in, you will be setting yourself up for a secure position in the near future.

Saturn Transiting your Tenth House

Circumstances demand or help you to establish, make stable or put into order issues concerning your career, status and reputation. This is a time of reckoning with regard to your position in the outside world. If you have been climbing steadily onwards and upwards, putting in good work and playing by the rules of your particular game, then you can expect either that those in power and authority will confer honours and rewards upon you, or that you will find favour with the general public. If you are entitled to success, then now is the time when it is most likely you will receive your 'laurels'. And if you are the one who is actually in authority, then it will be tested and then confirmed if you have whatever it takes to command respect from those under you. If, on the other hand, your way of reaching the top, or your manner of maintaining your position, has been questionable, then it is more than likely you will be caught out. This is a very important time regarding your standing in the world – and if you have let the grass grow under your feet and done little to establish or prove yourself here, then a feeling of purposelessness could affect you in some way. Put simply, this is a time when what you have truly earned is marked by what you actually get.

Saturn Transiting your Eleventh House

Circumstances demand or help you to establish, make stable or put into order issues concerning your friendships, group activities and any communal/political interests. This is not a time when you are advised or supposed to 'go it alone'. Teamwork is the watchword and recipe for success. Also, having something that goes beyond mere ambition – like aspirations and goals that further the social welfare of the sector of your concern – will give you a sense of position and purpose. Conversely, ignoring such things could find you alone and feeling meaningless – cast out, even. Friendships can be tested now, which is a good thing because often we abide others whose so-called friendship does not go very deep; it's good to know who you can trust, and you'll find out during this time. Any difficulty you have fitting into the collective of which you are a part could disadvantage you – so find out what reservations or inhibitions you have in this respect. Perhaps you are afraid of being or looking 'ordinary', but the paradox of ordinariness is that everyone has their peculiarities. Realizing that your humanness is the common factor can open up areas of security and stability that will surprise you. On the other hand, being too entrenched in your social group could prove suffocating and restrictive now.

Saturn Transiting your Twelfth House

Circumstances demand or help you to establish, make stable or put into order issues concerning 'behind-the-scenes' activities and what is more subtle and less obvious about life and yourself. This is, on the face of it, a time when loose ends have to be tied up, when unfinished business must be seen to. But such can run quite deep in their origins – going back to past lives (if you believe in reincarnation) or, at least, to events that happened very early on in your life, even in the womb, that set you on a course that now demands some kind of reckoning and reconciliation. If there is something stuck in your throat from the past, you won't be able to take in or on anything else until it has been cleared.

The areas that do breed immediate success or stability are those that relate to psychology and spirituality – that is, anything that looks within for the causes of things. External factors, be they people or things, may appear to be what are giving you trouble, but really they are simply symptoms of your internal landscape. Failing to realize this can lead to feeling confined and forced to contemplate your own life in more literal ways – such as a spell in hospital or some other institution. Or you may find yourself in such a place on somebody else's behalf, like spending time with a loved one. This is not exactly a time when you feel that life is getting anywhere in the usual sense of the expression, probably because our culture thinks of 'reality' as being mostly material or physical.

Saturn passing through your Twelfth House helps to make it plain that life is just as much a spiritual and mysterious thing – possibly more so. Failure to appreciate this can make it a depressing and unrewarding time, but if you see it as the necessary 'clearing of the decks' or 'paying off of debts', you will be rewarded eventually with a feeling that the world is resting more lightly on your shoulders – simply because you are willing to take responsibility. Ultimately, you appreciate that there is some Higher Power that is really looking after things – and you must do right by whatever you perceive such a thing to be.

Uranus House Ready-Reckoner (for 'Off-The-Peg' calculation only)

Your Birth Sign ↓ House Transited ↓ Page Number

Period	♈	♉	♊	♋	♌	♍	♎	♏	♐	♑	♒	♓
(Sign being transited)	Aries	Taurus	Gemini	Cancer	Leo	Virgo	Libra	Scorpio	Sagitt-arius	Capri-corn	Aquarius	Pisces
Jan 1 2007 to May 28 2010 (Pisces)	12th	11th	10th	9th	8th	7th	6th	5th	4th	3rd	2nd	1st
	p276	p275	p275	p274	p273	p273	p272	p272	p271	p271	p270	p270
May 28 2010 to Aug 14 2010 (Aries)	1st	12th	11th	10th	9th	8th	7th	6th	5th	4th	3rd	2nd
	p270	p276	p275	p275	p274	p273	p273	p272	p272	p271	p271	p270
Aug 14 2010 to Mar 12 2011 (Pisces)	12th	11th	10th	9th	8th	7th	6th	5th	4th	3rd	2nd	1st
	p276	p275	p275	p274	p273	p273	p272	p272	p271	p271	p270	p270
Mar 12 2011 to May 15 2018 (Aries)	1st	12th	11th	10th	9th	8th	7th	6th	5th	4th	3rd	2nd
	p270	p276	p275	p275	p274	p273	p273	p272	p272	p271	p271	p270
May 15 2018 to Jul 7 2025 (Taurus)	2nd	1st	12th	11th	10th	9th	8th	7th	6th	5th	4th	3rd
	p270	p270	p276	p275	p275	p274	p273	p273	p272	p272	p271	p271

♈	♉	♊	♋	♌	♍	♎	♏	♐	♑	♒	♓
Aries	Taurus	Gemini	Cancer	Leo	Virgo	Libra	Scorpio	Sagitt-arius	Capri-corn	Aquarius	Pisces

Uranus Transiting the Houses

Uranus Transiting your First House

Change or innovation, disruption or epiphany, or the unique, unusual, alternative or odd find their way into matters concerning your image, appearance and what constitutes your sense of presence in the world around you. So this is a wake-up call to the fact that there is no one else like you in the Universe, and you need to break away from anything or anyone that tries to keep you in some box or hole. Overdo this though and you could alienate yourself from others. Get it right and you will quite simply revolutionize yourself and your life. The unpredictable and unexpected are, you find, ways in which all this is implemented. Expect rebirth or reinvention of yourself.

Uranus Transiting your Second House

Change or innovation, disruption or epiphany, or the unique, unusual, alternative or odd find their way into matters concerning your finances, possessions, earning power, self-worth and sense of what has value for you. This usually means changing or updating your sense of self-worth and your manner of earning money. Taking a radical view or adopting a technological method is possible and advisable. If you are stuck in a rut in this respect, then expect to get tipped out of your comfort zone as you are no longer allowed to be complacent, and are made to renew your values. New or unusual ways of making money, and of looking at what is worth what is the key meaning and theme of this time.

Uranus Transiting your Third House

Change or innovation, disruption or ephipany, or the unique, unusual, alternative or odd find their way into matters concerning your everyday affairs and encounters, education, your relatives (especially siblings), and anything relating to communication. Day-to-day interactions and short trips may present you with the unexpected, showing you that the world is more than you know, or think you know. Technology or alternative subjects like astrology and symbolism enter into your way of thinking and relating to the world, and your way of communicating day-to-day affairs. Glitches or accidents will occur if you are hanging on to old ways of learning, communicating or looking at things, or if you are resisting the need for change to the point where something gets in the way or makes you jumpy. This time is about changing your mental attitude, and anything that happens, good or bad, is in aid of this.

Uranus Transiting your Fourth House

Change or innovation, disruption or epiphany, or the unique, unusual, alternative or odd find their way into matters concerning your home and family, and your sense of security and belonging. This can mean a home move, a change or disruption in domestic set-up, a family disturbance and/or revelation, or anything that gives you a keener idea of how your roots and background affect you. Home truths, no less. On a more mundane level, this could simply mean some kind of modernization in your home, possibly disrupting your daily living in the process – but even this would point to a more profound internal change in how you feel about your private place in the world.

Uranus Transiting your Fifth House

Change or innovation, disruption or epiphany, or the unique, unusual, alternative or odd find their way into matters concerning your manner of creative self-expression – and this includes everything from pastimes to romance, children to drama, partying to making anything that is a demonstration of your unique personality. One way or the other this should amount to your life being more stimulating and exciting as the main thrust of energy is about making something new happen. You may do this quite impulsively or unconsciously – like an affair out of the blue, an invention, or a chance event – in order to remind you that you are an extraordinary being with much to show the world. If you have children, this idea could find itself being expressed through them rather than yourself, or they may act up if their uniqueness is being denied or unnoticed. This is a time to express yourself in an original fashion, and allow certain others to do so too.

Uranus Transiting your Sixth House

Change or innovation, disruption or epiphany, or the unique, unusual, alternative or odd find their way into matters concerning work, co-workers, health, technical method and service to others. There is a strong likelihood that the feeling of being a 'slave' could surface now – that is, a slave to anyone or anything that seems to reward you insufficiently for your efforts. The truth, however, is that you are waking up to the difference between slavery and service. You may think you are dedicating yourself to some work or figure, but perhaps you are doing it to avoid something else that is possibly lacking in your life. Like service to yourself, for instance. The work ethic or work for its own sake is valid up to a point, but if you are past that point you will get signs of this now – like getting bored and frustrated with your job or co-workers. Failing this, it could show up in your health as your body rebels against what you are submitting it to in the name of work or service, or generally how you are literally keeping body and soul together. So, if any of these are the case, look to your true motivations for slaving away (guilt, for example) and do something about it. This means discovering what you really believe is worth the effort, or that you simply haven't found what that is yet. But you know you cannot carry on exhausting yourself for no good reason – or any reason, for that matter. This is like, or actually may be a case of, striking for better conditions. Also at this time, alternative health methods are likely to become an interest to you.

Uranus Transiting your Seventh House

Change or innovation, disruption or epiphany, or the unique, unusual, alternative or odd find their way into matters concerning relationships, your partner if you have one and your manner of relating to others. As relationships are often something which we get into for one reason when really it is another, this means that we have to confront the truth of why we are with someone – or why we are not. This is because security, perceived responsibility to others, or romantic illusions are usually to the fore in relationships, and freedom of expression and how we truly feel tend to get inhibited for the sake of peace and reliability. But now the desire to be yourself, to show your 'other side' comes surging forwards. If this urge is also repressed, then an external element – like a third party or a major break in routine – could occur in order to ring the changes and provide that emotional wake-up call.

The secret here is to be as open as possible with one another, without judging or giving in to childish insecurity and fears. The more possessive one person is, the more hotly the other will react now. A strong element amidst all this is the question of how much you are *friends* with your partner, rather than just emotionally and physically involved. The point here is that friends allow one another more latitude than lovers because there is an inherent respect for each other's individuality – and it is individuality within relationship that is the theme of this time. If you are not in a relationship – or even if you are – someone can appear out of the blue now, someone you would not expect to attract or be attracted by. Be careful not to reject the prospect because of this; you are, after all, exploring the other side of life and yourself now, which is a very important experience as it makes you more complete and interesting as a person, and brings you closer to being the individual that you truly are.

Uranus Transiting your Eighth House

Change or innovation, disruption or epiphany, or the unique, unusual, alternative or odd find their way into matters concerning other's resources and intimate involvements, be they emotional or financial, and any interest you might have in the hidden world or the 'other side'. Freedom and relying on others for money have long been uncomfortable bedfellows, so if this is the case for you, it will make for a difficult passage. Feeling beholden or dependent on something or someone means, by its very nature, that you are not 'free'. The trick here is to see such dependency as something that gives you the freedoms that you actually have, or should appreciate you have. Otherwise, extremely disharmonious situations can arise where there is no clear resolution. Such crises do, however, challenge you to eliminate deeply seated negative traits of character, while transforming them into something purer and higher, and more powerful. If you are lucky, something could happen that actually does provide you with freedom from someone else's resources – like an inheritance, for example. But this should not be banked upon!

All this includes that other area – intimate relationship – which is also rather inimical to freedom. Usually, when sexually committed to someone, exercising freedom to do what you want or go elsewhere is not welcome or allowed. This, of course, can be done in secret, another Eighth House matter, but as Uranus is all about openness and truth, expect to have your cover blown. Another of many alternatives to this conflicting Planet/House mix is that of freedom or experimentation within a sexual relationship, possibly involving one or more others. This can be very revealing and exciting, but also quite dangerous psychologically – but would still disclose where you and others are coming from sexually. This may possibly involve a more esoteric approach to sex, such as Tantra. In fact, this period can be one of awakening to the more metaphysical and occult side of life, either in proportion to how much you might already be interested in this, or quite unexpectedly, possibly owing to some sudden occurrence.

Uranus Transiting your Ninth House

Change or innovation, disruption or epiphany, or the unique, unusual, alternative or odd find their way into matters concerning travelling and seeking, higher education, covering new ground, finding laws and meanings, what you do or do not believe in, or generally broadcasting yourself to a wider audience. What all or any of this amounts to is the possibility of revolutionizing your world-view, and possibly that of others as well, if you are open to the evolutionary impulse to grow beyond what you have become so far. If, however, you resist this change (actually upgrade) in personal philosophy or opinion, then you are likely to attract the more negative aspects, like frustration, as growth is curtailed in the areas you want it, and possibly accidents and glitches occur as you try to get from A to B, or brushes with established religious or legal bodies as your unconscious tricks you into finding out that you are not as dyed-in-the-wool as your comfort zone would have you believe. Essentially, this time is about changing what you as an individual, or humanity as a whole, get particularly dogmatic about: what life, the Universe, and everything is all about.

Uranus Transiting your Tenth House

Change or innovation, disruption or epiphany, or the unique, unusual, alternative or odd find their way into matters concerning your career, status and reputation. Career moves or radical shifts are therefore likely. You may also find yourself rebelling against the rules and conditions of whatever authority or field you professionally operate in, as it appears to block or frustrate your progress or ambitions. Alternatively, some sudden or innovative development could be what revolutionizes your activities in the world at large. You may find that you have to consider what your longer-term goals are, and what your principles are, in the face of what seems a stifling and overly conservative arena. In truth, you have reached a point where your uniqueness as an individual is taking precedence over fitting in or toeing the party line. You are currently reinventing yourself with respect to what you amount to in life, so anything that gets in the way of this should not be put up with for too long because you may just blow a fuse and cause more damage to your reputation than is necessary or advisable.

Uranus Transiting your Eleventh House

Change or innovation, disruption or epiphany, or the unique, unusual, alternative or odd find their way into matters concerning your friendships, group activities and any communal/political interests. Quite possibly, a new and significant friend or group will come into your life now. This or some other social occurrence, like a seminar or workshop for instance, is in aid of presenting new ideals and aspirations so that you might look ahead or outside of what you regard as 'normal'. You are more inclined to side with the radical or different now, and this may mean rebelling against, or at least no longer feeling comfortable with the group you usually mix with. Generally, you are more inclined to refresh your social input and behaviour, and any events or upsets are best interpreted as helping this to happen.

Uranus Transiting your Twelfth House

Change or innovation, disruption or epiphany, or the unique, unusual, alternative or odd find their way into matters concerning 'behind-the-scenes' activities and what is more subtle and less obvious about life and yourself. This time can present you with all manner of strange, unaccountable, revealing, embarrassing or coincidental happenings. This is because you are currently subject to issues that you have either swept under the carpet some time in the past, or that you have simply forgotten about but need to be in touch with again. At a purely psychological level you may just get thoughts entering your head that seem intrusive or intriguing. However this influence affects you, your response should be to make the effort to understand what is happening, inside and/or outside your head. Using means that you might normally never entertain – like hypnosis, past-life regression or psychotherapy – to make such investigations is also a likelihood, and recommended too. On a more mundane level, you might unexpectedly find yourself concerned or involved with some form of institution, such as a hospital or prison – but probably not that directly. The point is that you are being put in touch with a side of life – and those who live it – that is not in your usual run of things. The purpose of such experiences is to clear out your closet of old memories and connections that are inhibiting your further progress. In the process you could well find some clue or interest that radically alters what you think life is actually about, eventually giving rise to some new outlook with a different path to match.

Neptune House Ready-Reckoner (for 'Off-The-Peg' calculation only)

Your Birth Sign ↓ House Transited ↓ Page Number

Period	♈	♉	♊	♋	♌	♍	♎	♏	♐	♑	♒	♓
(Sign being transited)	Aries	Taurus	Gemini	Cancer	Leo	Virgo	Libra	Scorpio	Sagitt-arius	Capri-corn	Aquarius	Pisces
Jan 1 2007 to Apr 4 2011 (Aquarius)	11th	10th	9th	8th	7th	6th	5th	4th	3rd	2nd	1st	12th
	p284	p283	p282	p281	p281	p280	p280	p279	p278	p278	p277	p284
Apr 4 2011 to Apr 5 2011 (Pisces)	12th	11th	10th	9th	8th	7th	6th	5th	4th	3rd	2nd	1st
	p284	p284	p283	p282	p281	p281	p280	p280	p279	p278	p278	p277
Apr 5 2011 to Feb 3 2012 (Aquarius)	11th	10th	9th	8th	7th	6th	5th	4th	3rd	2nd	1st	12th
	p284	p283	p282	p281	p281	p280	p280	p279	p278	p278	p277	p284
Feb 3 2012 to May 30 2025 (Pisces)	12th	11th	10th	9th	8th	7th	6th	5th	4th	3rd	2nd	1st
	p284	p284	p283	p282	p281	p281	p280	p280	p279	p278	p278	p277

♈	♉	♊	♋	♌	♍	♎	♏	♐	♑	♒	♓
Aries	Taurus	Gemini	Cancer	Leo	Virgo	Libra	Scorpio	Sagitt-arius	Capri-corn	Aquarius	Pisces

Neptune Transiting the Houses

Neptune Transiting your First House

Spirituality or illusion, subtle attunement or oversensitivity, inspiration or confusion find their way into matters concerning your image, appearance and what constitutes your sense of presence in the world around you. All of this can be experienced as anything from an identity crisis to feeling that you are the embodiment of or channel for something higher and greater than you. As ever with Neptune, the more you are consciously and deliberately endeavouring to attune to what your higher mind is picking up from the ether, then the more rewarding and less confusing it will be. So practises such as meditation, visualization, chanting, or any kind of creative expression or performance, are strongly recommended. If you leave this influence to its own devices, though, and do not meet it halfway, you are liable to receive and put out a lot of mixed messages. This is because in effect you are being put in touch with the many different impressions, energies and personas that are circulating in and around you. You may find yourself being one thing to one person, and someone totally different to another. You could also be inclined to heavily idealize people and situations, with subsequent disappointment. The reality behind reality – what the philosopher Immanuel Kant called the 'noumenon' – is trying to make itself known to you now – or rather *through* you. Like a high-frequency radio signal, it is wonderful if you tune in properly, but just lots of confusing static if you don't.

Neptune Transiting your Second House

Spirituality or illusion, subtle attunement or oversensitivity, inspiration or confusion find their way into matters concerning your finances, possessions, earning power, self-worth and sense of what has value for you. Basically then, you have the most spiritual and therefore non-material planet affecting that area of life which is the most tangible and materialistic. More often than not, this means that you will find that financial matters and issues of self-worth (which tend to be measured in terms of money or earning power) are destabilized or undermined in some way. For instance, any get-rich-quick scheme is bound to fail. This is Neptune's attempt to get you to look at material matters, and how you evaluate things, in a more spiritual or refined way. This would entail realizing that in the end everything is in the lap of the gods, and that putting too much emphasis on the material or physical side of life is misleading and unbalancing. At the extreme, the only way Neptune can make this point is to cause some sort of material loss so that you have to accept that possessions are a passing matter, that you 'can't take it with you'. Detaching from the desire or need to get and gain will give rise to more of a 'good Lord will provide' kind of philosophy, appreciating that true affluence is literally about being fluid, letting things flow in and flow out as requirements dictate. But as there is now an inclination to be too idealistic or fanciful with regard to money matters, it would be wise to 'trust in Allah but tie up your camel'.

Neptune Transiting your Third House

Spirituality or illusion, subtle attunement or oversensitivity, inspiration or confusion find their way into matters concerning your everyday affairs and encounters, education, your relatives (especially siblings), and anything relating to communication. This can be a time of wishful thinking or inspired thinking; deluded perception or psychic perception. It all depends on whether you are seeing life from a spiritual and metaphysical point of view, or are trying to make sense of it all in order to control what you see as your world. If you can imagine your mind as a radio receiver that tunes into thoughts and ideas, then your intercourse with those around you will take on a quality that is beyond the commonplace, elevating it out of the petty pace of everyday life. If you are oblivious to this, or in denial of there being something more to life than what meets the eye, then expect to be confused by the mean alternative as trivia turns into a meaningless mass of thoughts and words, wires get crossed and communications become farcical, or gossip takes on a more undermining or even scandalous quality. The saying, 'The world is more than we know,' is an apt one for this influence. Try to keep to what you (think you) know and you will be confounded. Keep open to the mysterious and unexplainable and you will be fascinated and put in touch with something that makes life far more interesting, uplifting and meaningful.

Neptune Transiting your Fourth House

Spirituality or illusion, subtle attunement or oversensitivity, inspiration or confusion find their way into matters concerning your home and family, and your sense of security and belonging. This time can, therefore, disclose whether or not you are comfortable with respect to where you live. If there is a bad feeling lurking, or things falling apart or not coming together, then it is saying that you need to review what it is that you want from your home and family life, why you are putting up with it or if you need to relocate. Or more metaphysically, where you live can be experienced as a projection of your own inner emotional state, or that of someone else living with you. This can be in the form of a strange occurrence, or one involving water in some way. Flooding and plumbing problems, for instance, would be a sign that there are emotional concerns surfacing that need to be 'mopped up' or seen to. At its most extreme this influence can be experienced as a haunting – but the same interpretation holds: it is reflecting some disturbance in your own being or that of another member of the household. Positively speaking, this influence can be experienced as a 'coming home', getting more in touch with the spirits of the house and home, and feeling a kind of communion with it all. More generally speaking, you feel psychically in touch with your roots – or long to be so – and/or with Nature herself.

Neptune Transiting your Fifth House

Spirituality or illusion, subtle attunement or oversensitivity, inspiration or confusion find their way into matters concerning your manner of creative self-expression – and this includes everything from pastimes to romance, children to drama, partying to making anything that is a demonstration of your unique personality. So this influence can manifest in quite a number of ways, but they would all be down to your wanting to make life more colourful, meaningful, romantic, glamorous, dramatic or creative. The downside is considerable because such could be experienced as falling hopelessly in love (or lust), idealizing someone out of all proportion to who they actually are – or having the same done to you – or investing yourself in some affair or scheme that goes belly up as your pipe dreams overwhelm any sense of reality. It can be a time when you do truly find a fine connection with someone, and one that is possibly even platonic as this can preserve the ideal more easily and create that high feeling of being spiritually involved with someone, like you have known one another before. Longings and sensitivities may find expression through children – your own or someone else's – with them embodying your ideals, your need for self-expression, or your weaknesses. Taking up or making more of any creative talent you have is one of the more fruitful and reliable ways of living out this influence because in this way you would be employing your imagination in its own area, rather than projecting it on to something or someone else.

Neptune Transiting your Sixth House

Spirituality or illusion, subtle attunement or oversensitivity, inspiration or confusion find their way into matters concerning work, co-workers, health, methodologies and service to others. It is probably with respect to health that you have to be most careful. This is because you are more susceptible, on the one hand, to picking up infections or developing allergies, and on the other, to letting your imagination get the better of you and actually making yourself ill. Then again, if you are unwell during this time it may be some strange or hard to diagnose complaint, or possibly psychosomatic. This latter point does not necessarily mean that there is nothing wrong with you, but that you are physically manifesting something that is bothering you on an unconscious or emotional level. It is also likely that during this period you will seek out complementary or alternative medical help, or actually seek to be a practitioner yourself. It is the subtler reasons for health or the lack of it that you are drawn to now – one way or the other. Likewise, nutrition or diet might become a concern, but again be careful that this does not become a problem in itself with fads posing as hard facts. At work, sensitivities, allergies and rumours could be an issue – but these too would be symptomatic of some underlying issue trying to make itself felt.

Neptune Transiting your Seventh House

Spirituality or illusion, subtle attunement or oversensitivity, inspiration or confusion find their way into matters concerning relationships, your partner if you have one, and your manner of relating to others. A common manifestation of this is falling in love – or falling prey to illusions of love. The human tendency to romanticize or idealize a loved one is really a way of being shown whether or not you can love genuinely or unconditionally, for during this time it is likely that you will encounter the weaker side of your partner – possibly as a health problem or some such other debilitating condition, or merely the side you hadn't, or wouldn't have fallen in love with had you encountered it in the first place. If you can love him or her through this, you have, as it were, passed Neptune's test and will be taken to a higher level of love and relatedness – possibly one that is platonic, temporarily or indefinitely. If, on the other hand, it's 'love's illusions' that were in play, then a painful, or at least embarrassing, parting of the ways is on the cards. Aside from this one-to-one relationship scenario, your dealings with others in general are best practised from the viewpoint of compassion and spiritual under-standing, or failing that, with an eye to seeing where the catch might be. Acceptance, looking at matters karmically, and turning the other cheek charac-terize the former, whereas taking things with a pinch of salt and reading the fine print characterize the latter.

Neptune Transiting your Eighth House

Spirituality or illusion, subtle attunement or oversensitivity, inspiration or confusion find their way into matters concerning others' resources and intimate involvements, be they emotional or financial, and any interest you might have in the hidden world or the 'other side'. By and large, all money or contractual issues should be heavily scrutinized because there is a possible element of deception, or at least misunderstanding born of not knowing all the facts. Guard against fanciful thinking or pie-in-the-sky projects, for such could find you undone. And yet, the more mystical or unquantifiable side of life could come into play regarding such things as inheritances or your financial dealings with others in a beneficial way – but you'd have to be quite finely attuned to how much one's fortunes are in the lap of the gods for this to be relied upon.

With respect to intimacy and sexuality, anything from the highest to the lowest, from the exotic to the bewildering, from the ecstatic to the denying can be part of your landscape here. Illusions regarding your attitude to sex, and anyone who is part of your sexual scenario, are likely to surface during this time, and they will need honestly confronting, refining and resolving if confusion is not to turn into rank chaos. A spiritual approach to sex, such as Tantra, could be an advisable route, or one that presents itself. As far as your spiritual life is concerned, this is a time when the reality and significance of death and the occult could play an important part in connecting you with the spirit world itself, and thereby with your more intense and undeniable feelings, and with helping you in a special or subtle way.

Neptune Transiting your Ninth House

Spirituality or illusion, subtle attunement or oversensitivity, inspiration or confusion find their way into matters concerning travelling and seeking, higher education, covering new ground, finding laws and meanings, or generally broadcasting yourself to a wider audience. The main theme of this influence is one of leading you to the realization that everything and everybody is *one*, that we all share the same source and fundamental nature as living creatures, and that indeed all things are sentient beings, from a flower to a mountain, from a human to an insect. Noble and fine, and a little 'hippy-like' as this all can be, there is a danger of taking an illusory or fanciful view of life with, paradoxically, a sense of moral superiority to go with it. At this point Neptune's influence goes some way to undermine such 'egotistical egolessness', the result being that we are left high and dry, the 'guru' turns out to be an all-too-human fake, and the heady dream of peace and love is confounded by the harsh realities of life as it actually is rather than as we have dreamt it to be. Be that as it may, such mystical excursions into what God, the universe and everything is about do lead to a certain elevation of your spiritual philosophy, contributing in some small degree to making a more wonderful and tolerant world. But you will probably have to get lost, literally or mentally or both, in the process.

Neptune Transiting your Tenth House

Spirituality or illusion, subtle attunement or oversensitivity, inspiration or confusion find their way into matters concerning your career, status and reputation. The way in which this can manifest varies considerably, but basically it is all about how much what you are doing in the world – by way of profession or amounting to something – has to do with a truer and more spiritual expression of who you are. If your position has more to do with a feeling of status, authority or wealth, then it is likely that some element will arise that sabotages this or undermines it in some way, or lays you bare. And as this would essentially be an ego issue, then it is quite likely that some other ego would come upon the scene – a figure of authority possibly – who 'gets your goat'. Fighting this blow for blow would be missing the point and lead to a thoroughly confusing and frustrating situation that ultimately found you the loser. This would be because you are not heeding or hearing the question that Neptune is posing through such an event or person: 'Is this what you really want to be doing, or at least, is this the way you want to be doing it?'

Another way that Neptune may pose this question is through you doing something on your own account – in the present or in the past – that undermines your position now. The positive expression of this influence is gained through satisfying Neptune's requirement that you do something in the world that is enlightening, relieving or entertaining. Alternatively, some pursuit or career that is in aid of such might present itself to you as an idea, opportunity or development, perhaps involving music, the metaphysical or theatre. In any event, it is what you are presently doing that uplifts or inspires others that is the true mark of your place in the world. Yet at the same time, be careful that your ego does not (again) get in the way by glorifying your role, for that too would lead to being undone, disillusioned or scandalized.

Neptune Transiting your Eleventh House

Spirituality or illusion, subtle attunement or oversensitivity, inspiration or confusion find their way into matters concerning your friendships, group activities and any communal/political interests. The beauty of such an influence can be experienced as feeling that you are really amongst kindred spirits or that you are involved in some movement that really is bound for glory or doing some good in the world. The trouble here is that if there is any illusion or snag, then with everyone concerned being under the same influence, there is the possibility that no-one will notice until the bubble bursts and what were idealistic convictions are seen to be no more than idealistic fancies – or that if they had been handled more subtly and mindfully then noble goals and aspirations would have been satisfied. Another expression of this transit can be one where compassion and unconditional love are given by, or given to a friend or group. In any event, honestly surrendering to the group's requirements, or your friend making some honest admission, is vital – otherwise matters could dissolve into disappointment and recrimination. Other expressions of this influence could be the attending of mystical groups, or simply being in a group that you find no longer 'does it for you' – or both. But group spiritual endeavour is the essence of this time, with all the highs and lows that such can engender.

Neptune Transiting your Twelfth House

Spirituality or illusion, subtle attunement or oversensitivity, inspiration or confusion find their way into matters concerning 'behind-the-scenes' activities and what is more delicate and less obvious about life and yourself. This is a doubly subtle influence – which means that you can either miss it altogether, or really reach a finer understanding of what you and life are all about from a spiritual perspective. But 'missing altogether' wouldn't be strictly true, because Neptune always goes round to the back door when it cannot get in the front – that is, it will draw your attention to the inner workings of life and your personality by bringing about something that you cannot explain or deal with in the usual objective, material or logical manner. There may be a sense that something or someone is missing, or that there is some part of you that is trying to make itself felt through the fog of activity and rationality with which you have surrounded yourself but take as being normal. Alternatively, it may register as some hard to treat or diagnose complaint, or something or someone may find their way into an area of your life or being without your invitation, so to speak. And so it is better by far to meet this influence with an investigation into your past or sense of mystery, into psychology or mysticism, and whatever your spiritual reality happens to be. In this way you will be talking Neptune's language and thereby forestall being confused by its more indirect approach. Issues concerning karma, womb-life and past lives are a possible and particularly fruitful area of investigation and experience – even if it is a case of doing so for the first time.

Pluto House Ready-Reckoner (for 'Off-The-Peg' calculation only)

Your Birth Sign ↓ House Transited ↓ Page Number

Period	♈	♉	♊	♋	♌	♍	♎	♏	♐	♑	♒	♓
(Sign being transited)	Aries	Taurus	Gemini	Cancer	Leo	Virgo	Libra	Scorpio	Sagitt-arius	Capri-corn	Aquarius	Pisces
Jan 1 2007 to Jan 26 2008 (Sagitarius)	9th	8th	7th	6th	5th	4th	3rd	2nd	1st	12th	11th	10th
	p291	p290	p290	p289	p288	p288	p287	p287	p286	p293	p292	p292
Jan 26 2008 to Jun 14 2008 (Capricorn)	10th	9th	8th	7th	6th	5th	4th	3rd	2nd	1st	12th	11th
	p292	p291	p290	p290	p289	p288	p288	p287	p287	p286	p293	p292
Jun 14 2008 to Nov 27 2008 (Sagitarius)	9th	8th	7th	6th	5th	4th	3rd	2nd	1st	12th	11th	10th
	p291	p290	p290	p289	p288	p288	p287	p287	p286	p293	p292	p292
Nov 27 2008 to Mar 23 2023 (Capricorn)	10th	9th	8th	7th	6th	5th	4th	3rd	2nd	1st	12th	11th
	p292	p291	p290	p290	p289	p288	p288	p287	p287	p286	p293	p292

♈	♉	♊	♋	♌	♍	♎	♏	♐	♑	♒	♓
Aries	Taurus	Gemini	Cancer	Leo	Virgo	Libra	Scorpio	Sagitt-arius	Capri-corn	Aquarius	Pisces

Pluto Transiting the Houses
Pluto Transiting your First House

Crises, deep transformations, fated occurrences and intense experiences find their way into matters concerning your image, appearance and what constitutes your sense of presence in the world around you. As this is characterized mainly by an intensification of what you see and feel to be actually happening, there can be a tendency, or even a compulsion, to control things because you suspect that things would overwhelm you if you didn't. The trouble is that this sets up a reaction from the environment and other people that kind of proves your suspicions correct. And so a negative spiral can ensue. It is therefore better by far to see this as an intensification of your *perception* rather than what you actually perceive. You might then see that the world is very much what you are making it as a result of impressions received earlier on in your life, or at the time of birth itself – or even before that. Further reflection could also lead you to realize that it is, in fact, you yourself who attracted such experiences by virtue of the way you come across to people, and again, by the way you have historically been inclined to view what is happening to you. Essentially, this amounts to the *empowering* of your persona, but a great deal depends on what it is that you use that empowered persona for. If you are using it to just get your own way and with little regard for others, then you would be attracting and building up animosity towards yourself. If, on the other hand, you see your powerful aura as a means to get closer to life and others in order to help, heal or entertain, then you will definitely be a presence to be sought out rather than avoided or abused.

Pluto Transiting your Second House

Crises, deep transformations, fated occurrences and intense experiences find their way into matters concerning your finances, possessions, earning power, self-worth and sense of what has value for you. Most fundamentally, this period has a huge impact on the merit we see ourselves being entitled to. A blow to your self-esteem or earning power – or any event during this time related to your worth – would really be a catalyst to make you review how you actually evaluate yourself and life, and the criteria you use to do this. One of the most ill-advised practises now would be trying to hang on to or hoard what you have got, for this would very likely attract a loss, simply because Pluto is saying 'you can't take it with you', that physical and material life is most definitely a transitory thing. If, on the other hand, you see yourself as being essentially an entity with an innate wealth that cannot be destroyed but only developed and transformed and used to help others, then you will invite Pluto's blessing through opportunities and encounters that enable you to make more of yourself.

Pluto Transiting your Third House

Crises, deep transformations, fated occurrences and intense experiences find their way into matters concerning your relatives (especially siblings), and anything relating to communication. Essentially, this is a period for the deepening of your mind, relative to how much you wish innately to look to the root causes of things. Your social and intellectual intercourse will therefore take on more probing and intense tones as you look for the reasons behind the reasons behind the reasons. Or if you are emotionally averse to getting to the bottom of things your mind and day-to-day life will become confused and overloaded. So, inevitably, you have to go looking for the more profound underpinnings of everyday existence, otherwise your mind will just become obsessed rather than convinced, your encounters with others dissatisfying rather than intriguing. So this could, or should, be a time when you get interested in psychology, astrology, numerology or anything that has a more profound take on reality. This could include maths, science or astronomy – or any serious course of education – as a means of getting a grip on reality as you perceive it.

Pluto Transiting your Fourth House

Crises, deep transformations, fated occurrences and intense experiences find their way into matters concerning your home and family, and your sense of security and belonging. So a good keyword for the underlying theme and essential meaning of this time is 'roots' – or more specifically, changes brought about by your being steeped in them or searching for them – perhaps compulsively. Dealings with your parents and home life have a quality which forces old issues out into the open, probably giving rise to power struggles, confrontations and upheavals. This process could also be reflected in your domestic life generally, with moves being symbolic of changes taking place deep within. You are searching for where you truly belong – and you may well find it – at least until you are required to search for an even deeper level of belonging. As part of this 'journey' you are also likely to become quite buried at home, tucked away from the world. With Pluto being the planet of endings and beginnings, this time could bring the passing of a parent of other family member – but this is by no means a certainty. If it does occur it is indicative of your 'rooting process' outstripping what were your earlier roots, rather like the rooting of an oak tree would see the comings and goings of the flora and fauna that exist in its midst.

Pluto Transiting your Fifth House

Crises, deep transformations, fated occurrences and intense experiences find their way into matters concerning your manner of creative self-expression – and this includes everything from pastimes to romance, children to drama, partying to making anything that is a demonstration of your unique personality. A powerful, even obsessive, sexual affair or romance can occur during this time – or an existing one goes through a crisis leading to greater intimacy and deeper understanding, or an end. Children could in some way figure, causing a more significant change than is usual. You should recognize that decisions made regarding children have a profound effect on your future and theirs now, so be very careful in your choices. Any pursuits you follow during this time are likely to be very absorbing, risky even. This is because you want to feel that you are doing or making something that has a profound effect upon yourself and others. The way in which you express yourself, and what it is about you that you do express, goes through certain changes – possibly as the result of events that you have no control over. For example, being made redundant and having to make something else of yourself.

Pluto Transiting your Sixth House

Crises, deep transformations, fated occurrences and intense experiences find their way into matters concerning work, co-workers, health, technical method and service to others. Obviously, it is the area of health that should be given priority now, considering Pluto's sometimes critical influence. So if there is some symptom, complaint or condition you have, be it mild or strong, it is during this time that it is likely to reach a stage where something fundamental has to be done about it, otherwise there could be cause for regret. At the same time, this is also one of the best influences for getting your mind and body back in shape through some form of regimen like yoga, working out, diet, etc. With respect to all of these possible scenarios, though, avoid becoming neurotic or obsessed for this could create a problem in itself. As Pluto is concerned with the deepest workings of things, it should now be appreciated that physical health actually originates in the deepest recesses of one's being. Becoming intimately involved with this area – through deep therapy like rebirthing, or shamanism, visualization or any discipline that recognizes and utilizes the intimate connection between mind and body – will breed incredibly positive results. You may have to go through some tough stuff to get there, but it will be worth it.

That other key area, work, is affected by Pluto in equally profound ways. On the negative side you could experience conflicts and power struggles at work or with co-workers. You might find your job just does not satisfy you or meet your requirements any more. But such events are not just negative. They are there to make you look deep within and discover what really is the right job for you or, on a less radical level, what technique or routine suits your requirements best. On a purely positive side, someone involved in your field could lend power to your elbow, or some kind of teaming up or retraining, improvement of method, or editing, could dramatically improve or facilitate what you are trying to do. In terms of the sort of work you get involved with now, it could well be Plutonian in nature, that is, regenerative, deeply cleansing or investigative.

Pluto Transiting your Seventh House

Crises, deep transformations, fated occurrences and intense experiences find their way into matters concerning relationships, your partner if you have one, and your manner of relating to others. As Pluto is the Lord of the Underworld, you may expect to encounter the deeper layers of your own and another's make-up. What you find there can be anything from thrilling and enthralling to profound and gut-wrenching. A great deal depends upon what kind of relationship you are already in or the kind you think you are looking for, set against what fate actually has in store for you. If you are in search of, or consciously need something that will affect you deeply and transform you, then you may expect that require-ment to be more than satisfied. If, however, you have been trying to keep things more superficial or uncommitted – whether you are aware of it or not – then it is very likely that you will experience something or someone that you cannot walk away from or explain away that easily. In any event, it is probable that there will be confrontations and power struggles as you thrash out what is important to you and where you agree or differ on serious issues. This will have the effect of either deepening a relationship or ending it. Trying to hover somewhere in between and not look into matters would result in a kind of slow death, however. You are likely to attract 'deep types', possibly powerful or probing by nature or in a professional sense.

Pluto Transiting your Eighth House

Crises, deep transformations, fated occurrences and intense experiences find their way into matters concerning others' resources and intimate involvements, be they emotional or financial, and any interest you might have in the hidden world or the 'other side'. So this can be a time when you are occasionally put in touch with the harder to fathom or explain away, or that which you cannot just walk away from. There are things in life you cannot avoid, like, as they say, death and taxes. Likewise, there are issues that force you to change in some profound or unmistakeable way; you are not allowed to just wing it. You have to get down to what the real score is, on whatever level you find yourself in deep. Power, in one or more of its forms, becomes an element in your dealings – so expect to be taken to extremes as struggles and breakthroughs occur. There may just be some sort of 'pay-off' or inheritance arising – but don't bank on this happening!

Pluto Transiting your Ninth House

Crises, deep transformations, fated occurrences and intense experiences find their way into matters concerning travelling and seeking, higher education, covering new ground, finding laws and meanings, or generally broadcasting yourself to a wider audience. Overall, then, this could be said to be a time when what you believe life is all about becomes a burning, even obsessive issue – possibly brought about by encountering some person, place or teaching that has a powerful effect upon you. Your previous philosophy or opinion may become insufficient for dealing with what confronts you now, or it is challenged by someone. Just mouthing what you believe in won't wash; you have to walk your talk – and you are actually given the opportunity to do that. The trouble can be that you still try to be academic rather than immerse yourself in the experience of life as distinct from mere theory. Alternatively, you may simply pick up with someone or something that appears to have what you are looking for with respect to a philosophy or system of belief. Even so, the inclination to get self-righteous, fundamentalist even, could blind you to the fact that one man's meat is another man's poison. The main objective of this influence is to give deeper meaning to your experience of life, ultimately giving you a far stronger sense of your own destiny and of the purpose of life on Earth. But if you begin to think that you have somehow taken possession of the ultimate moral philosophy or religion, then you are likely to be put in your place by a greater force than you – possibly the law itself, of whatever land or culture you find yourself living in or near.

Pluto Transiting your Tenth House

Crises, deep transformations, fated occurrences and intense experiences find their way into matters concerning your career, status and reputation. Effectively, you are now having to be your most authentic self with respect to what you are doing in the world, and how you strive to amount to something. You feel a power and urgency driving you to gain success and position. However, if you sacrifice integrity for material gain you could find yourself coming undone at a later stage, or running into people who are playing the same game – but have been doing it longer than you and are horribly ruthless. Paradoxically, though, a certain ruthlessness is required at this time – but really with yourself rather than others. If any habit or attachment is impeding your progress then you may well have to eliminate it, but again, be very careful who gets hurt here for it could backfire on you some way down the road. More likely, you will need to ascertain if you are in a position or on a path that is not really suited to you, and utterly detach yourself from that and cut any losses if necessary. There can be an inclination to obsess over your career now, which may reap rewards at first, but could cause other areas of your life, like home, family or relationships to suffer through neglect. Similarly, using underhand, secretive or even criminal means to get what you think you want can now be a temptation – but this too would ultimately land you in an awkward if not actually dangerous place. A lot can be gained and achieved during this transit, but a lot can be lost too!

Pluto Transiting your Eleventh House

Crises, deep transformations, fated occurrences and intense experiences find their way into matters concerning your friendships, group activities and any communal/political interests. A likely occurrence under this influence could be labelled 'Finding out who your friends are'. This is because genuine friendships are revealed and the fair-weather variety will be shown up as a result of some kind of crisis, large or small. Alternatively, or at the same time, the social values, principles or ideologies that you subscribe to can be brought into question, with you possibly having to review what you hold dear, along with anyone you were closely associated with in this respect. Then again, something might occur that forces you to decide which side you are on, and there may even be some cause you are willing to promote and make sacrifices for. At its most extreme this time could bring to mind what Martin Luther King once opined: 'If a man hasn't discovered something he will die for, he isn't fit to live.'

Pluto Transiting your Twelfth House

Crises, deep transformations, fated occurrences and intense experiences find their way into matters concerning 'behind-the-scenes' activities and what is more delicate and less obvious about life and yourself. Essentially, Pluto unearths what has been buried, which includes anything from the past that has been swept under the carpet for one reason or another. This also relates to certain aspects of your nature of which you are unconscious and/or disapprove, that now need to be brought into consciousness and come to terms with. The trouble here is that by their very nature, we are reluctant to have a good look at such things. And so events may occur that force you to look within, or as a mean alternative, tempt you to foolishly carry on denying your own role in a given matter. Fundamentally, once the shadow from your past, or that which is part of your own personality, has been confronted and dealt with, you will find what could be likened to a rush of fresh air entering the space that you had originally filled with the 'dark matter'. This time can therefore find you discovering dimensions to life and yourself that are enlightening, empowering or both. Additionally, subjects such as psychology and reincarnation may become of great or greater interest to you as you seek to plumb the depths of existence, be it your own, someone else's, or that of the collective. Effectively, then, this time can be like cleaning out the closet, giving you a feeling of having cleared the decks for something bright and new to enter your life when Pluto eventually leaves the Twelfth House and conjoins your Ascendant as it enters the First House. Carry on denying the existence and power of what dwells in your unconscious and you could be setting yourself up for a crisis at a later date that you can in no way sweep under the carpet, like for example an illness or physical loss.

APPENDIX 6

Hotspots: Peaks and Patterns

These are times for us to be more on our toes, when there is the greatest likelihood of something focal or significant happening with respect to one or more Planet-Waves, on both collective and personal levels. However, being conscious of a Planet-Wave's effect *throughout* its duration is still important for it will enable you to respond swiftly and appropriately whenever an unexpected flip of the Wave flicks the edge of your 'board'. This is in addition to the overall intention and effect of *Understanding The Future*, which is to *raise your consciousness* to a level that makes it possible for you to surf the Planet-Waves safely and successfully, to avoid their dangers and to benefit from what they are bringing.

Although there is no guarantee that something *will* actually occur during a Hotspot, these unexpected 'flips' are down to the fact that astrology, like quantum physics, meteorology, medicine and certain other subjects, is an *inexact* science. This means that they all require a degree of *judgement and imagination*. But probably most of all, they require *awareness and intuition*.

How We See It Is How We Make It

Hotspots are like highway intersections – or cross-currents – which are points where something is more likely to happen or be felt to happen. And so in the spirit of being co-creators of life and reality – which is the spirit of this book and this time – at these junctures we are more able to influence what will or will not happen. This is because we are being more influenced *by* them, for the 'wind' and 'current' are stronger. We can then set forth and avail ourselves of all the aids to Planet-Wave surfing given in this book with more 'weather awareness' than usual – and make more of a difference than usual! And remember that all this applies to your *personal* life as well as to global issues.

These are the two types of Hotspot listed below: Patterns and Peaks.

Patterns

These occur when a number of planets make significant patterns in the sky. When they involve New or Full Moons this makes them more powerful, and if they are Eclipses, even more so. Patterns can last anything from a few days to a week or more either side of the dates shown.

Peaks

These are simply when the two planets involved in a Wave are interacting most closely or intensely. (Technically speaking, this is when both planets are exactly aligned to a degree and minute of arc). Apart from anything else, these dates are recommended for practising any ritual you would like to do regarding that Wave, like using the relevant Planet-Wave Meditation for Major Storms and Favourable Winds at their peaks, which are always given below in **bold**.

Putting Them All Together

So here is an overview of all of the Hotspots, year by year, using the same symbols and codes:

❖ = Pattern

▲ = Major Storm or Favourable Wind Peak

✓ ▲ = Jupiter Booster Peak

Italics = Favourable Wind or Breeze blowing

Underlined = Grouping of Patterns occurs, strongly suggesting obvious events, or moods at least, for both individual and collective.

Shaded = When Hotspots occur on the same day or within a few days of one another, intensifying effects for good or ill.

Pages = Page numbers refer to Planet-Wave texts relevant to the Hotspot.

- On the page(s) indicated, simply look for any Planet-Wave occurring on or around the date of the Hotspot.
- The text will describe the energy of the Hotspot and what event, mood, warning or opportunity it could pose.
- Consider also any emphasis placed upon this energy by shading or underlining as described above.
- If the two planets of any Planet-Wave are both included in the planets mentioned in the 'Planet-Waves and/or Pattern' column of the Hotspot tables below, then this Planet-Wave should be paid special attention. For how we see it is how we make it.
- To gain further insights into what was, is or could be happening for any particular year in which a Hotspot occurs, consult also The Planet-Wave Year-by-Year Index on page 306.

2007 Hotspots

date	type	planet-wave and/or pattern	pages
Jan 13	❖	*Saturn/Pluto Pattern*	119, 123, 172
Jan 22	⚡▲	Jupiter/Uranus Minor Storm 2006–07	69
Feb 28	▲	**Saturn/Neptune Major Storm 2004–08**	135-69, 172-85
Mar 16	⚡▲	*Jupiter/Saturn Favourable Breeze 2007–09*	123, 173
May 6	⚡▲	*Jupiter/Saturn Favourable Breeze 2007–09*	123, 173
May 11	⚡▲	Jupiter/Uranus Minor Storm 2006–07	69
May 16	❖	*Jupiter/Saturn/Uranus Pattern*	69, 123, 173
May 16	❖	New Moon on Saturn/Neptune	135-69, 172-85
Jun 25	▲	**Saturn/Neptune Major Storm 2004–08**	123, 135–69, 172–85, 219
Jun 30	❖	Saturn/Neptune Pattern + Full Moon	123, 135–69, 172–85, 219
Jun 30	❖	*Saturn/Pluto Pattern + Full Moon*	*119, 172*
Aug 6	▲	***Saturn/Pluto Favourable Wind 2006–08***	119, 123, *172*
Aug 13	❖	New Moon on Saturn/Neptune	123, 135–69, 172–85
Aug 28	❖	Lunar Eclipse + Saturn/Neptune Pattern	123, 135–69, 172–85
Sep 11	❖	Solar Eclipse on Jupiter/Uranus/Pluto	27–80, 68
Sep 21	❖	Sun/Mars on Jupiter/Uranus/Pluto	27–80, 68
Oct 9	⚡▲	Jupiter/Uranus Minor Storm 2006–07	69, 220
Dec 11	⚡▲	Jupiter/Pluto Minor Storm 2007–08	69, 123
Dec 24	❖	Full Moon + Jupiter/Pluto Pattern	69, 123
Dec 24	❖	*Saturn/Pluto Pattern*	119, 123, 220

2008 Hotspots

date	type	planet-wave and/or pattern	pages
Jan 2	❖	Mars on Jupiter/Pluto	69, 123
Jan 21	✦ ▲	*Jupiter/Saturn Favourable Breeze 2007?2009*	123, 173, 220
Jun 18	❖	Full Moon Pattern on Uranus/Pluto	27–80
Aug 17	❖	Full Moon Pattern on Saturn/Neptune	123, 135–69, 172–85
Aug 17	❖	Uranus/Pluto Pattern	27–80
Aug 17	❖	*Jupiter/Saturn Pattern + Full Moon*	123, 173, 220
Sep 8	✦ ▲	*Jupiter/Saturn Favourable Breeze 2007–09*	123, 173, 220
Sep 8	❖	*Jupiter/Saturn Pattern*	123, 173, 220
Sep 8	❖	Sun on Saturn/Uranus	124, 173, 187–216
Nov 4	▲	**Saturn/Uranus Major Storm 2007–12**	123, 124, 187–216, 219–20
Nov 21	✦ ▲	*Jupiter/Saturn Favourable Breeze 2007–09*	123, 220
Nov 27	❖	Patterns + New Moon on Saturn/Uranus	123, 124, 173 174, 187–216, 219–20
Nov 30	❖	*Jupiter/Saturn Pattern*	123, 173, 220
Dec 12	❖	Mars/Full Moon on Saturn/Uranus	123, 124, 187–216, 219–20

2009 Hotspots

date	type	planet-wave and/or pattern	pages
Jan 26	❖	Solar Eclipse + Saturn/Uranus	123, 124, 187–216, 219–20
Feb 5	▲	**Saturn/Uranus Major Storm 2007–12**	123, 124, 187–216, 219–20
Mar 11	❖	Full Moon on Saturn/Uranus	123, 124, 187–216, 219–20
Apr 15	❖	Mars on Saturn/Uranus	123, 124, 187–216, 219–20

date	type	planet-wave and/or pattern	pages
Jul 7	❖	Full Moon on Uranus/Pluto	27–80
Aug 27	❖	Mercury/Mars on Uranus/Pluto	27–80
Sep 15	▲	**Saturn/Uranus Major Storm 2007–12**	123, 124, 187–216 219–20
Sep 18	❖	New Moon on Uranus/Pluto	27–80
Sep 18	❖	New Moon on Saturn/Uranus	123, 124, 187–216, 219–20
Nov 2	❖	Full Moon on Saturn/Pluto + Pattern	81–118, 123–24, 173, 220
Nov 15	▲	**Saturn/Pluto Major Storm 2008–11**	81–118, 123–24, 173, 220
Nov 16	❖	New Moon on Saturn/Pluto + Pattern	81–118, 123–24, 173, 220

2010 Hotspots

date	type	planet-wave and/or pattern	pages
Jan 30	❖	Full Moon Pattern + Saturn/Pluto	81–118, 123–24, 220
Jan 31	▲	**Saturn/Pluto Major Storm 2008–11**	81–118, 123–24, 220
Apr 4	❖	Saturn/Uranus/Pluto Pattern	27–118, 123–24, 173, 187–216 219–20
Apr 26	▲	**Saturn/Uranus Major Storm 2007–12**	123, 124, 173 174, 187–216 220–30
May 23	⚡▲	Jupiter/Saturn Minor Storm 2010–12	124, 221
Jun 8	⚡▲	Jupiter/Uranus Minor Storm 2010–11	69, 221
Jun 26	❖	Lunar Eclipse on Jupiter/Saturn/Uranus/ Pluto Pattern	69, 124, 221
Jul 25	⚡▲	Jupiter/Pluto Minor Storm 2010–11	69, 124
Jul 26	▲	**Saturn/Uranus Major Storm 2007–12**	123, 124, 187–216, 220–30

date	type	planet-wave and/or pattern	pages
Jul 26	❖	Full Moon + Jupiter/Saturn/Uranus/ Pluto Pattern	69, 124, 221
Aug 3	⚡▲	Jupiter/Pluto Minor Storm 2010–11	69, 124
Aug 10	❖	New Moon + Jupiter/Saturn/Uranus/ Pluto Pattern	69, 124, 221
Aug 16	⚡▲	Jupiter/Saturn Minor Storm 2010–12	124, 221
Aug 21	▲	**Saturn/Pluto Major Storm 2008–11**	81–118, 122–34
Sep 19	⚡▲	Jupiter/Uranus Minor Storm 2010–11	69, 221

2011 Hotspots

date	type	planet-wave and/or pattern	pages
Jan 4	⚡▲	Jupiter/Uranus Minor Storm 2010–11	69, 221
Feb 18	❖	Full Moon Pattern + Saturn/Uranus/ Pluto Pattern	69, 124, 221
Feb 25	⚡▲	Jupiter/Pluto Minor Storm 2010–11	69, 124
Apr 3	❖	New Moon Pattern on Saturn/Pluto	81–118, 122–34
May 28	⚡▲	Jupiter/Saturn Minor Storm 2010–12	124, 174, 221
Jul 7	⚡▲	*Jupiter/Pluto Favourable Breeze 2011–12*	69, 125
Sep 27	❖	New Moon Pattern on Uranus/Pluto	27–80
Oct 26	❖	*New Moon + Jupiter/Pluto*	70, 125
Oct 28	⚡▲	*Jupiter/Pluto Favourable Breeze 2011–12*	70, 125
Dec 24	❖	New Moon on Uranus/Pluto	27–80
Dec 24	❖	*New Moon + Saturn/Neptune*	135–69, 174–82
Dec 24	❖	*New Moon on Jupiter/Pluto*	70, 125

2012 Hotspots

date	type	planet-wave and/or pattern	pages
Mar 13	⚡▲	*Jupiter/Pluto Favourable Breeze 2011–12*	69
Mar 22	❖	New Moon on Uranus/Pluto	27–80
Mar 22	❖	*New Moon on Jupiter/Pluto*	69
May 20	❖	Solar Eclipse Pattern	27–80

date	type	planet-wave and/or pattern	pages
Jun 24	▲	URANUS/PLUTO MOTHER-WAVE 2007-20	27-80
Jun 25	◢ ▲	Jupiter/Neptune Minor Storm 2012	173
Aug 17	❖	New Moon + Pattern + Uranus/Pluto	27-80
Sep 19	▲	URANUS/PLUTO MOTHER-WAVE 2007-20	27-80
Sep 30	❖	Full Moon on Uranus/Pluto	27-80
Sep 30	❖	*Full Moon + Saturn/Neptune*	135-69, 174
Oct 11	▲	*Saturn/Neptune Favourable Wind 2010-13*	170-71
Dec 28	❖	Full Moon on Uranus/Pluto	27-80

2013 Hotspots

date	type	planet-wave and/or pattern	pages
Mar 22	❖	Uranus/Pluto Pattern	27-80
Apr 10	❖	New Moon Pattern on Uranus/Pluto	27-80
May 20	▲	URANUS/PLUTO MOTHER-WAVE 2007-20	27-80
Jun 11	▲	*Saturn/Neptune Favourable Wind 2010-13*	170-71, 174, 221
Jul 3	❖	*New Moon Pattern +Jupiter/Saturn/ Neptune Pattern*	170-71, 174
Jul 17	◢ ▲	*Jupiter/Saturn Favourable Breeze 2013-14*	173
Jul 18	◢ ▲	*Jupiter/Neptune Favourable Breeze 2013*	173
Jul 19	▲	*Saturn/Neptune Favourable Wind 2010-13*	170-71, 174
Jul 21	◢ ▲	Jupiter/Uranus Minor Storm 2013-14	70
Aug 7	◢ ▲	Jupiter/Pluto Minor Storm 2013-14	70
Nov 1	▲	URANUS/PLUTO MOTHER-WAVE 2007-20	27-80
Dec 13	◢ ▲	*Jupiter/Saturn Favourable Breeze 2013-14*	175
Dec 30	❖	Uranus/Pluto Pattern	27-80

2014 Hotspots

date	type	planet-wave and/or pattern	pages
Jan 1	❖	New Moon Pattern on Uranus/Pluto	27–80
Jan 21	❖	Jupiter/Uranus/Pluto Pattern	70
Jan 31	◢▲	Jupiter/Pluto Minor Storm 2013–14	70
Feb 26	◢▲	Jupiter/Uranus Minor Storm 2013–14	70
Apr 20	◢▲	Jupiter/Uranus Minor Storm 2013–14	70
Apr 20	◢▲	Jupiter/Pluto Minor Storm 2013–14	69
Apr 21	▲	**URANUS/PLUTO MOTHER-WAVE 2007–20**	27–80
Apr 21	❖	Jupiter/Uranus/Pluto Pattern	70
Jun 14	❖	Uranus/Pluto Pattern	27–80
Oct 8	❖	Full Moon Pattern on Uranus/Pluto	27–80
Oct 8	❖	*Full Moon Pattern on Jupiter/Uranus*	70
Oct 25	◢▲	*Jupiter/Uranus Favourable Breeze 2014–15*	70
Dec 15	▲	**URANUS/PLUTO MOTHER-WAVE 2007–20**	27–80

2015 Hotspots

Mar 3	◢▲	*Jupiter/Uranus Favourable Breeze 2014–15*	70
Mar 12	❖	Uranus/Pluto Pattern	27–80
Mar 17	▲	**URANUS/PLUTO MOTHER-WAVE 2007–20**	27–80
Apr 4	❖	Lunar Eclipse on Uranus/Pluto	27–80
Jun 22	◢▲	*Jupiter/Uranus Favourable Breeze 2014–15*	70
Jul 16	❖	Uranus/Pluto Pattern + New Moon	27–80
Aug 3	◢▲	Jupiter/Saturn Minor Storm 2015–16	175
Sep 17	◢▲	Jupiter/Neptune Minor Storm 2015–16	175
Oct 11	◢▲	*Jupiter/Pluto Favourable Breeze 2015–16*	70
Oct 13	❖	*New Moon + Jupiter/Pluto*	70
Oct 13	❖	New Moon + Uranus/Pluto	27–80

date	type	planet-wave and/or pattern	pages
Nov 25	❖	Full Moon Pattern on Saturn/Neptune	135–69, 175, 185
Nov 26	▲	**Saturn/Neptune Major Storm 2014–17**	135–69, 175, 185

2016 Hotspots

date	type	planet-wave and/or pattern	pages
Jan 10	❖	New Moon on Uranus/Pluto	27–80
Mar 16	⚊▲	*Jupiter/Pluto Favourable Breeze 2015–16*	70
Mar 23	⚊▲	Jupiter/Saturn Minor Storm 2015–16	175, 222
Mar 23	❖	Jupiter/Saturn/Neptune Pattern + Lunar Eclipse	175, 221–22
Mar 23	❖	Uranus/Pluto + Lunar Eclipse	27–80
Mar 23	❖	*Jupiter/Pluto + Lunar Eclipse*	70
Apr 7	❖	New Moon on Uranus/Pluto	27–80
May 21	❖	Full Moon Pattern on Jupiter/ Saturn/Neptune	175, 221–22
May 26	⚊▲	Jupiter/Saturn Minor Storm 2015–16	175, 222
Jun 5	❖	*New Moon Pattern on Jupiter/Saturn/Pluto*	70
Jun 18	▲	**Saturn/Neptune Major Storm 2014–17**	135–69, 175, 185
Jun 26	⚊▲	*Jupiter/Pluto Favourable Breeze 2015–16*	70
Sep 1	❖	Solar Eclipse on Saturn/Neptune	135–69, 175, 185
Sep 10	▲	**Saturn/Neptune Major Storm 2014–17**	135–69, 175, 185
Oct 16	❖	Uranus/Pluto Pattern + Full Moon	27–80
Nov 24	⚊▲	Jupiter/Pluto Minor Storm 2016–17	71
Dec 25	▲	*Saturn/Uranus Favourable Wind 2015–18*	176, 217–18
Dec 26	⚊▲	Jupiter/Uranus Minor Storm 2016–18	71, 222
Dec 29	❖	New Moon Pattern+Jupiter/Uranus/ Pluto Pattern	71, 222

2017 Hotspots

date	type	planet-wave and/or pattern	pages
Jan 12	❖	Full Moon on Jupiter/Uranus/Pluto Pattern	71, 222
Mar 3	∕ ▲	Jupiter/Uranus Minor Storm 2016–18	71, 222
Mar 30	∕ ▲	Jupiter/Pluto Minor Storm 2016–17	71
May 19	▲	*Saturn/Uranus Favourable Wind 2015–18*	126, 175, 217–18
Jun 30	❖	Jupiter/Uranus/Pluto Pattern	71
Jul 4	∕ ▲	Jupiter/Pluto Minor Storm 2016–17	71
Jul 23	❖	New Moon Pattern on Jupiter/ Uranus/Pluto Pattern	71
Jul 23	❖	*New Moon Pattern on Saturn/ Uranus Pattern*	217–18
Sep 28	∕ ▲	Jupiter/Uranus Minor Storm 2016–18	71–222
Oct 20	❖	Full Moon Pattern on Jupiter/ Uranus/Pluto Pattern	71–222
Oct 20	❖	*Full Moon Pattern on Saturn/ Uranus Pattern*	217–18
Nov 11	▲	*Saturn/Uranus Favourable Wind 2015–18*	126, 175, 217–18
Dec 3	∕ ▲	Jupiter/Neptune Favourable Breeze 2017–18	175
Dec 18	❖	*New Moon Pattern on Saturn/Uranus Pattern*	217–18

2018 Hotspots

date	type	planet-wave and/or pattern	pages
Jan 17	❖	New Moon Pattern on Uranus/Pluto	27–80
Mar 31	❖	Full Moon on Saturn/Pluto Pattern	81–118, 126
Jul 13	❖	Solar Eclipse Pattern + *Saturn/Uranus Pattern + Jupiter/Neptune*	126, 217–18
Jul 28	❖	Lunar Eclipse Pattern on *Saturn/ Uranus Pattern + Jupiter/Neptune*	126, 217–18
Oct 24	❖	*Full Moon Pattern on Saturn/Uranus*	126, 217–18
Nov 23	❖	Full Moon Pattern + Uranus/Pluto	27–80

2019 Hotspots

date	type	planet-wave and/or pattern	pages
Jan 21	❖	Lunar Eclipse + Saturn/Uranus/Pluto Pattern	27–80
Aug 30	❖	New Moon Pattern on Saturn/Uranus/Pluto Pattern	27–80, 81–118, 126–34
Oct 28	❖	Full Moon Pattern on Saturn/Pluto	81–118, 126–34
Dec 15	⚡▲	*Jupiter/Uranus Favourable Breeze 2019–20*	71

2020 Hotspots

date	type	planet-wave and/or pattern	pages
Jan 10	❖	Lunar Eclipse Pattern on Saturn/Uranus/Pluto Pattern	27–80, 71, 126, 187–216, 222–30
Jan 12	▲	**Saturn/Pluto Major Storm 2018–21**	81–118, 126–34
Jan 24	❖	New Moon on Saturn/Uranus/Pluto Pattern	27–80, 71, 126–34, 187–216, 222
Mar 5	⚡▲	Jupiter/Pluto Minor Storm 2020–21	71, 126
Apr 4	❖	Saturn/Uranus Pattern	187–216, 222
Apr 8	❖	Full Moon + Jupiter/Saturn/Uranus/Pluto Pattern	71, 126, 187–216, 222
Jun 30	⚡▲	Jupiter/Pluto Minor Storm 2020–21	71, 126
Jul 23	❖	New Moon on Jupiter/Saturn/Pluto Pattern	71, 126
Oct 16	❖	New Moon Pattern on Jupiter/Saturn/Pluto Pattern	71, 126
Nov 12	⚡▲	Jupiter/Pluto Minor Storm 2020–21	71, 126
Dec 21	⚡▲	Jupiter/Saturn Minor Storm 2019–21	126, 222

APPENDIX 7

The Planet-Wave
Year-by-Year Index

Year	Active Waves/Planet-Wave Weather + page where described
2007–2020	Introduction 1 The Planet-Wave Weather Chart 19 The Planet-Wave Timeline and Index 20 Uranus/Pluto Mother-Wave 27–80 The Dawning of the Aquarian Age 247
2007	**Uranus/Pluto Mother-Wave** 27–80 Jupiter/Uranus Minor Storm 69 Jupiter/Pluto Minor Storm 69
	Saturn/Pluto Favourable Wind 119–21 Saturn/Neptune Major Storm 122 Jupiter/Pluto Minor Storm 123 *Jupiter/Saturn Favourable Breeze* 123 Saturn/Uranus Major Storm 123
	Saturn/Neptune Major Storm 136–69, 172–85 *Saturn/Pluto Favourable Wind* 172 Jupiter/Saturn Favourable Breeze 173 Saturn/Uranus Major Storm 173
	Saturn/Uranus Major Storm 188–216, 219–30 Saturn/Neptune Major Storm 219 *Saturn/Pluto Favourable Wind* 220 Jupiter/Uranus Minor Storm 220 *Jupiter/Saturn Favourable Breeze* 220
2008	**Uranus/Pluto Mother-Wave** 27–80 Jupiter/Pluto Minor Storm 69
	Saturn/Pluto Favourable Wind 119–21 Saturn/Neptune Major Storm 122 Jupiter/Pluto Minor Storm 123 *Jupiter/Saturn Favourable Breeze* 123 Saturn/Uranus Major Storm 123
	Saturn/Pluto Major Storm 82–118, 121–34 *Jupiter/Saturn Favourable Breeze* 124 Saturn/Uranus Major Storm 124

Saturn/Neptune Favourable Wind 174–75 Saturn/Uranus Major Storm 174 Saturn/Pluto Major Storm 174 Jupiter/Saturn Minor Storm 175

Saturn/Uranus Major Storm 188–216, 219–30 Saturn/Pluto Major Storm 220 Jupiter/Saturn Minor Storm 221 Jupiter/Uranus Minor Storm 221 *Saturn/Neptune Favourable Wind* 221

2012 **Uranus/Pluto Mother-Wave** 27–80 *Jupiter/Pluto Favourable Breeze* 69

(Saturn/Pluto Major Storm) *Jupiter/Pluto Favourable Breeze* 125

Saturn/Neptune Favourable Wind 174–75 Saturn/Uranus Major Storm 174 Jupiter/Saturn Minor Storm 175 Jupiter/Neptune Minor Storm 175

Saturn/Uranus Major Storm 188–216, 219–30 Jupiter/Saturn Minor Storm 221 *Saturn/Neptune Favourable Wind* 221

End of Mayan Calendar 247

2013 **Uranus/Pluto Mother-Wave** 27–80 Jupiter/Pluto Minor Storm 70 Jupiter/Uranus Minor Storm 70

Saturn/Neptune Favourable Wind 174–75 *Jupiter/Saturn Favourable Breeze* 175 *Jupiter/Neptune Favourable Breeze* 175

(Saturn/Uranus Major Storm) *Saturn/Neptune Favourable Wind* 221

2014 **Uranus/Pluto Mother-Wave** 27–80 Jupiter/Pluto Minor Storm 70 Jupiter/Uranus Minor Storm 70 *Jupiter/Uranus Favourable Breeze* 70

Saturn/Neptune Major Storm 136–69, 172–85

2015 **Uranus/Pluto Mother-Wave** 27–80 *Jupiter/Uranus Favourable Breeze* 70 *Jupiter/Pluto Favourable Breeze* 70

Saturn/Neptune Major Storm 136–69, 172–85 Jupiter/Saturn Minor Storm 175 Jupiter/Neptune Minor Storm 175 *Saturn/Uranus Favourable Wind* 176

Saturn/Uranus Favourable Wind 221–22 Saturn/Neptune Major Storm 221 Jupiter/Saturn Minor Storm 222

2016 Uranus/Pluto Mother-Wave 27–80 *Jupiter/Pluto Favourable Breeze* 70 Jupiter/Pluto Minor Storm 71 Jupiter/Uranus MinorStorm 71

Saturn/Neptune Major Storm 136–69, 172–85 Jupiter/Saturn Minor Storm 175 Jupiter/Neptune Minor Storm 175 *Saturn/Uranus Favourable Wind* 176

Saturn/Uranus Favourable Wind 176 Saturn/Neptune Major Storm 221 Jupiter/Saturn Minor Storm 222 Jupiter/Uranus Minor Storm 222

2017 Uranus/Pluto Mother-Wave 27–80 Jupiter/Pluto Minor Storm 71 Jupiter/Uranus Minor Storm 71

Saturn/Neptune Major Storm 136–69, 172–85 *Saturn/Uranus Favourable Wind* 176 *Jupiter/Neptune Favourable Breeze* 176

Saturn/Uranus Favourable Wind 221–22 Saturn/Neptune Major Storm 221 Jupiter/Uranus Minor Storm 222

2018 Uranus/Pluto Mother-Wave 27–80 Jupiter/Uranus Minor Storm 71

Saturn/Pluto Major Storm 82–118, 121–34 *Saturn/Uranus Favourable Wind* 125

(Saturn/Neptune Major Storm) *Jupiter/Neptune Favourable Breeze* 176 Jupiter/Neptune Minor Storm 176

Saturn/Uranus Favourable Wind 221–22 Jupiter/Uranus Minor Storm 222 Saturn/Pluto Major Storm 222

2019 Uranus/Pluto Mother-Wave 27–80 *Jupiter/Uranus Favourable Breeze* 71

Saturn/Pluto Major Storm 82–118, 121–34 Jupiter/Saturn Minor Storm 126

(Saturn/Neptune Major Storm) Jupiter/Neptune Minor Storm 176

(Saturn/Uranus Major Storm) Jupiter/Saturn Minor Storm 223

2020 **Uranus/Pluto Mother-Wave** 27–80 *Jupiter/Uranus Favourable Breeze* 71 Jupiter/Pluto Minor Storm 71

Saturn/Pluto Major Storm 82–118, 121–34 Jupiter/Saturn Minor Storm 126 Jupiter/Pluto Minor Storm 126 Saturn/Uranus Major Storm 126

Saturn/Uranus Major Storm 188–216, 219–30 Saturn/Pluto Major Storm 222 Jupiter/Saturn Minor Storm 223

To zero in on 'hot dates' in any particular year, see also Hotspots on previous pages begininning with an explanation of how to use on page 294.